The Essential Guide to **London's Best Food Shops**

The Essential Guide to

London's Best Food Shops

Introduction by Antonio Carluccio

Photographs by John Freeman

NEW HOLLAND

First published in 2000 by
New Holland Publishers (UK) Ltd
London • Cape Town • Sydney • Auckland

24 Nutford Place, London W1H 6DQ, United Kingdom

80 McKenzie Street, Cape Town 8001, South Africa

Level 1, Unit 4, 14 Aquatic Drive, Frenchs Forest, NSW 2086, Australia

Unit 1A, 218 Lake Road, Northcote, Auckland, New Zealand

10 9 8 7 6 5 4 3 2 1

ISBN 1 85974 275 0

Editor: Christine Rista
Researchers: Brian Walker, Moya Gibbon
Writers: Silvija Davidson, Susan Fleming, Sarah Freeman,
Beverly LeBlanc, Susan Wolk, Jo Younger
Editorial Assistant: Melissa Lesson

Design: Roger Hammond
Cartography: William Smuts
Illustrations: Madeleine David
Production: Caroline Hansell

Editorial Direction: Yvonne McFarlane

Reproduction by PICA Colour Separation, Singapore
Printed and bound in Singapore by Kyodo Printing Co (Pte) Ltd

"If the 20th century can be characterized as the era of the industrialization of food, the 21st century may take on a different orientation. I see very contrary trends already... towards more local, diverse and less processed foods..."

Tim Lang,
Professor of Food Policy,
Thames Valley University

Contents

CENTRAL

CITY & EAST

WEST

NORTH-WEST

NORTH-EAST

SOUTH-EAST

SOUTH-WEST

Introduction by Antonio Carluccio

MY INTEREST IN food goes back a long time. I learned how to choose good food the hard way. In my teens, I wanted to contribute to the running of our large family and was often sent to the local shop for the ingredients for our evening meal. One day, I arrived home with the wrong cut of meat and my mother, an excellent cook, sent me straight back to the butcher. Reluctantly, and after much persuasion, he gave me the right cut.

With hindsight, I realise that, unbeknown to me at the time, this incident would prove to be the beginning of my gastronomic career. From that moment on, I made every effort to buy the best ingredients, always seeking out the finest produce, no matter how far I had to cycle to find it. During the summer and autumn months, my responsibility lay in preparing the dessert for our daily family meals – a dish which usually featured fruit. I took to following local farmers on my bicycle and, after a while, I knew exactly where to go for the best pears, apples, grapes, plums, peaches and chestnuts. It became a great joy to see my family's approval when I returned home with my prizes.

Sadly, I have never again tasted those divine *pesche di vigna*, small, misshapen peaches grown on little trees in vineyards, since they are not produced in quantity. Instead, precedence is given to varieties with a better yield, which are easy to cultivate, beautiful to look at, but, alas, which often taste of nothing. Fruit and vegetable growers all over the world are now geared to the demands of the supermarket buyers and the result is disappointing (albeit attractive looking) produce.

THE SUPERMARKET 'REVOLUTION'

Supermarkets claim that offering everything under one roof makes shopping easier and, they say, cheaper. Their so-called food revolution has led to the big chains being able to dictate to farmers and other suppliers what produce to provide to meet their demands. Thus, exactly the same cucumber or pepper or packet of salad leaves bought in a Cornish supermarket can also be found in the north of Scotland. Farmers, from home and abroad, cultivate huge quantities of carrots and potatoes, but they are the same size and shape and are only available in a limited range of varieties (mostly grown with high yield in mind): ultimately, quality suffers; certainly choice is limited. What is more, more often than not, prices are no cheaper than you will find in the local specialist shops. The neighbourhood greengrocer, fishmonger, butcher or cheese shop will be staffed by enthusiasts who know their suppliers and who are proud and enthusiastic about what they sell. They are usually more than willing to give advice about the taste or cooking methods for certain ingredients when asked, but try asking someone in a supermarket about which is the best potato for making mash or chips, what the difference in flavour is between a white peach and a yellow one, how to cook a parrot fish or a piece of beef topside, and you will be hard-pressed to find anyone with any knowledge (or interest) to help.

Another issue about which I feel quite strongly is the by now almost lost pleasure of eating food in season. In fact, I think we have lost all sense of seasonality when it comes to food. Roam round London's New Covent Garden wholesale market at Nine Elms at any time of the year and you get the impression of perennial seasons. Artificial cultivation, mostly in greenhouses, is to thank for this year-round availability – but at what price? Fruit and vegetables not cultivated in open-air, organic conditions rarely have much taste – who wants to eat cherries or grapes in winter if they have no taste? And which of us cannot recall that delicious sense of anticipation we felt as children when we looked forward to sun-ripened, scented summer and autumn fruits, real new potatoes or quality cheese?

This book is a showcase for London's specialist food suppliers. It will be an invaluable reference for Londoners and visitors to the city alike (whether from the UK or abroad). Dedicated lovers of good food will use it to select the very best shops for the range of produce they require. Often it is possible to shop for fruit, meat, fish and vegetables and delicatessen goods in one small area – I think of the Fulham Road area, or Turnham Green Terrace, for example – where you can find all you need in very close proximity. Or it may be necessary to travel around a bit, depending on what ingredients you are looking for.

Certainly, supermarkets will always be necessary to accommodate the huge distribution of produce of all kinds that modern society needs. But perhaps we should consider them as suppliers of certain basic ingredients only, and look elsewhere for the food we most value, for fresh and seasonal produce, handmade foodstuffs and specialities locally produced and from abroad. In the smaller, specialized and, usually, independent food shops, there is an excellent range of quality foods accompanied by, no less importantly, customer care and advice. The excitement of entering a specialist shop – whether selling cheeses from all over the world, properly kept and properly sold, or the very freshest of fish bought and sold with quality in mind, selected fruit and vegetables, not to mention perfectly reared and hung meats – is wonderful.

No other city in the world has such a variety and concentration of food shops specializing in ingredients of the world's cuisines. Decades of immigration as well as improved communication with even the remotest countries has resulted in the astonishing variety of produce available for cooks living in and visiting London. The increase in foreign travel and the interest generated by top chefs from all over the world with their cookery books and television programmes have also increased demand for ingredients unknown to the British cook a decade ago – from balsamic vinegar to galangal, cavolo nero and wasabi. Through foreign travel, people gather new impressions about culinary customs, they taste new food and see strange ingredients in the shops and markets.

Once home, they want to recreate what they have eaten abroad, and this is where the ethnic and foreign food suppliers can offer what the supermarkets cannot. Europe is not far away, and fresh, seasonal produce can often be ordered and delivered from small, individual producers on the continent. Even from the Far East, Australia and Africa, regional delicacies can easily be imported and made available.

Conversely, Britain is also gaining a reputation for good food in its own right, and many visitors from abroad visit London to shop for special items of food. The success of the Neal's Yard Dairy, for example, is, as I knew it would be from the start, overwhelming. Before it opened, even most British customers were unaware that Britain could offer such a variety of artisan cheeses, and now foodie tourists stop here en route home to France or Italy to buy a truckle of the best English stilton or cheddar. Our own shop, Carluccio's, with its own carefully selected and imported range of top Italian foods, has been very successful and has become a Mecca for lovers of real Italian food. But it did not happen overnight. It took my wife, Priscilla, and me nine hard-working years to achieve such success. The award, 'by appointment' as supplier to the royal family, is the icing on our cake.

THE AFTERMATH OF BSE

Perhaps the single most significant fact in recent years which wrought a profound change in attitudes to food production in this country was the BSE crisis which began in the early Nineties and which blighted the remainder of the decade. The consequences were catastrophic for livestock farmers in Britain. Sales of meat plummeted, the export of beef ceased entirely and is only now becoming possible again. In the interim period, during which there have also been various other food-linked crises associated with food poisoning, the food professionals and the British public have been forced to confront serious health issues. More recently, the general and widespread public aversion to genetically modified food has drawn further attention to the plethora of dangers related to cheap mass-produced food on a global scale. The result is that a new, consumer-led revolution is under way. The clamour for better quality food, more naturally produced, under sustainable conditions, for more choice and more variety (and above all, for more organic produce) can be heard from the rooftops.

One striking innovation as a reaction to this has been the emergence of farmers' markets on a national scale. Here, local suppliers sell their own produce direct to consumers. Of course, these have been a popular feature of the continental and American food scene for many years, but they are new to Britain and are springing up all over the country (they can now be found in all our main cities as well as in towns and villages the length and breadth of the land, from Inverness to Glastonbury). By the end of 1999, I'm told, there were almost 60 operating in the UK.

In the London area, new farmers' markets seem to appear weekly (see page 140 for more details of how to find one in your area). What can be more fun than being able to buy ultra-fresh ingredients for the meals ahead direct from the producers themselves? As a general rule, it is possible to find everything from meat, poultry and game to fresh, seasonal fruit and vegetables, plus cheeses and dairy produce, beers, wines, ciders and fruit cordials, not to mention home-made preserves and chocolates, bread and cakes. At a farmers' market, the eggs will be at most, two days old, not two weeks.

In the last 25 years, since I first came to London, I have seen food fashions come and go and leave their own perceptible mark. For British chefs, this has been a time to experiment with a multitude of new ingredients and a kind of wonderful 'fusion cuisine' have evolved.

I think it is sensational that a book about shops where one can buy good and special ingredients can be published at all! It would have been unthinkable 20 years ago. In the new millennium, *The Essential Guide to London's Best Food Shops* will be compulsory reading for anyone interested in good food.

Wanting to eat good food is not about snobbery or high fashion: good food is essential for good health and happy living. We owe it to ourselves to obtain not only nourishment, but also pleasure from what is one of the most important human activities. By taking just a little time to find the best produce, we really can make a difference to our own lives, and to the environment.

Happy shopping and *buon appetito*!

How to use this guide

OUR AIMS

Written for people who love good food in all its guises - from haute cuisine, French or Italian cooking, to ethnic peasant dishes – this book guides readers to the best retail suppliers in Greater London. It tells you where to go to buy quality ingredients from knowledgeable staff – whether you are looking for organic produce or not. We have also included our (doubtless controversial) list of the food shops which we would single out as the very best in London (page 14).

In the course of our researches on your behalf we have visited hundreds of retailers and dozens of markets. Our decision to include a particular entry was based on the quality of the produce on offer, its diversity, the knowledge and enthusiasm of the people running the shop or store, as well as the service it provides in areas where quality food outlets are rarer than is the case in more central parts of London.

So, while on the superficial level it may seem a little strange that a book claiming to be the essential guide to London's best food shops includes food halls ranging in style (and price) from Harvey Nichols to Wing Yip, or from Luigi's or Mortimer and Bennett to Thalad Thai, Green Street Market and Borough Market, in truth such a broad selection is completely valid to today's discerning cook or food shopper.

In many cases the shops also will sell wines and spirits, but food has been our focus in this first edition. The trend towards food-to-go (aka traiteur food or take away dishes) is on the increase - much-needed boon for the busy urban cook as are the catering facilities offered by many of these outlets.

STRUCTURE

This guide divides London into 7 sections: Central, The City and East, West, North-West, North-East, South-East and South-West.

At the beginning of each section a map gives a geographical reference to the areas covered. Each section has entries arranged alphabetically in each neighbourhood. Interspersed among the shop entries are relevant quotes from food personalities, various food features and cookery-related shops in the area.

THE MAPS

The stylised maps, which should be used in conjunction with a good London street atlas, give a general overview to the areas covered.

How to use this guide

THE ENTRIES

At the top of each main entry you will find the full name of the shop, the address, including post code, telephone and fax numbers, followed by details on opening and closing hours, public transport and payment. Alongside each entry description there are symbols which provide at-a-glance information about specialities.

THE PHOTOGRAPHS

The photographs show a selection of shops and markets which are particularly photogenic and illustrate the diversity of outlets all over London. They are not an indicator of hierarchy.

MAIL ORDER & DELIVERY SERVICES

Businesses which are exclusively mail order have been listed at the back of the book, in a separate section. All their food is either sent by post or delivered; in some cases you have the option to go and collect it yourself, but that is more unusual. Shops which offer mail order services have been listed under the main entries, and this facility has been indicated, but they are not listed in the mail order section.

INDICES

At the end of the book there is a general index of all shops, listed alphabetically, and one of all the mail order and delivery services, also listed alphabetically. There is also an index of shops listed under specialities, and the one for delicatessens and grocers has been further subdivided into various national specialities.

READERS' REPORTS

If you have any comments - good or bad - on any of the products or services provided by any of the places listed in this guide, including your opinion of the taste and quality of the product, the service, value for money and the efficiency of the mail-order service, if appropriate, we would love to hear from you. There is a Readers' Report Form at the back of the book (see page 200).

Similarly, if you would like to recommend shops not listed here for inclusion in future editions, please send full details (including name, exact postal address and telephone number).

Thank you, and happy shopping.

Christine Rista
Editor

Best in town

FRENCH

Bagatelle Boutique 52

GREEK

T. Adamou & Son 72
Athenian Grocery 18

INDIAN

V.B. & Son 130
Wembley Exotics 130

ITALIAN

I. Camisa 50
Carluccio's 29
Fratelli Camisa 31
G. Gazzano & Sons 60
Lina Stores 50
Luigi's 23

JAPANESE

Atari-Ya 113

JEWISH

Panzer's 128
Rogg's 69

MIDDLE EASTERN

Green Valley 38
Le Maroc 96
Reza Pâtisserie 88
Super Bahar 89

PORTUGUESE

Lisboa Delicatessen 97

SOUTH-EAST ASIAN

Loon Fung 26
Talad Thai 180
Wing Yip 112

SPANISH

R. Garcia & Sons 93

TURKISH

Yasar Halim 136

BAKERIES

Baker & Spice 33
& Clarke's 86
De Gustibus 38
Maison Blanc 127

Best in town

BUTCHERS

Butcher & Edmonds 56
Enzo Tartarelli 131
Frank Godfrey 136
Freeman's Butchers 113
Kingsland Master Butchers 95
C. Lidgate 84
A.S. Portwine & Son 31
Randalls 80

CHEESE SHOPS

Barstow & Barr 86
La Fromagerie 137
Neal's Yard Dairy 30
Paxton & Whitfield 47

CHOCOLATIERS

Ackermans 129
Rococo 25
Theobroma Cacao 75

COFFEE SHOPS

Algerian Coffee Stores 47
A. Angelucci 49
H.R. Higgins (Coffee Man) 41
Monmouth Coffee House 29

DELICATESSEN

The Cooler 146
Fortnum & Mason 44
Harvey Nichols 34
Limoncello 139
Mortimer & Bennett 75
Villandry 32

FISHMONGERS

Aberdeen Sea Products 154
Blagden Fishmongers 36
Chalmers & Gray 91
Condon Fishmongers 175
Cope's 79
fish! 154
H.S. Linwood 58
Steve Hatt 143

GREENGROCERS

M & C 74
Michanicou 85
The Olive Tree 120

PATISSERIES

Bagatelle Boutique 52
Harrods 34
Maison Blanc 127
Villandry 32

SPICE SHOP

The Spice Shop 102

TEA SHOPS

Fortnum & Mason 44
Harrods 34

WHOLEFOOD AND ORGANIC SHOPS

Oliver's Wholefood Store 178
Planet Organic 19
Portobello Wholefoods 101

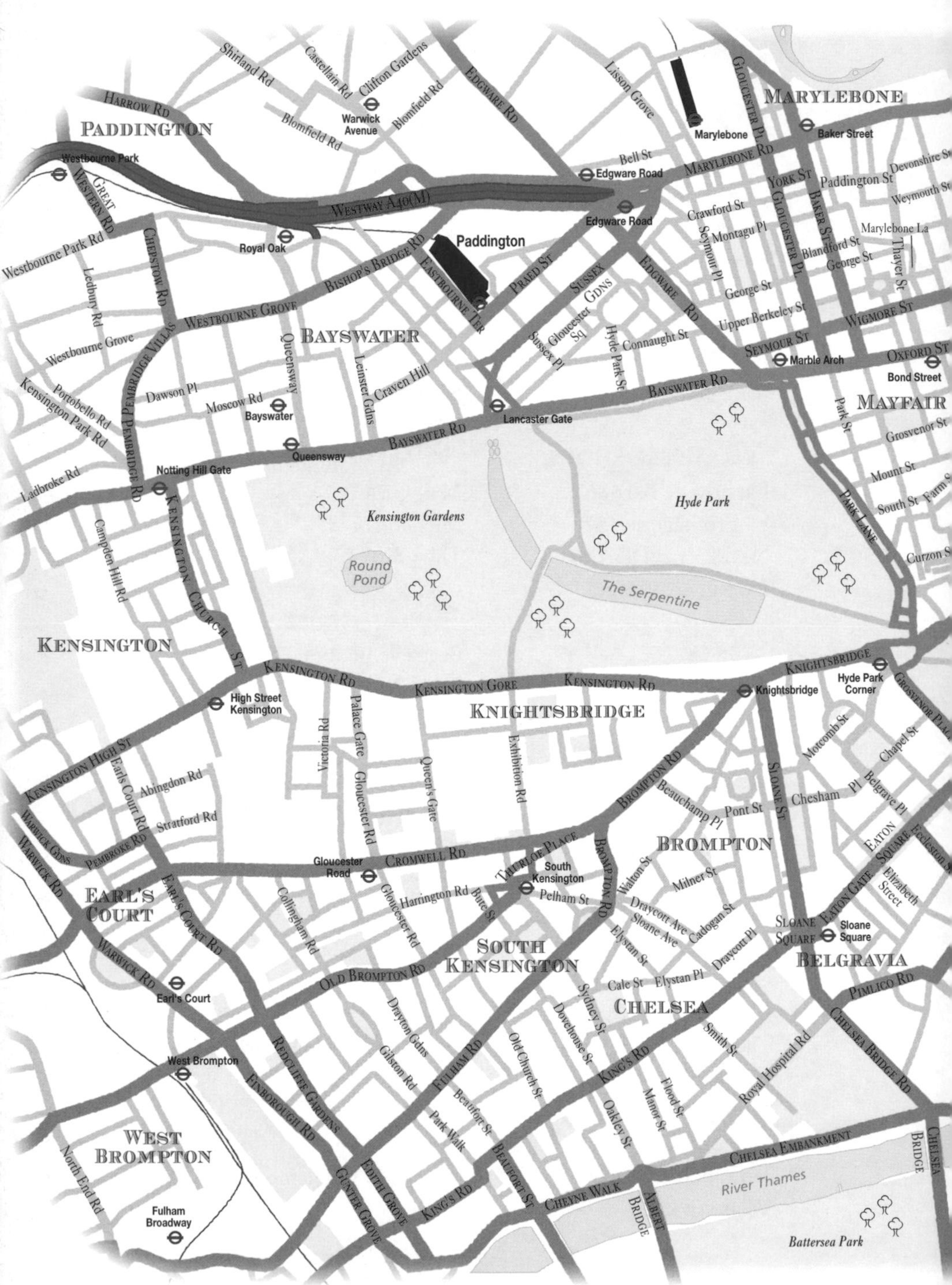

Shirland Rd
Castellain Rd
Clifton Gardens
Blomfield Rd
Edgware Rd
Lisson Grove
Gloucester Pl
Marylebone
Harrow Rd
Paddington
Warwick Avenue
Blomfield Rd
Marylebone
Baker Street
Westbourne Park
Great Western Rd
Bell St
Edgware Road
Marylebone Rd
York St
Paddington St
Devonshire St
Weymouth St
Westway A40(M)
Edgware Road
Crawford St
Gloucester Pl
Baker St
Marylebone La
Westbourne Park Rd
Royal Oak
Paddington
Seymour Pl
Montagu Pl
Blandford St
George St
Thayer St
Chepstow Rd
Ledbury Rd
Bishop's Bridge Rd
Eastbourne Ter
Praed St
Sussex Gdns
Edgware Rd
George St
Westbourne Grove
Upper Berkeley St
Wigmore St
Westbourne Grove
Bayswater
Queensway
Gloucester Sq
Sussex Pl
Hyde Park St
Connaught St
Seymour St
Marble Arch
Oxford St
Pembridge Villas
Leinster Gdns
Craven Hill
Bond Street
Portobello Rd
Kensington Park Rd
Dawson Pl
Moscow Rd
Bayswater
Bayswater Rd
Mayfair
Lancaster Gate
Park St
Grosvenor St
Pembridge Rd
Bayswater Rd
Queensway
Ladbroke Rd
Notting Hill Gate
Mount St
Hyde Park
Park Lane
South St
Kensington Gardens
Campden Hill Rd
Round Pond
The Serpentine
Curzon St
Kensington Church St
Kensington
Kensington Rd
Knightsbridge
Hyde Park Corner
Kensington Gore
Kensington Rd
Knightsbridge
High Street Kensington
Knightsbridge
Grosvenor Pl
Kensington High St
Victoria Rd
Palace Gate
Exhibition Rd
Motcomb St
Chapel St
Earls Court Rd
Abingdon Rd
Gloucester Rd
Queen's Gate
Brompton Rd
Beauchamp Pl
Chesham Pl
Belgrave Pl
Stratford Rd
Pont St
Sloane St
Warwick Gdns
Pembroke Rd
Gloucester Road
Cromwell Rd
Thurloe Place
Brompton
Eaton Square
Eccleston
Warwick Rd
South Kensington
Brompton Rd
Walton St
Milner St
Elizabeth Street
Eaton Gate
Earl's Court
Earl's Court Rd
Collingham Rd
Gloucester Rd
Harrington Rd
Bute St
Pelham St
Draycott Ave
Sloane Ave
Cadogan St
Sloane Square
Sloane Square
Elystan St
Draycott Pl
South Kensington
Belgravia
Warwick Rd
Old Brompton Rd
Earl's Court
Cale St
Elystan Pl
Pimlico Rd
Drayton Gdns
Sydney St
Chelsea
Dovehouse St
Old Church St
Smith St
Chelsea Bridge Rd
West Brompton
Redcliffe Gardens
Gilston Rd
Fulham Rd
King's Rd
Royal Hospital Rd
Finborough Rd
Beaufort St
Flood St
Manor St
Park Walk
Oakley St
Chelsea Embankment
Chelsea Bridge
West Brompton
North End Rd
Gunter Grove
Edith Grove
King's Rd
Beaufort St
Cheyne Walk
Albert Bridge
River Thames
Fulham Broadway
Battersea Park

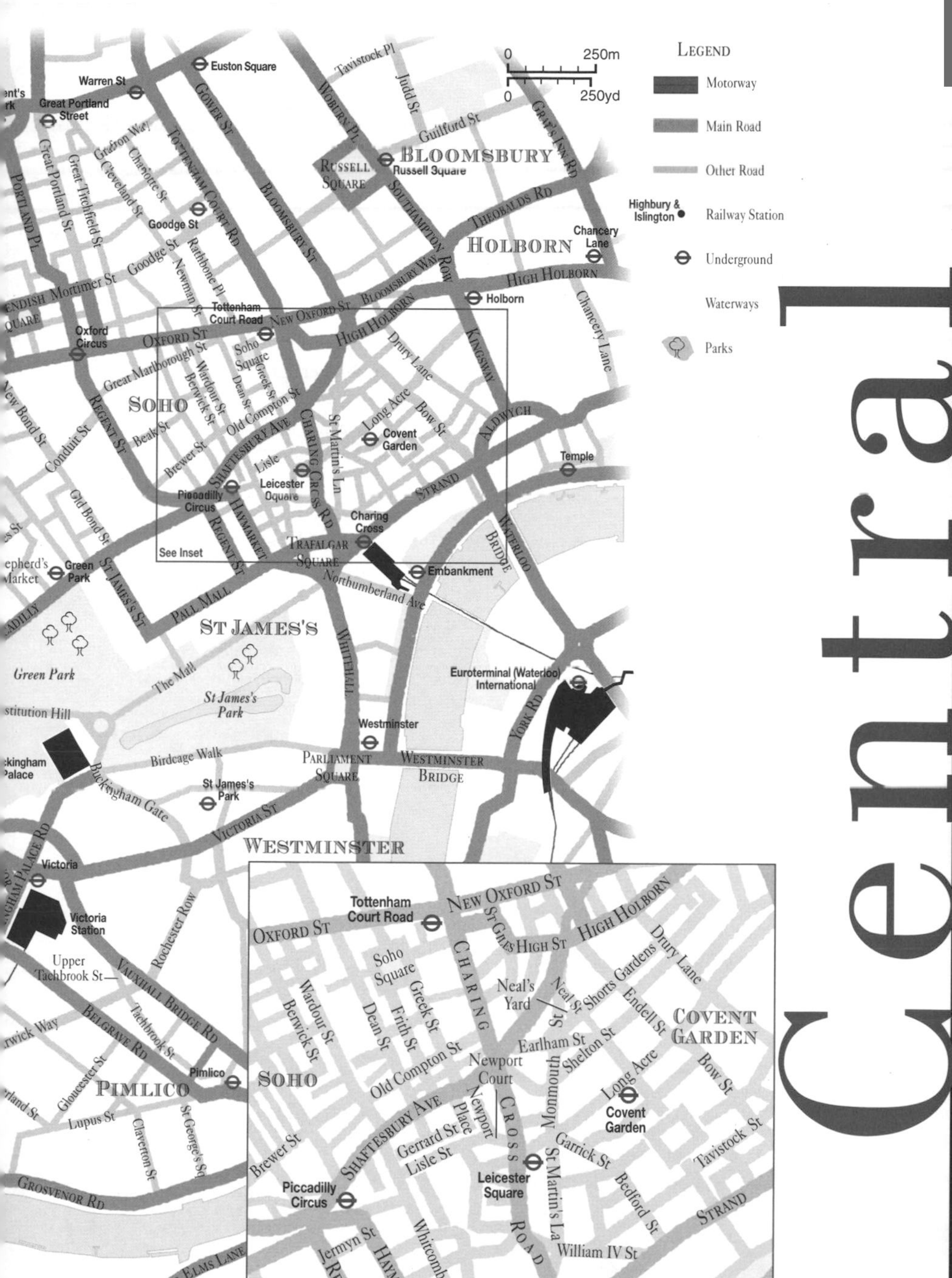
Central
LEGEND
Motorway
Main Road
Other Road
Railway Station
Underground
Waterways
Parks
Highbury & Islington
0 250m
0 250yd
Euston Square
Warren St
Great Portland Street
Tavistock Pl
Judd St
Woburn Pl
Gower St
Tottenham Court Rd
Grafton Way
Cleveland St
Charlotte St
Great Titchfield St
Great Portland St
Portland Pl
Goodge St
Rathbone Pl
Newman St
Mortimer St
Guilford St
Gray's Inn Rd
Russell Square
BLOOMSBURY
Southampton Row
Bloomsbury St
Bloomsbury Way
Theobalds Rd
HOLBORN
Chancery Lane
High Holborn
Holborn
Tottenham Court Road
New Oxford St
Oxford St
Oxford Circus
Great Marlborough St
Soho Square
Wardour St
Berwick St
Dean St
Greek St
Old Compton St
SOHO
Regent St
Conduit St
New Bond St
Beak St
Brewer St
Shaftesbury Ave
Lisle
Leicester Square
Charing Cross Rd
St Martin's Ln
Long Acre
Covent Garden
Drury Lane
Bow St
Kingsway
Aldwych
Temple
Strand
Piccadilly Circus
Haymarket
Charing Cross
Trafalgar Square
See Inset
Waterloo Bridge
Embankment
Northumberland Ave
Old Bond St
Green Park
St James's St
Pall Mall
ST JAMES'S
Whitehall
Green Park
The Mall
St James's Park
Constitution Hill
Euroterminal (Waterloo) International
York Rd
Westminster
Birdcage Walk
Parliament Square
Westminster Bridge
Buckingham Palace
Buckingham Gate
St James's Park
Victoria St
WESTMINSTER
Buckingham Palace Rd
Victoria
Victoria Station
Rochester Row
Upper Tachbrook St
Vauxhall Bridge Rd
Tachbrook St
Belgrave Rd
Warwick Way
Gloucester St
Pimlico
PIMLICO
Lupus St
Claverton St
St George's Sq
Grosvenor Rd
NINE ELMS
Nine Elms Lane
Tottenham Court Road
New Oxford St
Oxford St
St Giles High St
High Holborn
Soho Square
Charing Cross
Neal's Yard
Neal St
Shorts Gardens
Drury Lane
Endell St
COVENT GARDEN
Wardour St
Berwick St
Dean St
Frith St
Greek St
Earlham St
Shelton St
Monmouth St
Old Compton St
Newport Court
Newport Place
Long Acre
Bow St
SOHO
Covent Garden
Shaftesbury Ave
Gerrard St
Lisle St
Garrick St
Tavistock St
Brewer St
Leicester Square
St Martin's La
Bedford St
Piccadilly Circus
Strand
Jermyn St
Regent St
Haymarket
Whitcomb St
Road
William IV St
Trafalgar Square
Charing Cross

Bayswater

Greek Cypriot Grocer Delicatessen

★ ATHENIAN GROCERY

16a Moscow Road, London W2 7AX
Tel: 020 7229 6280
Open: Mon-Sat 8.30am-7pm, Sun 9.30am-1pm, Bank holidays 10am-1pm **Closed:** 25, 26 Dec.
Tube: Bayswater, Queensway
Bus: 70 **Payment:** cash, cheques

Dating from 1952 and located near the Greek Orthodox Cathedral, this popular corner shop is painted in the blue and white colours of the Greek flag. Along with Greek and Cypriot seasonal produce (figs, pomegranates and cactus fruit in early autumn, and bunches of bitter endive, which the Greek boil quickly and dress with olive oil and lemon for a salad, in summer), you'll find everything for creating Mediterranean meals - loose feta, fresh filo, haloumi, taramasalata, olive oils, breadsticks, freshly baked bread with sesame seeds, honey, coffee and good-value bunches of rocket and other salad greens. When you don't feel like cooking, try the frozen meals, such as haloumi-stuffed ravioli and olive turnovers. Manager Kimon Kyprianides proudly explains how Greeks and Greek Cypriots come from all over London and the southeast to shop here on weekdays, and from as far away as Scotland on weekends. Friendly assistants readily give advice.

Coffee

MARKUS COFFEE CO.

13 Connaught Street, London W2 2AY
Tel/Fax: 020 7723 4020
Open: Mon-Fri 8.30am-5.30pm, Sat 8.30am-1.30pm **Closed:** Sun and Bank holidays **Tube:** Marble Arch **Bus:** 6, 7, 15, 16, 16a,17, 23, 36, 98 **Payment:** cash, cheques, Amex, Delta, MasterCard, Switch, Visa
Catalogue, delivery, mail-order, retail and wholesale

A popular small coffee shop, which has been established since 1957. They offer 22 different blends, and to ensure that their coffees are supplied in the freshest and best possible condition, they roast every day, and deliver to their customers within 24 hours (sometimes even sooner). They also offer a selection of coffee-making equipment, sugars and teas.

Our aim at Planet Organic is to be the market leader in customer service, quality products and education.

Renée Elliott, founder and Managing Director of Planet Organic

Wholefood Organic Food Hall

★PLANET ORGANIC

42 Westbourne Grove, London W2 5SH
Tel: 020 7221 7171
Fax: 020 7221 1923
Open: Mon-Sat 9am-8pm, Sun 11am-5pm **Closed:** Some Bank holidays **Tube:** Bayswater **Bus:** 7, 23, 27, 70 **Payment:** cash, cheques, Delta, MasterCard, Switch, Visa
Catering, delivery service, food-to-go.

Possibly London's largest organic supermarket, Planet Organic is committed to the environment and a healthy way of life. Although not all the stock is organic, a large part of it is – vegetables, fruit, meat, fish, cheese and a variety of tinned and jarred products, as well as organic wines and beers – and the range and quality are excellent and as natural as possible. They also offer a wide range of gluten-, wheat-, yeast- and dairy-free products to suit customers with with special dietary needs. As well as good food you can also buy flowers, books, petfoods, health and beauty products and supplements (with advice on beauty and nutrition to boot), and enjoy an organic coffee or fruit juice in-store. Plans are afoot to open more branches over the coming months. Delivery is by bicycle (for those within a four-mile range).

South-East Asian Grocer

TAWANA

18-20 Chepstow Road, London W2 5BD
Tel. 020 7221 6316
Open: every day, incl. Bank holidays, 9.30am-8pm **Tube:** Bayswater, Notting Hill Gate **Bus:** 7, 28, 31, 70, 328 **Payment:** cash, cheques

The stock is extremely varied in this packed South-East Asian shop, which specializes in Thai ingredients, plus a broad stock of items from across East Asia: China, Malaysia, Indonesia, Korea, Singapore, Japan and the Philippines. Thai fresh fruit, herbs and vegetables such as jackfruit, lychees, rambutans, grass jelly, sugar cane and fresh young coconut are imported directly every Wednesday and Sunday, and so is their frozen fish. In the fridge, on the day we visited, were vegetables such as purple yams, banana leaf, chok fui, and Thai basil leaf. The range of dried fish included dried mackerel, tiny anchovies, squid and shrimps. The frozen fish was abalone, sharks fins, shrimps, squid and prawns. Also in the freezer were Chinese leeks, sping roll pastry, sweet potato leaves and some made-up dishes, mud fish, fish from Mekong valley in China and prepared fish cakes, as well as fresh tofu and noodles.

Belgravia

Chocolate

THE CHOCOLATE SOCIETY

36 Elizabeth Street,
London SW1W 9NZ
Tel: 020 7259 9222
Fax: 020 7259 9666
Open: Mon-Fri 10am-5pm, Sat 10am-3pm **Closed:** Sun and Bank holidays **Tube:** Victoria, Sloane Square **Bus:** C1 **Payment:** cash, cheques, Delta, MasterCard, Switch, Visa
Catalogue, café, catering, delivery, gift service, mail-order

This shop, which also operates as a café, is the public face of the Chocolate Society and its manufacturing and mail-order service, based in North Yorkshire. Join the society for £55, receive a badge, a hamper of chocolates and a discount on mail order - learn that chocolate really is good for you! Shelves are packed with drinking chocolate, biscuits, sauces and truffles. Chocolate bars include the full Valrhona range, and also own-label 40%, 64%, 66%, 70%, and even 100% cocoa solids styles. They also make a chocolate bar from pure Criollo cocoa beans.

Cheese shop
Delicatessen

JEROBOAMS

51 Elizabeth Street, London
SW1W 9PP
Tel: 020 7823 5623

Main shop: see Holland Park, page 83

Bloomsbury

Bakery
Cheese shop

BLOOMSBURY CHEESES

61b Judd Street, London
WC1H 9QT
Tel/Fax: 020 7387 7654
Open: Mon-Fri 10am-7pm, Sat 10am-5.30pm, Sun 10am-1.30pm **Closed:** Bank holidays **Tube:** King's Cross, Russell Square **Bus:** 10, 30, 68, 73, 91, 168, 188 **Mainline station:** King's Cross **Payment:** cash, cheques, Delta, Electron, MasterCard, Solo, Switch, Visa

A beautifully designed little shop showcasing a wonderful selection of British and French cheeses in tip-top condition; the joint venture of cheese-loving Parisian musician Christiane Ten-Hoopen and architect Hugh Cullum. Everything is both pristine and perfectly presented, from the crottins in glass-covered wooden boxes, to Mediterranean yellow and green terracotta bowls filled with glistening olives, and bags of frivolous, colourful pasta shapes hung from the pink washed walls. Apart from the olives, there is a wide range of chargrilled, bottled vegetables, principally from Seggiano, who also produce the honeys and seasonal panforte and panettone. Breads are selected as carefully as the cheeses: the best of Baker & Spice (see page 33), & Clarke (see page 86), Bakoven and St John Bakery (see page 62); as, indeed, is the small but fine range of wines supplied by Les

Caves des Pyrénées, complete with tasting notes and cheese-matching suggestions. The 7pm closing time allows King's Cross commuters and British Library readers to make a quick purchase for supper.

Chelsea

Fishmonger

BIBENDUM CRUSTACEA AND FISHMONGER

Michelin House, 81 Fulham Road, London SW3 6RD
Tel: 020 7589 0864
Open: Mon-Sat 9am-7pm
Closed: Sun **Tube:** South Kensington **Bus:** 14, 49, 345
Payment: cash, cheques, Amex, Delta, MasterCard, Switch, Visa
Bespoke delivery, catering, food-to-go

At the entrance to the Michelin building, with its wonderfully tiled forecourt, a colourful flower stall spills out on to the pavement, opposite a smart fish and shellfish stall. The most succulent oysters from France are a speciality, but superb quality seasonal fish and other crustaceans are available too.

Food Hall

BLUEBIRD FOODSTORE

350 Kings Road, London SW3 5UU
Tel: 020 7559 1153
Fax: 020 7559 1111
Open: Mon-Wed 9am-8pm, Thu-Sat 9am-9pm, Sun 12pm-6pm (Charcuterie, Traiteur and Bakery: Mon-Fri 8am-10pm, Sat 8am-9pm, Sun 12pm-6pm)
Closed: 25, 26 Dec., Easter Sunday **Tube:** Sloane Square **Bus:** 11, 19, 22, 49, 211, 319, 345 **Payment:** cash, cheques, Amex, Delta, MasterCard, Switch, Visa
Catering, local delivery, food-to-go, mail-order

Another garage conversion to add to the burgeoning Conran empire (see The Oil and Spice Shop, page 153, and Le Pont de la Tour Foodstore, page 152). This Foodstore is part of what has been christened the Bluebird Gastrodome, and indeed Bluebird is an epicurean experience for lovers of food and drink. Inspired by Sir Terence's memories of the food markets of France and Italy, it encompasses a large foodstore, a wine merchant, flower market, kitchen shop, traiteur, bakery and pâtisserie, with an outdoor fruit and vegetable market, alongside a restaurant, café, bar and private dining club. The fruit and vegetables on offer are largely organic, and come from small, often family-run, suppliers. There is a wide range of free-range, organic meats and poultry, with many preserved meats cooked in the Bluebird kitchens. Seafood is delivered daily. Fresh pasta and breads are made on the premises every day, and there is a wonderful display of seasonal cheeses (apparently over three whole wheels of Parmesan are sold every week). Own-label Bluebird jams, vinegars, oils, chocolates, biscuits, teas and wines are available, as are many daily traiteur dishes produced by executive chef Andrew Sargent and his team.

South African Delicatessen

FINNS OF CHELSEA GREEN

4 Elystan Street, London
SW3 3NS
Tel: 020 7225 0733
Open: Mon-Fri 8am-7pm, Sat 8am-2pm **Closed:** Sun and Bank holidays **Tube:** Sloane Square, South Kensington **Bus:** 11, 14, 19, 22, 49, 211, 319, 345
Payment: cash, cheques, Delta, MasterCard, Switch, Visa
Catalogue, catering, food-to-go

A gourmet food and catering business, run by Julia Bannister from a small, uncluttered shop. It has a good selection of cheeses, pickles, a variety of salts, and a few South African specialities. The principal line though, is the food-to-go, which is cooked daily in the kitchen behind the shop, using the best-quality ingredients. The catalogue lists many favourites which might be on offer depending on season and availability of ingredients, from hot and cold soups, wonderful salads, grilled and roasted vegetables, a selection of hot and cold meat and poultry dishes, sandwiches, and luscious desserts. These can be bought in situ or ordered in advance. Cold and hot canapés can enhance your drinks party, and if you're lazy, you can even get them to prepare a picnic for you, from a choice of four menus! Service is friendly, helpful and discreet.

Party cakes

JANE ASHER PARTY CAKES

24 Cale Street, London
SW3 3QU
Tel: 020 7584 6177
Fax: 020 7584 6179
Open: Mon-Sat 9.30am-5.30pm
Closed: Sun and Bank holidays
Tube: South Kensington, Sloane Square **Bus:** 11, 14, 19, 22, 211, 319 **Payment:** cash, cheques, Amex, Delta, MasterCard, Switch, Visa
Catalogue, mail-order

This cake shop to end all cake shops sells over 2,000 cakes a year, all made to order on the premises. Clients can specify the design, or choose from a portfolio, and the shop window is illustrative of the range of ideas that can be transformed into edible fantasies - from a Gucci shoe or Prada handbag, to a summer straw hat or Van Gogh self-portrait. Allow seven days for a simpler idea, up to a month for a wedding cake. The shop also provides everything you are likely to ever want or need for decorating a cake yourself - nozzles, cake boards, cutters and moulds, recipe books and candles. Personalised cakes can also be courier-delivered anywhere in the country (Intercake as opposed to Interflora).

Fishmonger

LA MARÉE

76 Sloane Avenue, London
SW3 3DZ
Tel: 020 7589 8067
Open: Mon-Sat 8am-6pm
Closed: Sun and Bank holidays
Tube: South Kensington **Bus:** 14, 49, 345 **Payment:** cash, cheques, Amex, Delta, MasterCard, Switch, Visa
Catering, food-to-go

A tiny shop which sells very fresh, high-quality fish and shellfish. They offer a variety of sea fish in season, as well as oysters, scallops, crabs, lobster, four types of Iranian caviar, smoked salmon, eel, mackerel and cod's roe. They can prepare and cook whole fish (or portions) to order: poached wild or farmed salmon or turbot, baked or roast sea bass or John Dory. There are always some home-made sauces on offer to go with your fish - tartare, dill, hollandaise or rouille - and they can also supply organic chickens and game in season.

Italian Delicatessen

★ LUIGI'S

349 Fulham Road, London
SW3 3DZ
Tel: 020 7352 7739
Open: Mon-Fri 9am-9.30pm, Sat 9am-7pm **Closed:** Sun and Bank holidays **Tube:** Fulham Broadway **Bus:** 14, 49, 345
Payment: cash, cheques, Amex, Delta, MasterCard, Switch, Visa
Catering, food-to-go

This well-established shop, owned by Luigi Molinaro from Montecatini in Tuscany, and run with the help of his friendly manager, Anna, is one of the very best Italian delis in town in terms of quality, breadth of stock and service. It has a deservedly large and loyal local customer base. The window displays fresh breads including *Pugliese, ciabatta*, corn bread, *focaccia* and the like, as well as fresh fruit, vegetables and herbs. Inside the shop, the cheese counter contains well over a dozen types of pecorino, smoked mozzarella di bufala,

Chelsea Organic Market

Duke of York's Headquarters, King's Road, London SW3
Open: Fri 10am-6pm **Tube:** Sloane Square **Bus:** 11, 19, 22, 49, 211, 319, 345

This small organic market sells mainly British produce: there are good vegetables, bread, meat, dried fruit and nuts and chocolate. Everything is organic. The same market stalls can be found in Notting Hill, on Portobello Road, under the Westway, on Thursdays, from 11am-6.30pm.

scamorza as well as the other more usual Italian cheeses. The food-to-go range, cooked on the premises, is fabulous - Italian chickens (boned, stuffed and roasted), homemade soups, roasted meat, cooked sauces and roasted vegetables. Luigi's homemade pasta sauces are a speciality and include a sensational porcini sauce. The deli meat counter is similarly impressive, with more unusual hams such as *Carpegna Prosciutto San Leo* and *San Daniele Reserva* (cured for 18 months) as well as a big range of salume, speck, bresaola, smoked pancetta and *lardo salato* (salted lard for cooking). Offcuts are sold loose for use in cooking (or for eating as is). Towards the back of the shop is the counter selling freshly made pasta (*tortelloni, ravioli*, noodles) as well as trays of marinated, roasted or grilled vegetables: artichokes, peppers, mushroom, garlic and courgettes. The wall-to-floor shelving on all sides of the shop groans with dried pasta, Italian coffee cakes, biscuits and preserves (we saw lovely jars of *Baba Positanesi* - tiny rum babas preserved in lemon liquor, a speciality of Positano). They also stock organic Italian ice cream, wines and an interesting range of liqueurs and amari.

MAISON BLANC

French
Bakery
Pâtisserie

11 Elystan Street, London
SW3 3NT
Tel: 020 7584 6913

303 Fulham Road, London
SW10 9QH
Tel: 020 7795 2663

Main shop: see St John's Wood, page 127

MEAT CITY

Butcher
Game dealer

421 Kings Road, London
SW10 0LR
Tel/Fax: 020 7352 9894
Open: Mon-Sat 7.30am-6pm
Closed: Sun and Bank holidays
Tube: Sloane Square **Bus:** 11, 22,
Payment: cash, cheques

This hidden gem at the World's End of the King's Road comes recommended by food writer, Miriam Polunin, who although a vegetarian herself has friends

HANSENS KITCHEN EQUIPMENT

306 Fulham Road, London SW10 9ER
Tel. 020 7351 6933

In the Area

From its showroom on the corner of Ifield Road, this shop and design consultancy (also known as The Chef's Shop) is aimed squarely at professionals, but will appeal to very serious amateur cooks, too. Hansens design and supply top kitchens around the country and abroad (Oxo Tower, Mirabelle, Bank to name a few). Here you will also find espresso machines, heavy-duty mincers, stainless steel tables and state-of-the-art premier range cookers.

and family who highly commend the place for the quality of the produce and friendliness of the service. Spanish-speaking purveyors of high-quality meat and game (both fur and feather), they also sell bronze turkeys and free-range geese at Christmas, and baby lamb, suckling pig, kid and Spanish foie gras to order, in season. The meat counter usually includes marinated chicken, lamb kebabs, albondigas (meatballs made with veal and pork) and chicken Kiev, all prepared daily on the premises. Around Christmas, in addition to quality serrano ham, they also stock Lacon Gallego (cured shoulder of pork on the bone). Spanish sausages for cooking include morcilla, chorizo (hot and mild), fuet and even sobrasada de Mallorca (a soft, paprika-flavoured pork sausage for spreading on bread). Spanish cheeses include tetilla, Cabrales and manchego. The shelves in the mini-market area groan with jars of preserves from France, Spain, and Italy, as well as a useful array of dried, tinned and packeted goods.

Chocolate

★ ROCOCO
321 Kings Road, London SW3 5EP
Tel: 020 7352 5857
Fax: 020 7352 7360
Open: Mon-Sat 10am-6.30pm, Sun 12am-5pm **Tube:** South Kensington, Sloane Square **Bus:** 11, 19, 22, 49, 211, 319, 345
Payment: cash, cheques, Amex, Delta, Electron, JCB/Solo, MasterCard, Switch, Visa (minimum £10 spend)
Catalogue, mail-order

Owned and run by Chantal Coady since 1983, this chocolate shop is possibly the most interesting in London. Small, with an original Victorian frontage, it is stocked from floor to ceiling with all sorts of chocolate and chocolate delicacies, many produced in their kitchens in Vauxhall. For their own-brand products, the chocolate used is Valrhona Grand Cru, and you can buy it in rough-hewn bars for cooking or in chocolate bars for eating; choose from Manjari (pure Criollo, 64% cocoa solids), Guanaja (a blend of 4 beans, 70%) or Caraïbe (pure Trinitario, 66%). Many of their chocolate bars are flavoured with organic essential oils, such as cardamom, juniper and lavender; the best-seller amongst customers is orange and geranium, but another great favourite, perhaps surprisingly, is chilli pepper! You can also buy made-up boxes of chocolates or fresh cream truffles, beautifully packaged, or chocolate dragées, almonds, raisins and coffee beans, Valrhona cocoa powder and, at Christmas and Easter (when they are extraordinarily busy), marrons glacés and candied fruit.

Chinatown

Chinese
Bakery
Pâtisserie

FAR EAST

13 Gerrard Street, London
W1V 7LJ
Tel: 020 7437 6148
Open: Mon-Sun 10.30am-7pm
Tube: Leicester Square **Bus:** 14, 19, 22, 24, 29, 38, 176 **Mainline station:** Charing Cross **Payment:** cash, cheques

On the main drag in Chinatown, this unassuming looking Chinese bakery claims to offer some of the freshest and most delicious traditional Chinese cakes and pastries in London, and the huge number of regulars that visit the shop seem to be evidence to this fact. The cakes, buns and rolls are all simply stacked on baking trays in the window and along the counter. The most popular with westerners is the mooncake, a sweet bun made from lotus seed and red bean, with a salted duck egg in the middle. There are pork rolls, curry puffs, coconut buns (which literally melt in the mouth), crusted red bean rolls and raisin toasts. At the weekends there are more varieties of cake to choose from. During the day the bakery doubles as a tea-shop, and at night it turns into a restaurant.

Chinese
Grocer
Greengrocer

GOLDEN GATE GROCERS

16 Newport Place, London
WC2H 7JS
Tel: 020 7437 6266
Open: Mon-Sun 10am-8pm
Closed: Bank holidays **Tube:** Leicester Square **Bus:** 14, 19, 22, 24, 29, 38, 176 **Payment:** cash, cheques, Amex, MasterCard, Switch (£10 minimum), Visa

There is another branch of this grocer in Lisle Street, just around the corner, and both sell mainly Chinese products, though they also stock South-East-Asian spice pastes. They are a major stockist of exotic fruits - durian, mangosteen, fresh longans and lychees and carambola - and seasonal tropical vegetables like green carrots, ridged gourds, bitter melons, Taiwanese bok-choy and other greens that do not have English names.

Branch: 14 Lisle Street, London
WC2H 7BE
Tel: 020 7437 0014

Chinese
Food Hall

★ LOON FUNG

42-44 Gerrard Street, London
W1V 7LP
Tel: 020 7437 7332
Fax: 020 7439 1585

Shopping in Chinatown

TERRY TAN

The hub of shopping activity in London's Chinatown centres on Gerrard Street, spilling out on to Gerrard Place, Newport Place and Lisle Street mainly. Here the 'Big Five' are Loon Fung, See Woo Hong, Golden Gate, Loon Moon and Newport Supermarket.

At first glance, to the western eye, they all seem to stock much the same Chinese products, seemingly arranged higgledy-piggledy and with no particular order in mind. This is one aspect of ethnic supermarkets that can be a bugbear for people not familiar with the culinary culture, but thankfully seems to be slowly coming to some sort of order. Vegetables and fruits spilling out on to the pavement have almost become a characteristic of the area, and this has become a draw in itself.

Loon Fung is the largest and busiest of the group, with its focus squarely on Chinese products. The two branches of Golden Gate (one in Lisle Street, one in Newport Place, just around the corner), are basically smaller versions of Loon Fung, though with more emphasis on South-East Asian products. See Woo also sells some Vietnamese ingredients, and Loon Moon claims to specialise in foods from virtually the whole of South-East Asia and the South Pacific! The Newport Supermarket, although the smallest of the group, does stock some items unobtainable elsewhere.

Dotting Gerrard Place and at the end of Newport Place, are little Chinese teashops that sell Chinese pastries, cakes, fresh dumplings like char siu pow, siu mai, curry puffs, chiffon pandan cakes, beancurd jellies, lotus seed and red bean paste buns.

Open: Mon-Sat 10am-8pm, Sun 10am-4pm **Closed:** Bank holidays **Tube:** Leicester Square **Bus:** 14, 19, 22, 24, 29, 38, 176 **Payment:** cash, cheques, MasterCard, Switch (£5 minimum), Visa

The focus here is squarely on Chinese products with the addition of a resident butcher, but pork and pork spare parts are the only meats available. The way pork is cut by Chinese butchers differs radically from the British way, and you get spare ribs and streaky belly slices with the ratio of fat and thin in the correct balance. Offal including spleen, heart, lungs and even coagulated blood is available, as it is integral to much Chinese cooking. There is a wide range of processed fish products ranging from fish balls to fish cakes, squid balls and shellfish; frozen fish and shellfish are imported, as are rare vegetables and fruits. A separate section stocks a bewildering variety of spice pastes, dry noodles, flours, sauces, canned pickles, dried spices, Chinese utensils and crockery.

Branch: see Tottenham page 147, Wembley page 130

South-East Asian Greengrocer Grocer

NEW LOON MOON

9a Gerrard Street, London W1V 7LJ
Tel: 020 7734 3887
Fax: 020 7439 8880
Open: Mon-Sun 10.30am-8pm
Closed: 25, 26 Dec. **Tube:** Leicester Square **Bus:** 14, 19, 22, 24, 29, 38, 176 **Mainline Station:** Charing Cross **Payment:** cash, cheques, Delta, MasterCard, Switch, Visa
Bespoke delivery

Right across from Loon Fung in Gerrard Place, this little food hall boldly advertises that it specialises in Malaysian, Chinese, Japanese, Korean, Vietnamese and Filipino products. And they deliver on that promise, for it is the best place for such esoterics as water convolvulus, fresh turmeric, pandanus leaves, Vietnamese salad greens, Filipino spice pastes and pickles, processed Thai curry pastes, a wide range of tofu products, Korean kimchee and Malaysian sambals and korma pastes.

Chinese Grocer Greengrocer

NEWPORT SUPERMARKET

28-29 Newport Court, London WC2H 7PQ
Tel: 020 7437 2386
Open: Mon-Sun 10.30am-8pm
Closed: 25, 26 Dec. **Tube:** Leicester Square **Bus:** 14, 19, 22, 24, 29, 38, 176 **Payment:** cash only

This, basically a scaled-down version of Loon Fung (see page 26), is the smallest of the Chinatown food shops. Like all the others, it has a wide range of Chinese canned vegetables and fruits, pickles, snacks and biscuits. They do, however, also stock unusual items like pickled sour bamboo shoots, fresh tropical fruits and vegetables, herbs and other aromatics.

Chinese Vietnamese Grocer Greengrocer

SEE WOO HONG

19 Lisle Street, London WC2H 7BA
Tel: 020 7439 8325 or 020 7734 4468
Open: Mon-Sun 10am-8pm
Closed: 25 Dec. **Tube:** Leicester Square **Bus:** 14, 19, 24, 29, 38, 176 **Payment:** cash, cheques, Delta, Electron, Switch

With a purple façade and no visible English name, this shop is similar to many others in Chinatown, but also sells a select range of Vietnamese canned pickles, processed fish products, sauces, and hard-to-find vegetables such as Chinese chive flowers, jungle beans and sweet turnips (vital in spring rolls). They sell fresh galangal and lemongrass, plus a range of fresh red and green chillies. Downstairs you will find steamers, woks of various sizes and even Taoist artefacts.

Covent Garden

Italian Delicatessen

★ CARLUCCIO'S

28a Neal Street, London
WC2H 9PS
Tel: 020 7240 1487
Fax: 020 7497 1361
Open: Mon-Sat 11am-7pm, Sun noon-6pm **Closed:** Bank holidays. **Tube:** Covent Garden **Bus:** 14, 19, 24, 29, 38, 176 **Payment:** cash, cheques, Amex, Delta, Electron, MasterCard, Solo, Switch, Visa
Catering, food-to-go, mail-order service

Possibly the prettiest Italian deli in town, and a cornucopia of all delicious things Italian. Most are exclusively imported from the various regions, and personally selected by the owners, Priscilla and Antonio Carluccio. The high-quality fare includes dried mushrooms, fresh wild mushrooms (in season), Parma ham, speck, salume, aged Parmesans, organic fruits, vegetables and herbs, a huge variety of pasta, extra virgin olive oils, balsamic vinegars, sauces (including a sweet syrup, Saba, made from the reduced must of the Trebbiano grape), rice and confectionery. There is an excellent range of freshly baked Italian breads, just inside the door, opposite a tasting table usually featuring a variety of oils. They produce a Christmas gift catalogue and a year round mail order service of their seasonal wares, and offer attractively wrapped foodie gift ideas, boxes and hampers.

Coffee

★ MONMOUTH COFFEE HOUSE

27 Monmouth Street, London
WC2H 9DD
Tel: 020 7836 5272
Fax: 020 7240 8524
Open: Mon-Sat 9am-6.30pm
Closed: Sun and some Bank holidays, 25, 26 Dec., 1 Jan. **Tube:** Covent Garden, Tottenham Court Road **Bus:** 14, 19, 24, 29, 38, 176 **Payment:** cash, cheques, Amex, Delta, MasterCard, Switch, Visa
Catalogue (with Neal's Yard Dairy), mail-order

The shop is labelled 'House', but trades in a wholesale sense as the Monmouth Coffee Company, supplying most of London's restaurants - and many further afield - with delicious and unusual coffees. Their wares are available to the public as well: you can buy freshly roasted and ground beans, to taste in the little sampling room at the back, or to drink an espresso or cappuccino in the café. They

ELIZABETH DAVID COOKSHOP
3 North Row, Covent Garden WC2E 8RA
Tel. 020 7836 9167

Attractive, if slightly cramped, two-floor shop in the heart of Covent Garden market. Packed with culinary gadgets, cookbooks, tableware and utensils.

offer around ten to twelve varieties of beans, and a few basics are always available (single estates from Costa Rica, Colombia and Kenya, say). A speciality, though, is seeking out coffees with a difference, perhaps a small crop from somewhere more unusual, which will sell out fairly quickly. One of these is southern Ethiopian beans, from a small town called Yirgacheffe; the locals pick the beans from the wild - coffee is thought to have originated in this part of the world - then clean and process them in situ. Another potential buy could perhaps be the most expensive coffee in the world: the beans grow in the cleared jungles of St Helena, in the middle of the Atlantic, hundreds of miles from anywhere. Chocolates made near Lyons can be bought in the winter months.

British
Bakery
Organic

NEAL'S YARD BAKERY

6 Neal's Yard, London
WC2H 9DP
Tel: 020 7836 5199
Fax: 020 7379 1544
Open: Mon-Sat 10.30am-5pm
Closed: Sun and Bank holidays
Tube: Covent Garden **Bus:** 14, 19, 24, 29, 38, 176 **Payment:** cash only

A wonderful, primarily whole-wheat, bread shop in the centre of Covent Garden's alternative health quarter. Everything including a three-seed loaf (sesame, linseed and poppy) and cheese and herb loaf is hand-baked on the premises daily, using the highest quality materials, free-range eggs and organic flours and vegetables. There is a characterful tea-room above the bakery in which you can have lunch or tea, or buy a snack to take away.

> "BSE was the single event that made everyone think about the food we eat and where it comes from."
>
> Patrick Holden,
> director of the Soil Association

Branch: see Borough, page 156

British
Cheese shop

★ NEAL'S YARD DAIRY

17 Short's Gardens, London
WC2H 9AT
Tel: 020 7379 7646
Fax: 020 7240 2442
Open: Mon-Sat 9am-7pm, Sun 10am-5pm **Closed:** Bank holidays **Tube:** Covent Garden
Bus: 14, 19, 24, 29, 38, 176
Payment: Delta, MasterCard, Switch, Visa
Export, mail-order, wholesale

This is one of the country's finest and most famous cheese shops, stocking almost exclusively British cheeses which are unpasteurised - a passion of the owner, Randolph Hodgson, a former chairman of the Specialist Cheesemakers' Association. All the cheeses - among them Cheddar, Lancashire, Double Gloucester and a host of lesser-known varieties - are hand-made on farms throughout the country, using traditional methods, and they are often selected and bought directly from the farms by the Dairy. Many of the cheeses are matured and ripened in the Dairy's own cellars in Borough (where there is a second Neal's Yard Dairy). The shop also sells cream, yoghurt, butter and bread, fresh northern oatcakes and fabulous cheese straws from & Clarke's (see page 86). Service is immaculate and informed, and you can have a taste before you decide. You can buy wholesale - one visitor saw an Italian buy a whole Stilton here to take home! - and there is an excellent world-wide mail-order service.

Branch: see Borough, page 156

Pâtisserie

PÂTISSERIE VALERIE
8 Russell Street WC2 5HZ
Tel: 020 7240 0064

Main shop: see Soho, page 51

British
Butcher
Organic

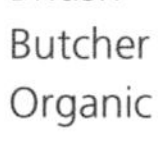

★ A.S. PORTWINE & SON
24 Earlham Street,
London WC2H 9LN
Tel: 020 7836 2353
Fax: 020 7813 0313
Open: Tue-Thu 7.30am-5pm, Fri 7.30am-5.30pm, Mon and Sat, 7.30am-2pm **Closed:** Sun and Bank holidays **Tube:** Covent Garden, Leicester Square **Bus:** 14, 19, 24, 29, 38, 176 **Payment:** cash, cheques, Amex, Delta, Diners, MasterCard, Switch, Visa
Wholesale

Graham Portwine claims this is the oldest butcher's shop in London still trading in the original family. It specialises in British free-range, organic and drug-free meats, many of which are from pure and rare breeds. Meaty joys are endless, and they include beef from Scotland, lamb and real mutton (ideal for Middle Eastern dishes and bought by the Tunisian restaurant round the corner), bacon cured in a variety of ways and with a variety of tantalising flavours, chickens, turkeys, ducks, and a legion of sausages, including haggis, *boudin blanc* and black pudding.

Fitzrovia

Italian
Delicatessen

★ FRATELLI CAMISA
53 Charlotte Street, London W1P 1LA
Tel: 020 7255 1240
Open: Mon-Wed, Fri-Sat 9am-6pm, Thurs 9am-2pm **Closed:** Sun and Bank holidays
Tube: Goodge Street **Bus:** C2, 10, 24, 29, 73, 134, 135
Payment: cash, cheques, JCB, MasterCard, Solo, Switch, Visa
Catalogue, delivery, mail-order, website

The first Fratelli Camisa (now alas gone) was established in

1929, in Soho, and now the family serves Fitzrovia its especial blend of all things Italian. Boxes of loose sun-dried tomatoes and fried porcini perfume the air. The stock ranges from fresh cheeses (provolone, taleggio, Parmesan, grana padano, and buffalo mozzarella among them), fresh pastas, home-made sauces, olives, breads, sausages and salume, to tins and jars of pesto and artichokes and bottles of aged balsamic vinegar and various grades of olive oil. At Christmas the shop is festooned with boxes of panettone and other festive Italian delights. Occasionally, you can find such esoteric items as Parmesan cheese cutters; a Camisa paperback cookery book is also available. The service is friendly and helpful, and there are good sandwiches on offer at lunchtime.

French Food Hall

★ VILLANDRY

170 Great Portland Street, London W1N 5TB
Tel: 020 7631 3131
Fax: 020 7631 3030
Open: Mon-Sat 8.30am-10pm, Sun 11am-4pm **Tube:** Great Portland Street **Bus:** C2, 7, 8, 10, 25, 55, 73, 98, 135, 176 **Payment:** cash, cheques, Amex, Delta, MasterCard, Switch, Visa.
Catering, food-to-go, mail-order, restaurant

From smaller beginnings in Marylebone High Street, Villandry, one of London's best, mainly French, delis has become a large and irresistible operation. Jean-Charles Carrarini is a restless seeker after the finest, most striking produce that Europe, the States, and occasionally the Southern Hemisphere, have to offer. At least 50% of the produce is now organic, and ranges from beech-smoked goose breast, Italian salume, French pâtés and rillettes (don't miss the wide range of charcuterie from Cougard in Brittany) via unique lines of dairy produce (sheep's milk drain-it-yourself faiselle, and sheep's milk yoghourt with chestnut purée) to crispbreads, biscuits and confectionery of British, French, German and Australian origin. There is a good, exclusive range of 'Bonneterre' frozen ready-meals, though the pride and joy of the organic range must be the fresh fruit and vegetables delivered from France on Thursdays (soon to be twice a week). Non-organic ranges tend to be of sound artisanal origin and scarcely less desirable: impeccable cheeses from Philippe Olivier, wood-smoked harengs doux from La Tréport, wonderful smoked tuna, kipper and wild salmon fillets from the Woodcock smokery in Cork. The fresh bread and pâtisserie that tempt passers-by via the plate glass window are largely baked on the premises; the apple feuilletées and frangipane fruit tarts have won wide acclaim. Prices are steep, and stock is volatile, but each visit offers the excitement of a fresh discovery.

Knightsbridge

Bakery
Delicatessen
Pâtisserie

★ BAKER & SPICE

46 Walton Street, London SW3 1RB
Tel: 020 7589 4734
Fax: 020 7823 9148
Open: Mon-Sat 7am-7pm, Sun 8.30am-2pm (reduced hours on bank holidays) **Closed:** Easter Bank holiday, 3 weeks in August, 1 week at Christmas
Tube: Knightsbridge, South Kensington **Bus:** C1, 14, 49, 74, 345 **Payment:** cash, cheques, Delta, Switch, Visa
Catering, food-to-go

This extremely popular bakery-cum-traiteur was established by Gail Stephens in 1995, but the two gigantic, subterranean, brick baking ovens have been in situ since 1902, still miraculously operating after only a few modifications, and where all the food of the shop is cooked or baked daily (and nightly). Dan Lepard is the master baker here, and he is passionate about bread and all its possibilities. His sourdough breads, some flavoured with caramelised garlic, some with potato and rosemary, have become the shop's speciality, many of the recipes researched in the British Library. Also on sale are wonderful croissants, Parmesan-and-pistachio biscuits, foot-long cheese straws, fig, plum or pear tarts, muffins, Danishes, chocolate-and-pecan and carrot-and-walnut cakes. Food to take away, currently with a Middle Eastern slant, is prepared on the premises daily, the organic, seasonal ingredients bought by Gail Stephens, mostly at New Covent Garden Market. Available on the day of our visit were wild rice and other salads, chicken legs in rosemary, baked peppers, baked squashes and a variety of home-made soups. You can eat on the premises (there are three minuscule tables with chairs on the pavement outside the shop) or take away; buy some of their jams, coffees or olive oils, or ask them to prepare you a feast for a reception (they'll even rent the marquee for you). Gail Stephens is planning to open another branch in Queen's Park in the next few months.

Belgian
Pâtisserie
Bakery

DE BAERE

5-6 William Street, London SW1X 9HL
Tel: 020 7235 4040

Main shop: see Notting Hill, page 91

Food Hall

★ HARRODS

Brompton Road, London
SW1X 7XL
Tel: 0207 730 1234
Fax: 0207 893 8945/581 0470
Open: Mon, Tue, Sat 10am-6pm, Wed, Thu, Fri 10am-7pm
Closed: Sun and Bank holidays
Tube: Knightsbridge **Bus:** 14, 19, 22, 52, 74, 137, C1 **Payment:** cash, cheques, Amex, Delta, Harrods card, MasterCard, Visa

Bespoke delivery, bespoke hampers and picnics, catalogue, catering, food advisory service, food-to-go, mail-order

This mammoth Knightsbridge department store is famous the world over, and has been situated in the Brompton Road since 1849. Like Fortnum & Mason, it originated as a grocer rather than as a draper, which emphasises that food, then and now, is a major player in the success and profitability of the business. The store holds three Royal Warrants, one of which is Suppliers of Provisions and Household Goods to Her Majesty the Queen. The Food Hall itself, covering a major part of the ground floor (nearly 24,000 square feet), is magnificent, boasting wall and ceiling decorations, light fittings and Doulton tiles, many of which date from the turn of the century. The displays of foods are spectacular and colourful, particularly that of wet fish, which incorporates a new design every day. It is all a feast for the eyes, as well as for the shopping basket, with over 350 types of cheese on offer, 150 types of bread, 150 varieties of tea (many single estate garden teas), wines and spirits, charcuterie, smoked fish, pastas, exotic fruits and vegetables. Scottish beef is available, as well as venison and lamb, some of it from the chairman's Belugavan estate. There are treats galore, many of which can be packaged especially as gifts. Enjoy a break in your shopping day by having a snack or meal at one of Harrods' nineteen bars and restaurants.

Food Hall

★ HARVEY NICHOLS

Knightsbridge, London
SW1X 7RJ
Tel: 020 7235 5000
Fax: 020 7235 5020
Open: Mon-Tue, Thu-Sat 10am-7pm, Wed 10 am-8pm, Sun 12pm-6pm **Tube:** Knightsbridge
Bus: C1, 14, 19, 22, 52, 74, 137
Payment: cash, cheques, Amex, Diners, Electron, JCB, MasterCard, Solo, Switch, Visa

Christmas hamper brochure, delivery, food-to-go, mail-order, picnic hampers

Now one of the sights of foodie London, the food store, on the very top of the building, is a mecca for wonderful food treats. Laid out on metal display racks beneath acres of piping are esoteric packets and jars of sauces and relishes, pastas and noodles, grains and oils, from every corner of the earth. Many of the products are sold under Harvey Nichols' own label, and are beautifully packaged. For the lazy or novice cook, there are 'kits' for dishes such as risotto and *pasta e fagioli.* A serious wine shop at one end abuts a sushi bar with moving counter; the perimeter of the room is lined with bread, fish, charcuterie and fresh meat counters; butchers are on hand to cut joints to order. Huge baskets of fruit and vegetables, all good quality and many organic, form a colourful display at one side, with an impressive array of wild mushrooms, in season. Have a coffee before you fight your way down the escalators (or, better still, use the express lift), or enjoy a meal at the rated Fifth Floor Restaurant.

Italian Delicatessen

LA PICENA

5 Walton Street, London SW3 2JD
Tel: 020 7823 9971
Fax: 020 7589 4993
Open: Mon-Fri 7am-7pm, Sat 7.30am-7pm, Sun 8am-6pm **Closed:** Christmas and Easter holidays **Tube:** Knightsbridge, South Kensington **Bus:** C1, 14, 49, 74, 345 **Payment:** cash, cheques, Amex, Delta, MasterCard, Switch, Visa
Catering, food-to-go

Lina de Angelis hails from Ascoli La Picena, and named her shop after her home town when she opened in 1974. With her faithful aides, Maria and her husband, Antonio (who have been with her for over 20 years), she does all the buying and runs this friendly deli and traiteur with enormous pleasure and pride. The front window displays the butchery side of the business, with Italian favourites such as fresh calves' liver, breaded veal escalopes, chicken Kiev, veal chops, veal roast, *osso buco* and free-range chicken. As well as stocking all the usual ingredients for Italian cooking, their excellent homemade pasta sauces include pesto, fiery arrabiatta (with and without radicchio), vongole, bolognese, plus mushroon-with-porcini and a walnut sauce. Seasonal fruit and vegetables are imported from Italy (look out for the small peaches in mid-summer) and there is a small, but high-quality range of salad ingredients including vine tomatoes, radicchio, endive and chicory. Downstairs the fridges groan with food-to-go for the busy city-dweller: stuffed aubergines and peppers, cannelloni, lasagne, gnocchi, sausage stew, cooked chicken, a variety of salads and finger foods. All the meat and cooked dishes are prepared daily by Antonio.

French Pâtisserie

PÂTISSERIE VALERIE

25 Brompton Road, London SW3 2EJ
Tel: 020 7823 9971

Main shop: see Soho, page 51

Marylebone

Sausages

BIGGLES

66 Marylebone Lane, London W1M 5FF
Tel: 020 7224 5937
Open: Mon 10am-2pm, Tue-Fri 9.30am-6pm, Sat 9.30am-4.30pm **Closed:** Sun and Bank holidays **Tube:** Bond Street **Bus:** 6, 7, 10, 12, 13, 15, 23, 73, 94, 98, 113, 135, 137, 139, 159, 189 **Mainline station:** Marylebone
Payment: cash, cheques, Delta, MasterCard, Switch, Visa
Delivery depending on quantity; special orders with notice

Colin Bailey, the owner of one of central London foodies' favourite haunts, makes his sausages in the basement of this small shop just minutes from bustling Oxford Street. Since 1989 he has built up a following of loyal customers, especially ex-pat South Africans who come specifically for his boerewors - they say it's the best in town. Bailey claims to be the only sausage-maker in London not to use bread additives or MSG in his recipes, which are also gluten-free. They capture the flavours of almost every sausage-producing country in the world. Garlic-flavoured Toulouse sausages are popular, but you also find traditional British bangers, along with Greek, Hungarian, American, Italian, French and Middle Eastern varieties. If you have a long trip home, look for the frozen ones.

★ BLAGDEN FISHMONGERS

Fishmonger
Game
Dealer

65 Paddington Street, London W1M 3RR
Tel/Fax: 020 7935 8321
Open: Mon-Fri 7.30am-5pm, Sat 7.30am-1pm **Closed:** Sun and Bank holidays **Tube:** Baker Street **Bus:** 2, 13, 18, 27, 30, 74, 82, 113, 139, 189, 274 **Payment:** cash, cheques
Delivery, free recipes and advice

A mouth-watering display of a multitude of fish, nicely iced and parsleyed, is open to Paddington Street, an ice-machine churning noisily away inside. This stands next to the long chilled counter, usually holding a selection of game birds (including grouse in August, as the shop is a licensed game dealer), free-range chickens or ducks, free-range eggs, quails' and gulls' eggs, Loch Fyne and Manx kippers and huge tubs of peeled

ANYTHING LEFTHANDED

57 Brewer Street, London W1R 3FB
Tel: 020 7437 3910

In the Area

Amid the quirky implements and gadgets that fill this shop you will find a good selection specifically designed for left-handed cooks. They cater for all the areas where one would expect a left-handed person to encounter difficulties, ranging from corkscrews to peelers and grapefruit knives. There is a range of fish-knives and ladels, as well as pastry slicers, can-openers and kitchen scissors.

shrimps. The fish are on offer seasonally, and they include Scottish salmon, Colchester oysters, Salcombe crabs, West Country mackerel ('best when gooseberries are about') and Suffolk and Norfolk geese, guinea fowl and turkey. This is one of the few place you can find samphire in season, and they also offer a selection of French fish soups in jars, as well as rouille, dill sauce and salmon roe. A monthly newsletter always includes a favourite recipe or two.

Chocolate Wedding cakes

CHOCCYWOCCYDOODAH
47 Harrowby Street,
London W1H 5HF
Tel/Fax: 020 7724 5465
Open: Tue 10.30am-6pm, Wed-Fri 11am-7pm, Sat 10am-6pm **Closed:** Mon, Sun and Bank holidays **Tube:** Edgware Road, Marble Arch **Bus:** 6, 7, 15, 16, 23, 36, 98 **Payment:** cash, cheques
Nationwide deliveries for wedding cakes, catalogue

A shop that relies on (rapidly growing) reputation rather than passing trade – though easily found off the Edgware Road, it is not located on any shopping thoroughfare – Choccywoccydoodah is well worth a visit, if only to see the fantastic display of doric-column based fantasy wedding cakes. You can, meanwhile, drink in the wonderful Belgian chocolate aroma, nibble on a violet-rum cream and walk away

Church Street Market

Open: Tue-Sat 9am-5pm **Closed**: Sun, Mon, Bank holidays **Tube:** Edgware Road **Bus:** 6, 7, 8, 15, 16, 16a, 23, 36, 98

Although not far from Regent's Park and Madame Tussaud's, very few tourists come to this good value local street market, and its buyers are principally locals from the estates off Lisson Grove and Arabs who have made their homes around Edgware Road. During the week, several fruit and veg stalls congregate at the Edgware Road end, but on Fridays and Saturdays there can be over 200 stalls selling fruit, vegetables, cheap packeted and tinned foods, wholefoods such as dried pulses, fruit and nuts, plants and herbs, spankingly fresh fish and raw or cooked shellfish. You can also find general household goods and bric-à-brac.

WORTH A DETOUR

The Sea Shell, 49-51 Lisson Grove, Tel: 020 7723 8703 - best fish and chips in London with a bag of truffles (Belgian truffles are imported, British style chocolates – rose and violet creams, Bucks fizz truffles and white chocolate coated ginger – are home-made at the Brighton base). But wedding cakes and favours are the thing, and the selection process is aided by a plush red-cushioned sofa, and glass coffee table strewn with lifestyle magazines. 'Towering Rococo tiers, baroque cherubic fantasies, decadent gothic gargoyles, rose strewn country garden columns' are all illustrated, as described, in the colourful catalogue but seem even more improbable and imposing in 3-dimension reality. The cakes are made entirely of chocolate, the centre a ganache-layered, dense chocolate cake, sculptural elements white and dyed chocolate, and are the work of Christine Taylor, a graphic designer by training. Her wedding favours display similar wit in design, and include plenty with child appeal.

Branch: 27 Middle Street, Brighton, Sussex BN1 1AL

Bakery

★ DE GUSTIBUS

53 Blandford Street,
London W1H 3AF
Tel/Fax: 020 7486 6608
Open: Mon-Fri 7am-4.30pm, Sat 9am-3pm **Closed:** Sun and Bank holidays **Tube:** Baker Street **Bus:** 2, 13, 30, 74, 82, 113, 139, 189, 274 **Payment:** cash, cheques
Food-to-go

Dan Schickentanz is a name to reckon with in the world of bread. Passionate about sourdough, he started selling his loaves from an Oxford stall, and from there he has progressed to supplying some of the finest restaurants in the country with bread (Raymond Blanc was one of the first to show and voice his appreciation). We can enjoy his breads at market stalls still - notably at Borough Market (see page 158.) and various food fairs - but his superb breads (baked in Abingdon, Oxfordshire) are also available from this little shop. You could have a six-day sourdough, an organic sourdough, an Old Milwaukee rye loaf, a bagel, an olive focaccia or a date-and-walnut loaf. You can also enjoy a sandwich, soup, fresh juice or cup of coffee, eating it inside or at the few tables outside on the pavement.

Middle Eastern Food Hall

★ GREEN VALLEY

36 Upper Berkeley Street,
London W1H 7PG
Tel: 020 7402 7385
Fax: 020 7723 2545
Open: every day 8am-midnight
Tube: Edgware Road, Marble Arch **Bus:** 6, 15, 16, 23, 36, 98
Payment: cash, cheques, Delta, MasterCard, Visa, Solo, Switch
Catering (specialities big parties, Christmas, Ramadan), food-to-go

There can be few people who work harder than Green

> "I always thought there would be a significant change, that organic food would one day come of age, but I never imagined it would be quite this sudden."
>
> Patrick Holden, director of the Soil Association

Valley's Lebanese owner, Hayam Beany, who originally opened up in adjoining premises in 1986 - on hand at all hours, good humouredly helping staff and customers, now in her vastly enlarged new shop. At the front of the shop are the fresh fruit and veg, (deliveries come in from Cyprus, Jordan and the Lebanon) and in season you will find quince, fresh olives, all variety of salad greens and fresh herbs, dates, figs, watermelons, and delicious tomatoes. Among the more unusual items are trimmed, cored courgettes, small cucumbers and purple carrots ready for stuffing with meat or rice. Opposite are displayed Middle Eastern pastries and sweets, alongside which is a good range of dried and salted nuts. En route to the back of the store are barrels of pickles and at least nine types of olives. Next come fresh fish and meat – look out for their homemade lamb sausages, flavoured with chillies and spices or pine nuts, and the bastourma - cured, dried beef fillet flavoured with herbs. At the back is a fine array of take-away dishes (prepared in the downstairs kitchens) – tabbouleh, kibbeh, vegetable salads, falafel, filled sanbusak pastries, real Greek sheep's feta, Syrian and Lebanese plaited cheese, and the highly flavoured shankish from northern Lebanon; also raw lamb kebabs and kofte (all halal meat of the highest quality) flavoured with herbs and spices, ready for grilling. Then there are dried and tinned goods, as well as grenadine and pomegranate molasses and dried limes for Iranian cooking. Surely the best shop of its kind in central London.

INTERNATIONAL CHEESE CENTRE

Cheese shop

5 Marylebone Station,
Melcombe Place, London
NW1 6JJ
Tel: 020 7724 1432

Main shop: see The City, page 58

Middle Eastern Butcher Grocer

LA BELLE BOUCHERIE
3–5 Bell Street, London
NW1 5BY
Tel: 020 7258 0230
Open: Mon-Sat 9am-9pm, Sun 11am-9pm **Tube:** Edgware Road **Bus:** 6, 16, 98 **Mainline station:** Marylebone, Paddington
Payment: cash, cheques

Just off the Edgware Road, this small, bustling, Algerian-owned butcher-cum-grocer stocks a good range of foods for Middle Eastern cookery. Their highly recommended homemade merguez sausages are available in two versions, hot and normal, and stocks of quality halal meat, including spicy kofte ready for the grill. Couscous and burghul are sold loose in various grades. Also available: pure honey (costly) from Pakistan and the Yemen, green tea, preserved lemons, apricot leather, Turkish delight, good-value extra virgin olive oil from Crete and pomegranate molasses (for Iranian dishes). They also sell couscousières and tagines.

Pâtisserie

PÂTISSERIE VALERIE
105 Marylebone High Street
London, W1M 3DB
Tel: 020 7935 6240

66 Portland Place, London
W1N 4AD
Tel: 020 7631 0467

Main shop: see Soho, page 51

Wholefoods Organic

WHOLEFOODS ORGANIC
24 Paddington Street, London
W1M 4DR
Tel: 020 7935 3924
Fax: 020 7486 2756
Open: Mon-Thu 8.30am-6pm, Fri 8.30am-6.30pm, Sat 8.30am-1pm **Closed:** Sun and Bank holidays **Tube:** Baker Street **Bus:** 2, 13, 18, 27, 30, 74, 82, 113, 139, 189, 274 **Payment:** cash, cheques, MasterCard, Visa

One of the first wholefood and organic shops in London, opened in the 1960s with the blessing of the Soil Association. Everything is organic - vegetables, fruit, pasta, cereals, and meat - and many items are labelled as gluten-free, wheat-free etc. The book section sports a large selection of healthy titles.

Mayfair

Butcher Game dealer

ALLEN & CO.
117 Mount Street, London
W1Y 6HX
Tel: 020 7499 5831
Fax: 020 7409 7112
Open: Mon-Fri 4am-4pm, Sat 5am-12.30pm **Closed:** Sun and Bank holidays **Tube:** Green Park **Bus:** 2, 8, 9, 10, 14, 16, 19, 22, 36, 38, 73, 74, 82, 137, 137a
Payment: cash, cheques
Bespoke deliveries within central London

Worn mosaic entrance tiling, deeply concave butchers' blocks and no-mod-cons

Mr Christian's

Notting Hill – *see page 98*

Reza Pâtisserie

Kensington – *see page 88*

Golden Gate Grocers

Chinatown – *see page 26*

Atari-Ya Food

Finchley – *see page 113*

payment via a sliding window at the back of the shop are just some of the signs that confirm the venerable age (some 150 years) of this well-established Mayfair butcher. This is no place for browsing, or selecting a delicate fillet: window displays tend to consist of an array of whole carcases, braces of gamebirds in full plumage, plus winches and meat hooks of grand proportions. But you can of course request fillet of grass-fed, four-week-hung Scotch beef (though rib joints, with their creamy yellow fat marbling, suggest themselves more strongly). Pork and lamb have equally fine pedigree, while the range of game is perhaps unmatched, as one might expect of suppliers to the Ritz and other top London restaurants. While anything from teal to foie gras may be found here, according to season, you should, however, phone through any unusual requests to assure supply. If you live locally, you can benefit from free delivery.

Chocolate

CHARBONNEL ET WALKER

1 The Royal Arcade,
28 Old Bond Street, London
W1X 4BT
Tel: 020 7491 0939
Fax: 020 7495 6279
Open: Mon-Fri 9am-6pm, Sat 10am-5pm **Closed:** Sun and Bank holidays **Tube:** Green Park **Bus:** 9, 14, 19, 22, 38 **Payment:** cash, cheques, Amex, Delta, MasterCard, Switch, Visa
Mail-order

Now with a branch at Royal Exchange in EC3, Charbonnel et Walker has been established as Britain's Master Chocolatiers since 1875. In that year, King Edward VII (the Prince of Wales) encouraged Mme Charbonnel to leave a chocolate house in Paris to come to London. The royal connection continues today, in that they hold a Royal Warrant as manufacturers of chocolates to the Queen. Luscious hand-made chocolates in every hue and flavour can be bought in a variety of glamorous boxes, fit for every celebratory occasion. Drinking chocolate and tubs of truffle sauce are available as well.

Branch: see The City, page 57

Belgian
Pâtisserie
Bakery

DE BAERE

3 Shepherd Street, London
W1Y 7LN
Tel: 020 7408 1991

Main shop: see Notting Hill, page 91

Coffee
Tea

★ HR HIGGINS (COFFEE-MAN) LTD

79 Duke Street,
London W1M 6AS
Tel: 020 7629 3913 or 020 7491 8819
Open: Mon-Wed 8.45am-5.30pm, Thu-Fri 8.45am-6pm, Sat 10am-5pm **Closed:** Sun **Tube:**

Bond Street **Bus:** 6, 7, 10, 12, 13, 15, 23, 73, 94, 98, 113, 135, 137, 139, 159, 189 **Payment:** cash, cheques, MasterCard
Mail-order

If you want to know anything about teas or coffees this is the place. The Higgins family has been running this friendly business for three generations, and today it offers one of the largest selections in London-more than 40 coffees and 25 teas. The coffee specialities include a mocha and mysore blend ('rich and smooth with a subtle aftertaste') and Vienna blend ('a smooth background with a subtle edge of strength'), but the list also includes the ever-popular Jamaica Blue Mountain and decaffeinated varieties. When you buy 2.5 kg or more the delivery is free in the UK and you can select a 100g sample. If shopping in nearby Bond Street has tired you out, pop in for a pick-me-up cuppa in the small café.

Afro-Caribbean Coffee

JAMAICAN BLUE MOUNTAIN COFFEE SHOP

18 Maddox Street, London W1R 9PL
Tel: 020 7408 2272
Open: Mon-Fri 8am-10pm, Sat-Sun noon-10pm **Closed:** 25 Dec., Bank holidays **Tube:** Oxford Circus **Bus:** 3, 6, 8, 12, 13, 15, 23, 53, 88, 94, 139, 159 **Payment:** cash, cheques, Amex, Delta, MasterCard, Switch, Visa
Bespoke deliveries within W1, London-wide hamper service, mail-order (coffee only)

The name, in fact, is 'shops', signifying the aim to be the first of many. The opening hours reflect the venue's new identity as a Caribbean cultural centre-cum-café, and even something of a nightclub. Its main purpose, however, is to serve and sell the world famous coffee – often mooted as the best coffee in the world – shipped directly from coffee farms in the Blue Mountains. The blend is exclusive to the UK and the price somewhat less (barring impostors, which do exist) than that of Blue Mountain coffees sold elsewhere – currently £28/lb. There is also Blue Mountain cake, cheesecake and muffins to take away or sample at the café. Interesting Caribbean sandwiches include callaloo and chicken, ackee and saltfish, jerk chicken, and there are other moist and delicious cakes, too: rum and tropical fruit; Jamaican ginger and coconut drops among them.

Fishmonger

JAMES KNIGHT OF MAYFAIR

8 Shepherd Market, London W1Y 7HT
Tel: 020 7499 2664
Fax: 020 7495 6301
Open: Mon-Fri 8am-6pm, Sat 8.30am-10.30am **Closed:** Sun, Bank holidays **Tube:** Green Park **Bus:** 8, 9, 14, 19, 22, 38 **Payment:** cash, cheques, MasterCard,

Switch, Visa
Bespoke deliveries within central London

A delightful shop in the somewhat run-down, but now reviving, Shepherd Market enclave of Mayfair. From the newly marble tiled floor, to the classical background music and charming, Irish-humoured reception by the Doyle brothers, the experience is an unusually pleasurable one. A good range of fish is fresh as one would expect from a Royal Appointment (HRH Prince of Wales) fishmonger -- there is a wholesale arm in Islington, open to the public in the early hours. What attracts the eye, however – apart from the window-tank lobsters which, be warned, are named pets - is the fine range of ready-prepared fishy products: lobster butter, fish soups and 'fonds', colourful fish terrines designed for dinner parties, Equinox Seafare seaweeds and, of course, caviar. Downstairs is an Aladdin's cave, full of the unexpected: artisanal confits, dried mushrooms, vanilla pods, innovative salad dressings, and not least, glass cabinets-ful of Ellie-Arnaud Denoix Cognacs, Eaux de Vie and Grappas in elegant bottles. A further touch of charm comes via rescued filing cabinets out of Paddington Station. An altogether intriguing little enterprise.

Branch: see Cecil & Co., Highbury page 136

Oxford Street

SELFRIDGES

Food Hall

400 Oxford Street, London W1A 1AB
Tel: 020 7629 1234
Fax: 020 7495 8321
Open: Mon-Wed 10am-7pm, Thu-Fri 10am-8pm, Sat 9.30am-7pm, Sun 12pm-6pm **Closed:** 25 Dec. **Tube:** Bond Street, Marble Arch **Bus:** 2, 6, 7, 10, 12, 13, 15, 16A, 23, 30, 73, 74, 82, 94, 98, 113, 135, 137, 137A, 139, 159, 189, 274 **Payment:** cash, cheques, Amex, Delta, MasterCard, Switch, Travellers cheques, Visa
Catering, delivery, food-to-go, mail-order

The extensive food hall, featuring ingredients and prepared dishes from all over the world, occupies part of the ground floor of the general department store, and has several eating areas, a Yo Sushi, Prêt-A-Manger, oyster bar and salt beef bar. Everything is in sections, each offering a huge variety of foods. The fresh fruit and vegetable section is perhaps the smallest, but it is of good quality, with a range of wild mushrooms in season. There is a deli counter, with a biltong special offer on the day of visiting, a myriad salume, hams, cooked meats, mini quiches and pies. The fishmonger's counter offers yabbies from Australia, fresh conger and sea urchin, and the butcher has bowls of chicken hearts, livers and gizzards, trays of osso buco, calf's tails and crocodile (the essence of Australia), as well as good quality pork, lamb and beef. At the traiteur you can find everything you might want for a quick dinner party, from cooked lobster to smoked salmon mousse, from terrines and salads to stuffed mussels ready to grill. There are smoked salmon, caviar, cheese, pasta, pâtisserie, bread and kosher counters, with plenty of other areas specialising in international tins, jars, bottles and special offers. For those with a sweet tooth, a bright and multi-coloured confectionery section abuts the main part of the food hall.

Piccadilly

Food Hall

★ FORTNUM & MASON

181 Piccadilly, London
W1A 1ER
Tel: 020 7734 8040
Open: Mon-Sat 9.30am-6pm
Closed: Sun and Bank holidays
Tube: Piccadilly Circus, Green Park **Bus:** 9, 14, 19, 22, 38
Payment: cash, cheques, Amex, JCB, MasterCard, Switch, Visa,
Bespoke delivery, catalogue, catering, food-to-go, mail-order

The food hall of this famous store, which was established as a grocery in 1707, is one of the gustatory wonders of London. It is like wandering through a very up-market perfume or designer clothes section in a spacious, highly expensive department store (which Fortnum has indeed since become), but everything on the ground floor is foodie, and luscious, and you want to buy everything in sight. There are decorative tins of teas (a choice of over 120), jars of a multitude of vegetables and other groceries, boxes of confectionery, and a very special and aromatic chocolate section. There is also a huge selection of wines, spirits and cigars. The displays of regional British foods are spectacular, featuring butters, hams, smoked salmon and kippers from some of the best producers in the country. The cheese counter offers an unusually fine selection of seasonal British and international cheeses. Hampers can be prepared for travelling feasts, and canapés may be ordered for parties.

Japanese Food Hall

JAPAN CENTRE, NATURAL HOUSE FOOD SHOP

212 Piccadilly, London
W1V 9LD
Tel: 020 7434 4218
Fax: 020 7287 1082
Open: Mon-Sat 10am-7.30pm, Sun, Bank holidays 10am-6pm
Closed: 25 Dec **Tube:** Piccadilly Circus **Bus:** 9, 14, 19, 22, 38
Payment: cash, cheques, MasterCard, Switch, Visa
Catering, mail-order

The Japan Centre offers this Japanese mini-supermarket, as well as a bookshop and a travel service. They try to stock all the groceries one would expect to find in a food store in Japan, from extra-thinly sliced beef and pork for sukiyaki, to the ingredients for sushi (from fresh fish to rolling mats). They also sell a wide range of basics such as tea, rice, miso, soy sauce and instant noodles, and make their own lunchboxes to go.

Japanese Confectioners

MINAMOTO KITCHOAN

44 Piccadilly, London W1V 9AJ
Tel: 020 7437 3135
Fax: 020 7437 3191
Open: Sun-Fri 10am-7pm, Sat 10am-8pm **Closed:** Bank holidays **Tube:** Piccadilly Circus **Bus:** 9, 14, 19, 22, 38 **Payment:** cash, cheques, Amex, Delta, MasterCard, Switch, Visa
Catalogue, catering

The second best thing to actually visiting this Japanese sweet shop is poring over its catalogue, which is packed with items of confectionery and pâtisserie either imported or made on the premises, most of them extraordinary to the Western eye, but infinitely desirable to all Japanese with a sweet tooth. There are *wagashis* made with healthy ingredients such as red kidney beans, glutinous and powdered rice, sweet potatoes, sesame and agar-agar, allied with natural unrefined sugar. Speciality No.1 is a whole muscat wrapped inside a sweet rice cake and sprinkled with sugar. Speciality No. 3 is a whole peach coated with Japanese-style seaweed jelly whose stone has been replaced with a green baby peach, so you can eat the whole thing. Sample any of these treats on the premises with some green tea, or take away in beautiful packaging.

Chocolate

PRESTAT

14 Princes Arcade, Piccadilly, London SW1Y 6DS
Tel: 020 7629 4838
Fax: 020 7928 8485
Open: Mon-Sat 9.30am-6pm
Closed: Sun and Bank holidays
Tube: Piccadilly Circus **Bus:** 9, 14, 19, 22, 38 **Payment:** cash, cheques, Amex, MasterCard, Switch, Visa
Bespoke delivery, catalogue, mail-order

A tiny chocolate shop, established in 1902, which is one of London's oldest and finest, and an appointed purveyor of chocolates to Her Majesty the Queen. It was the outright winner in The Times 1999 Easter Egg Consumer Survey. The shelves are crammed with luscious chocolates of every description (plus marrons glacés and real Turkish Delight), and the shop guards zealously the secret recipe for their Napoleon III truffles, all hand-made and cocoa dusted and available by mail order.

Pimlico

Bakery
Pâtisserie

BONNE BOUCHE

38a Tachbrook Street, London SW1 2JS
Tel: 020 7630 1626
Open: Mon-Sat 8.30am-6pm
Tube: Pimlico, Victoria **Bus:** 2, 24, 36, 185 **Payment:** cash, cheques

A narrow bakery/pâtisserie which is part of a catering and bakery chain. The products are baked in a central kitchen, but the breads - plain, tomato and olive ciabattas, rye and wholemeal, French sticks among them - are wonderfully fresh, as are the meringue bases and vol-au-vent cases. Luscious sandwiches, made on the premises, are on offer at lunchtime.

Branches: too numerous to list here, please consult your local telephone directory

Italian
Delicatessen

GASTRONOMIA ITALIA

8 Tachbrook Street, London SW1 1SH
Tel: 020 7834 2767
Open: Mon-Fri 9am-6pm, Sat 9am-5pm **Closed:** Sun and Bank holidays **Tube:** Pimlico, Victoria **Bus:** 2, 24, 36, 185 **Payment:** cash, cheques

A busy little delicatessen and sandwich shop, with wonderful homemade pizza at lunchtime, run by Mario d'Annunzio. Fresh cheeses, marinated olives, home-made pesto and plump salamis galore in the chill cabinet, jars, packets, tins and bottles of every possible Italian product on the shelves, including a selection of wines. Sit at one of the tables outside and enjoy a cappuccino on a sunny day.

Cheese shop

INTERNATIONAL CHEESE CENTRE

41 The Parade, Platform 14-19 Victoria Station, London SW1V 1RJ
Tel: 020 7828 2886

Main shop: see The City, page 58

Cheese shop

RIPPON CHEESE STORES

26 Upper Tachbrook Street, London SW1V 1SW
Tel: 020 7931 0668 for 24 hour answering service, 020 7931 0628 for shop
Fax: 020 7828 2368
Open: Mon-Sat 8am-6.30pm
Closed: Sun and Bank holidays
Tube: Pimlico, Victoria **Bus:** 2, 36, 185, 24 **Payment:** cash, cheques, Delta, MasterCard, Switch, Visa
Mail-order

A spankingly clean shop run by Philip and Karen Rippon. Close to Tachbrook Street market, it stocks more than 500 types of cheeses in chillers behind plastic strips. An ideal place for the food lover, chef and caterer to view, taste and buy a wide range from the United Kingdom, and Ireland, as well as products from France, Italy, Germany,

Scandinavia, Holland, Spain and Switzerland.

Fishmonger

SEA HARVEST FISHERIES

16 Warwick Way, London SW1V 1RX
Tel: 020 7821 5192
Open: Tue-Sat 10am-6pm
Closed: Mon, Sun **Tube:** Victoria
Bus: 2, 24, 36, 185 **Payment:** cash, cheques

A busy fishmonger which offers many seafood delights, including on the occasion of our visit, sprats, soft roe, cuttlefish, tiny squid, monkfish, whole Scottish salmon, Scottish mussels, and fresh, raw, seawater prawns. Smoked salmon comes from Scotland as well, and the small packets of smoked salmon offcuts are extremely good value.

St James's

Cheese shop

★ PAXTON & WHITFIELD

93 Jermyn Street, London SW1Y 6JE
Tel: 020 7930 0259
Fax: 020 7321 0621
Open: Mon-Fri 9.30am-6pm, Sat 9am-5.30pm **Closed:** Sun and Bank holidays **Tube:** Piccadilly Circus, Green Park **Bus:** 3, 6, 9, 12, 13, 14, 15, 19, 22, 23, 38, 53, 88, 94, 135, 159 **Payment:** cash, cheques, Amex, Delta, MasterCard, Switch, Visa
Catalogue, mail-order

One of London's best-known shops, established in St James's over 200 years ago, and now has branches in Bath and Stratford-upon-Avon. The emphasis is, of course, on cheese, and there are some superb examples of British, Irish and French artisan products, stacked up on the counter. There are always a couple of cheeses on special offer, and the shop runs a mail-order tasting club, sending members a selection of cheeses every month. They also organise cheese tasting in the shop. But there are other delights on offer as well: accessories, port and Stilton gift boxes, smoked salmon, hams, pies, teas, coffees, biscuits, preserves and foie gras.

Soho

Coffee
Tea

★ ALGERIAN COFFEE STORES

52 Old Compton Street, London W1V 6PB
Tel: 020 7437 2480
Fax: 020 7437 5470
Open: Mon-Sat 9am-7pm
Closed: Sun and Bank holidays
Tube: Leicester Square, Piccadilly Circus **Bus:** 14, 19, 22, 24, 29, 38, 94, 176 **Payment:** cash, cheques, Amex, Delta, MasterCard, Switch, Visa
Catalogue, mail-order, wholesale

An old-fashioned shop, one of the leading coffee and tea retailers/wholesalers in London, which is famous world-wide and has been established since 1887. The rich, enticing smell of

Berwick Street Market

Open: Mon-Sat 8am-6pm **Closed:** Sun **Tube:** Piccadilly Circus **Bus:** 3, 6, 12, 13, 14, 15, 19, 22, 23, 38, 53, 88, 94, 39

Soho, the cosmopolitan area roughly bounded by Oxford Street, Tottenham Court Road, Shaftesbury Avenue and Regent Street, has long been associated with food (as well as sex). A haven for many refugees - primarily French Huguenots, Greeks, Italians and Jews - from the seventeenth century onwards, it became known firstly for its international restaurants, then as a source of exotic foodstuffs. The market in Berwick Street, if no longer particularly international or exotic, still retains much of the louche flavour of old Soho, although it has diminished in size in recent years due to local council demands. Now one side of the street only is crammed with fruit and vegetable stalls, supplying Soho inhabitants, Soho workers and the multitude of local restaurants. If the volume of trade is high, so is the volume of the stallholders advertising their wares! Prices are generally reasonable, and scoops of tomatoes, avocados or bananas can be had for the bargain price of £1. There are also good individual fish, cheese, herb and bread stalls (the latter run by the same people who run The Breadstall shop in Portobello Road, see page 90).

WORTH A DETOUR

- Leon Jaeggi & Sons, 77 Shaftesbury Avenue, Tel: 020 7434 4545, high-class catering/kitchen suppliers
- Pages, 121 Shaftesbury Avenue, Tel: 020 7379 6334, high-class catering/kitchen suppliers,
- Denny's, 55a Dean Street, Tel: 020 7494 2745, food service and chefs' wear

coffee filters out on to the pavement whenever the door opens, and it's like an olfactory fix inside. Over 100 types of coffee are on offer, from the familiar South American and African, to organic coffee from Papua New Guinea. Beans come whole, roasted or ground to specification and even coated in chocolate! There are over 160 teas available as well, including the familiar Indian blacks and Formosa greens, and the less familiar black China fruit-flavoured teas and herbal teas. For the sweet-toothed, there's a luscious range of chocolates and other confectionery, and for the practical, a huge selection of coffee-making jugs and machines, both for domestic and commercial use.

Italian
French
Pâtisserie

AMATO

14 Old Compton Street,
London W1V 5PE
Tel: 020 7734 5733
Open: Mon-Sat 8am-10pm, Sun 10am-8pm **Tube:** Tottenham Court Road **Bus:** 14, 19, 22, 14, 29, 38, 94, 176 **Mainline station:** Charing Cross **Payment:** cash, cheques, Amex, Delta, MasterCard, Switch, Visa
Mail-order

This brightly lit French/Italian café and pâtisserie entices you in with a wonderful display of cakes and pastries. Everything is made on the premises under the close eye of the chef and proprietor Ugo Amato, so is really fresh and of high quality. Their speciality is *cannoli siciliani,* delicate pastries made with white wine and filled with ricotta and chocolate. Choose from the focaccia, a quiche of the day, salads or generously filled club sandwiches. But the cakes are the crowning glory, with *palmiers, tartes au citron* and *tartes aux pommes,* daring you to eat them. They also offer celebration cakes made to order and will endeavour to make anything you wish.

“Stepping into Angelucci's for my coffee beans.”

From Dire Straits' song
Wild Wild West End

Coffee

★ A. ANGELUCCI

23b Frith Street,
London W1V 5TS
Tel: 020 7437 5889
Open: Mon, Tue, Wed, Fri, Sat 9am-5pm, Thu 9am-1pm
Closed: Sun **Tube:** Tottenham Court Road, Leicester Square
Bus: 7, 8, 10, 14, 19, 24, 29, 38, 73, 176 **Mainline station:** Charing Cross **Payment:** cash, cheques
Mail-order

This tiny coffee shop, in the heart of Soho, has changed little, if at all, since 1929 when it first opened. As you walk inside there is the wonderful, all pervasive smell of freshly ground coffee. On the counter sits a huge red enamelled set of old scales where they weigh your beans (they weighed some for President de Gaulle when he visited during wartime) and an old red enamelled grinder noisily grinds the coffee to your specifications. You can choose from 36 different types of coffee, all in great bags piled round the shop, including Angelucci's own blend, Mokital, a medium dark roast blend used by the famous Bar Italia, just a few doors up from Angelucci. Regular customers are greeted by name by Mr Angelucci, the son of the founder. It is a real Soho institution.

Japanese Grocer

ARIGATO'S

48-50 Brewer Street, London W1R 3HN
Tel/Fax: 020 7287 1722
Open: Mon-Sat 10am-9pm, Sun 11am-8pm **Closed:** 25, 26 Dec., 1 Jan. **Tube:** Piccadilly Circus **Bus:** 3, 6, 12, 13, 14, 15, 19, 22, 23, 38, 53, 88, 94, 139 **Payment:** cash, cheques, Delta, MasterCard, Switch, Visa
Catering, food-to-go

Brewer Street has become the province of the immigrant Japanese, with several little supermarkets like Arigato, and a number of restaurants. This cramped but bright little shop does in fact have seating, where you can choose to eat some of the home-made sushi selection others take away. There are lunch boxes too, made on the premises. The shelves are packed with gaudy packets and jars imported directly from Japan. These contain all the elements for a Japanese feast at home - soy sauces, ready-made miso and soup mixes, every type of dried seaweed and noodle, and over 50 types of *sakè* (rice wine). They also sell the freshest of raw fish in case you want to make your own sushi at home.

Italian Delicatessen

★ I. CAMISA

61 Old Compton Street, London WIV 5PN
Tel: 020 7437 7610
Open: Mon-Fri 8.30am-6pm, Sat 8am-6pm **Closed:** Sun and Bank holidays **Tube:** Piccadilly Circus, Leicester Square **Bus:** 14, 19, 22, 24 , 29, 38, 94, 176 **Payment:** cash, cheques

This long-established Italian deli is tiny, dark and cramped, and smells wonderful, a mixture of coffee, cheese and spice. They sell every type of Italian speciality possible: San Daniele and wild boar ham, pancetta, the best Parmesan and many other cheeses, fresh and packaged Italian sausages, salume, olives in bowls or tins, marinated artichokes, beans, olive oils, vinegar, pasta fresh and dried, and Italian truffles and truffle pastes - a rare source of reliable supply. There is an extensive range of fresh pasta with homemade sauces to match.

Italian Delicatessen

★ LINA STORES

18 Brewer Street, London W1R 3FS
Tel: 020 7437 6482
Open: Mon-Fri 7am-5.30pm, Sat 7am-5pm **Closed:** Sun and Bank holidays **Tube:** Piccadilly Circus, Leicester Square **Bus:** 14, 19, 22, 38, 94 **Payment:** cash, cheques, Amex, Delta, Diners Club, MasterCard, Switch, Visa

Another superb, long-established Italian delicatessen, where service is helpful and friendly, and you can get everything you need in one place. Every square inch - and it's not a large shop - is crammed with Italianate delights such as breads, packets of dried pasta, tins and jars of olives, bunches of fresh basil, tomatoes, artichoke hearts, oils, vinegar etc. Chill cabinets hold a variety of Italian cheeses, including fresh ricotta, pancetta, salami, buckets of various olives, and fresh Italian sweet and hot pork sausages. Dried porcini dangle from the ceiling along with boxes of panettone. Fresh pasta is a speciality, made daily on the premises (look out for the pumpkin tortellini), and the shop won a Pasta Retailer of the Year award in 1998. Occasionally they can offer bottarga (salted, dried grey mullet roe) fresh porcini and truffles.

French Pâtisserie

MAISON BERTAUX

28 Greek Street, London W1V 5LL
Tel: 020 7437 6007
Open: Mon-Sun 8.30am-8.30pm **Closed:** Bank holidays **Tube:** Tottenham Court Road **Bus:** 7, 8, 10, 14, 19, 24, 25, 29, 38, 55, 73, 98, 176 **Mainline station:** Charing Cross **Payment:** cash, cheques

A wonderful display of pastries, savouries and some of the best croissants in town line the front window of this little French pâtisserie and tea-room. Founded in 1871, this charming Soho institution has changed very little over the years. They have a band of regulars who come just for pastries or to while away some time in the café. Michelle Wade, the proprietor, runs things charmingly and creates a cosy and welcoming atmosphere. They specialise in *croque-en-bouche* (French wedding cakes made with piles of profiteroles) and will make things to order.

Pâtisserie

PÂTISSERIE VALERIE

44 Old Compton Street, London W1V 5PL
Tel: 020 7437 3466
Open: Mon-Fri 7.30am-10pm, Sat 8am-10pm, Sun 9.30am-7pm **Closed:** Bank holidays **Tube:** Leicester Square **Bus:** 14, 19, 24, 29, 38, 176 **Payment:** cash, cheques, Amex, Delta, MasterCard, Switch, Visa
Catalogue

The original and, many say, the best of the burgeoning chain. Founded by the Belgian Madame Valerie, it has sold cakes, tarts, eclairs and gateaux to the rich, famous, poor and unknown of Soho since 1926. Breakfast in Valerie's is very special: treat yourself to a good coffee and delicious croissants. Wedding cakes are a speciality, made with white and dark chocolate, as is a *croque-en-bouche* sculpture of profiteroles, cream and spun sugar.

Branch: see Covent Garden,

page 31, Knightsbridge page 35, Marylebone page 40

Sausages

SIMPLY SAUSAGES
93b Berwick Street, London W1V 3PP
Tel: 020 7287 3482

Main shop: see Clerkenwell, page 63

South Kensington

French Bakery Pâtisserie Delicatessen

★BAGATELLE BOUTIQUE
44 Harrington Road, London SW7 3NB
Tel: 020 7581 1551
Fax: 020 7591 0517
Open: Mon-Sat 8am-8pm, Sun and Bank holidays 8am-6pm
Closed: 25 Dec **Tube:** South Kensington **Bus:** 49, 70, 74
Payment: cash, cheques, Amex, Delta, MasterCard, Switch, Visa
Catalogue, catering, delivery, food-to-go

All the breads and pastries sold in this useful shop - it's open virtually every day - are baked in their Wembley factory, using flour from France, and no additives or preservatives. They supply many restaurants, but in the shop, delivered twice daily, the public can buy the freshest baguettes, croissants and *pains au chocolat*, as well as delectable items of pâtisserie, including Bagatelle (vanilla *bavarois* and bitter chocolate mousse topped with caramelised almond biscuit) and Raspberry *Napoléon* (caramelised *millefeuille* with a raspberry compote). For a special occasion such as a wedding you could order a *croque-en-bouche* (to feed from 12 to 200!), or a *bûche de Noël* or *galette du Roi* at Christmas. They sell chocolates as well, made in Paris by a small specialist producer. A charcuterie counter displays pâtés of every possible permutation, along with French hams, sausages and foie gras. They stock smoked salmon, some French cheeses and, in season, regional dishes such as *choucroûte* (both ready-made and still to cook).

Butcher

BUTE STREET BOUCHERIE
19 Bute Street, London SW7 3EY
Tel: 020 7581 0210
Open: Mon-Sat 7.30am-6pm
Closed: Sun, Bank holidays **Tube:** South Kensington **Bus:** 14, 49, 70, 74, 345, C1 **Payment:** cash, cheques, Amex, Delta, MasterCard, Switch, Visa
Bespoke deliveries locally

Well established in the 'French quarter' of South Kensington, this is nonetheless a quintessentially English butcher, employing British cutting techniques, supplying Norfolk chicken, English free-range eggs, Scotch beef (curiously, hung for two weeks' only). But the guinea fowl is French, as is the duck breast and, of course, the *foie gras*; and the veal is continental. Perhaps more interesting is the range of very French tins and conserves: Castelnaudary pork cassoulet, duck confit, duck fat, veal quenelles plus likely accompaniments: *choucroûte*, cooked lentils, bottled flageolets and *petits pois*, even vac-pacs of ready-to-cook endives and beetroot. Pasta is from Savoie and Alsace, there is a good range of ubiquitous LU biscuits, and condiments include Tunisian hot pepper and French-labelled balsamic vinegar.

Belgian
Bakery
Pâtisserie

DE BAERE

24 Bute Street, South Kensington, London SW7 3EX
Tel: 020 7591 0606

Main branch: see Notting Hill, page 91

French
Delicatessen
Special diet

THE MONTIGNAC BOUTIQUE

160 Old Brompton Road, London SW5 0BA
Tel/Fax: 020 7370 2010
Open: Mon-Fri 8.30am-10pm; Sat 8.30am-6pm, Sun 10am-5pm **Closed:** fortnight at Christmas, Bank holidays **Tube:** South Kensington, Gloucester Road **Bus:** C1 **Payment:** cash, cheques, Amex, Delta, MasterCard, Switch, Visa
Food-to-go, local delivery, mail-order

At first sight a rather smart café, this French-concept 'boutique' is in fact the English dietary centre of 'Eat Yourself Slim' guru Michel Montignac. Don't let that put you off, however: while the idea behind the foods on offer – both conserved and freshly prepared – is that they have a low 'glycaemic index' whilst being nutritionally valuable, they are mostly very delicious. The café/traiteur section offers typically French goodies such as duck confit, celeriac mash, lentils vinaigrette and some surprisingly indulgent cakes and puds: dark, flourless chocolate cake and Tiramisu, plus a small selection of French cheeses. The range of labelled Montignac 'products' (Fauchon-style glossy, but generally artisan prepared) includes wood-fire toasted muesli; organic pulses, pastas and grains; very French condiment-sauces along the lines of sorrel purée; superbly concentrated fruit compotes, preserves and coulis (including less usual varieties like rosehip), biscuits and toasts and high cocoa content chocolate. Virtually all are suitable for diabetics. Their pride and joy, however, is the organic, wholegrain, sourdough, wood-fire baked breads flown in from Savoie almost daily which have, on occasion, earned the accolade of 'best bread in London'. Prices generally reflect the 'gourmet' and 'cure' aspects of the enterprise.

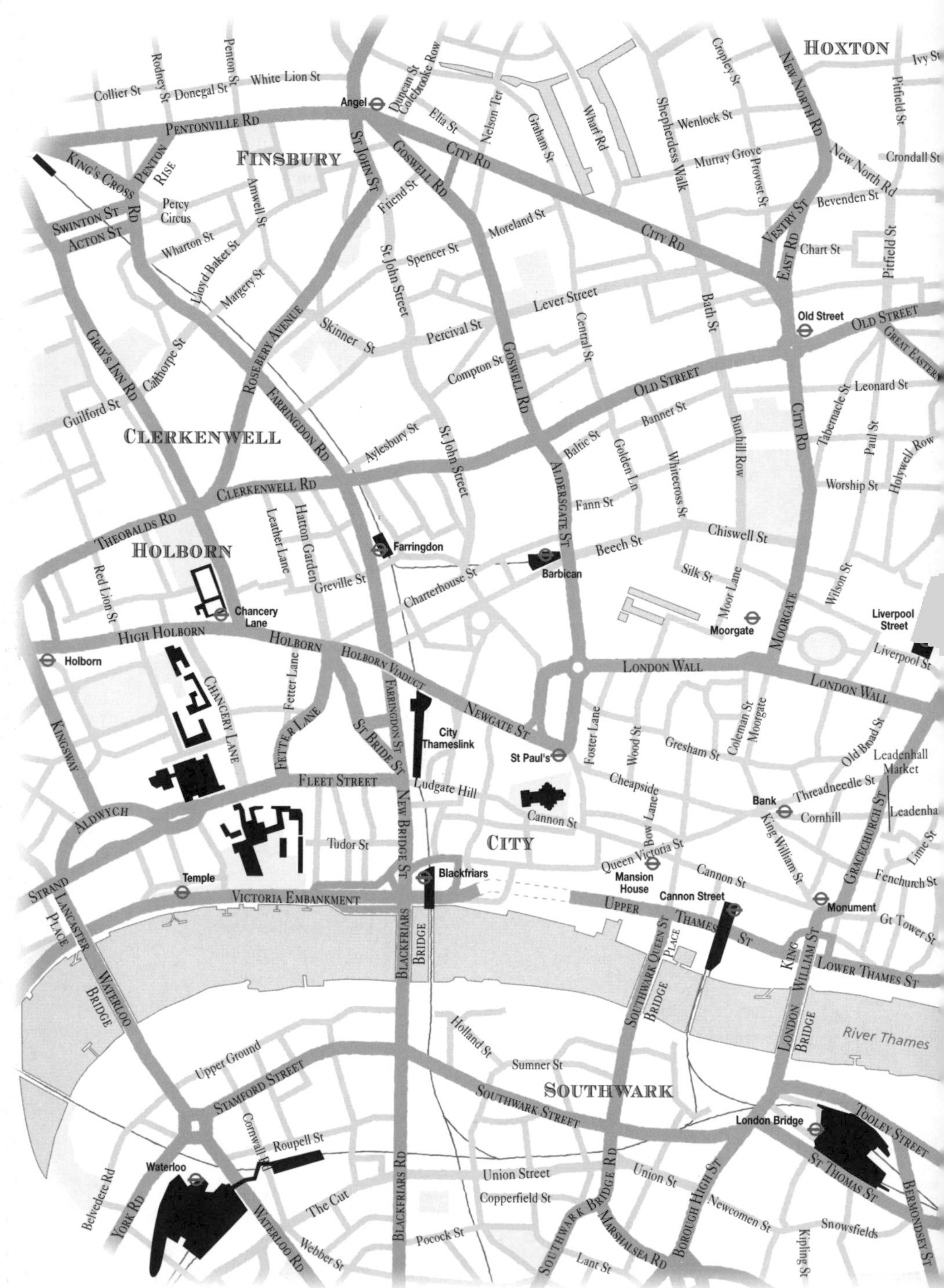

HOXTON
FINSBURY
CLERKENWELL
HOLBORN
CITY
SOUTHWARK
River Thames
Angel
Old Street
Farringdon
Barbican
Chancery Lane
Holborn
Moorgate
Liverpool Street
City Thameslink
St Paul's
Bank
Temple
Blackfriars
Mansion House
Cannon Street
Monument
London Bridge
Waterloo
Pentonville Rd
King's Cross Rd
Penton Rise
City Rd
Goswell Rd
St John St
Old Street
Clerkenwell Rd
Theobalds Rd
High Holborn
Holborn Viaduct
Newgate St
London Wall
Fleet Street
Ludgate Hill
Victoria Embankment
Upper Thames St
Lower Thames St
Blackfriars Bridge
Waterloo Bridge
Southwark Bridge
London Bridge
Southwark Street
Stamford Street
Tooley Street
Union Street
Farringdon Rd
Rosebery Avenue
Gray's Inn Rd
Kingsway
Aldwych
Strand
Chancery Lane
Aldersgate St
Moorgate
New North Rd
Cheapside
Cannon St
Queen Victoria St
King William St
Gracechurch St
Borough High St
Blackfriars Rd
Waterloo Rd
York Rd
Southwark Bridge Rd
Marshalsea Rd
Bermondsey St
St Thomas St
New Bridge St
Farringdon St
St Bride St
Fetter Lane
Lancaster Place
Southwark Queen St Place
East Rd
Vestry St
Great Eastern St

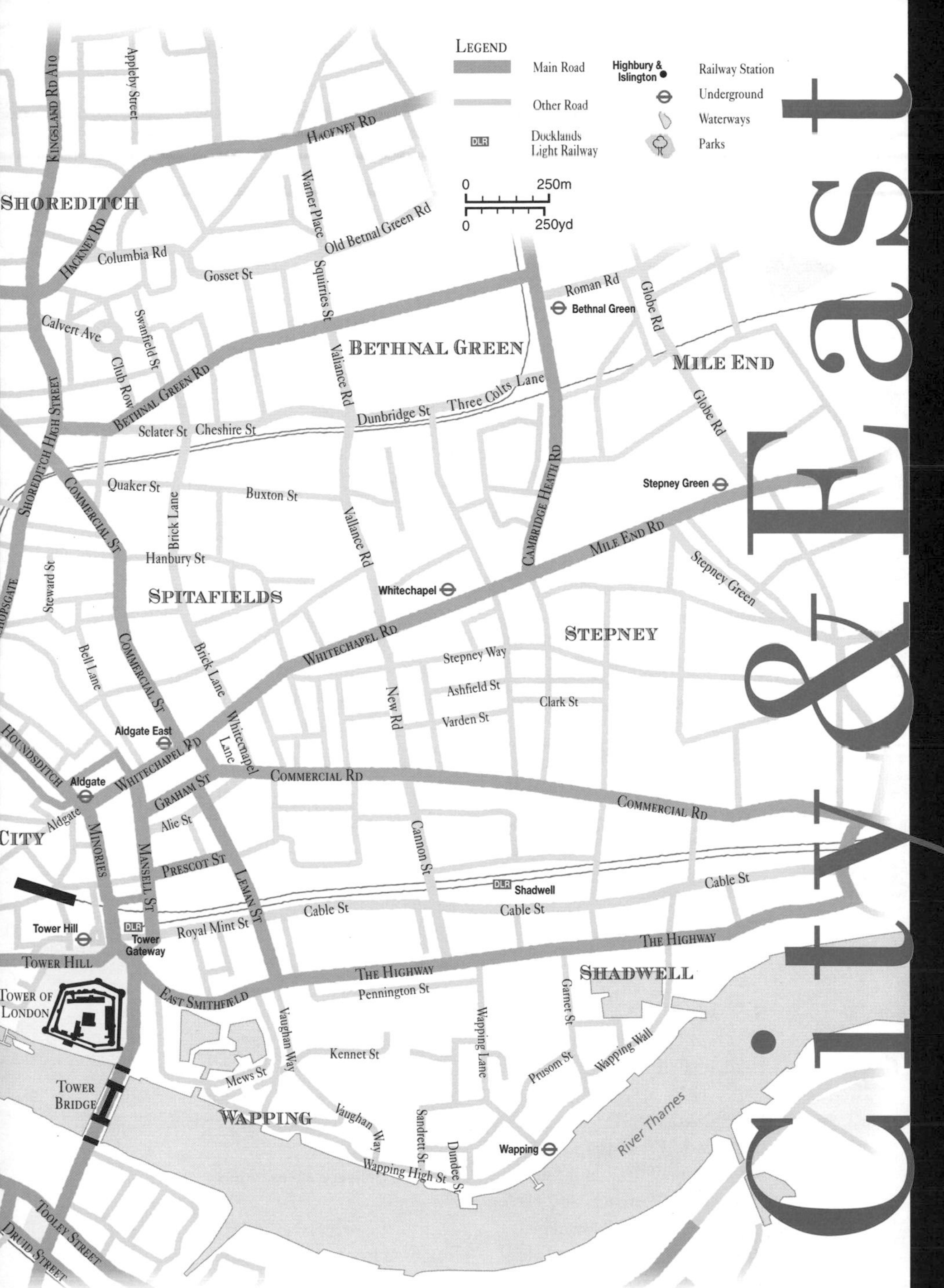
City & East
Legend
Main Road
Other Road
Docklands Light Railway
DLR
Highbury & Islington
Railway Station
Underground
Waterways
Parks
0
250m
0
250yd
Shoreditch
Bethnal Green
Mile End
Spitafields
Stepney
City
Shadwell
Wapping
Kingsland Rd A10
Appleby Street
Hackney Rd
Warner Place
Old Betnal Green Rd
Hackney Rd
Columbia Rd
Gosset St
Squirries St
Roman Rd
Bethnal Green
Globe Rd
Calvert Ave
Swanfield St
Club Row
Valiance Rd
Bethnal Green Rd
Three Colts Lane
Dunbridge St
Globe Rd
Sclater St
Cheshire St
Shoreditch High Street
Cambridge Heath Rd
Commercial St
Quaker St
Buxton St
Brick Lane
Vallance Rd
Stepney Green
Mile End Rd
Hanbury St
Steward St
Stepney Green
Whitechapel
Bell Lane
Commercial St
Brick Lane
Whitechapel Rd
Stepney Way
Ashfield St
Clark St
New Rd
Varden St
Aldgate East
Houndsditch
Whitechapel Rd
Whitechapel Lane
Aldgate
Graham St
Commercial Rd
Commercial Rd
Aldgate
Minories
Alie St
Cannon St
Mansell St
Prescot St
Leman St
Shadwell
Cable St
Cable St
Cable St
Tower Hill
Tower Gateway
Royal Mint St
Tower Hill
The Highway
The Highway
Pennington St
Tower of London
East Smithfield
Garnet St
Vaughan Way
Wapping Lane
Kennet St
Prusom St
Wapping Wall
Mews St
Tower Bridge
Vaughan Way
Sandrett St
Dundee St
Wapping
River Thames
Wapping High St
Tooley Street
Druid Street

Bethnal Green Road Market

Open: Mon-Wed, Fri-Sat 8am-6pm
Closed: Thu, Sun and Bank holidays
Tube: Bethnal Green **Bus:** 8
Mainline station: Bethnal Green

At the side of the main road to points north and east, between Vallance Road and Wilmot Street, this characterful East End street market continues to thrive, particularly at weekends. Most of the stalls offer traditional and reasonably priced fruit and vegetables, but you can also buy Afro-Caribbean foods, cut-price foods, household goods and clothes.

City

Butcher

R.S. ASHBY

4-5 Grand Avenue, Leadenhall Market, London EC3V 1LR
Tel: 020 7626 3871
Open: Mon-Fri 5am-4pm **Closed:** Sat, Sun, Bank holidays **Tube:** Monument, Bank **Bus:** 8, 25, 26, 35, 47, 48, 149, 242 **Mainline station:** Fenchurch Street
Payment: cash, cheques, Delta, MasterCard, Switch, Visa
Bespoke delivery, takes orders

A long-established butcher supplying a wide range of cooked meat products, as well as sound basic cuts of meat from the likes of 2-week hung Angus beef and Scotch lamb. A number of the sausages are homemade, notably 'Fred's Specials', cocktails and chipolatas. City shoppers with no time to cook will also find ready-cooked chickens, smoked duck breast, Rougié foie gras, haggis and a selection of pâtés and cold meats. Those inclined to wield a frying pan will find a useful range of Englert stocks, both meat and game. To round off your dinner party, choose from a fair range of cut cheeses or take home an impressive truckle.

Butcher
Game dealer

★ BUTCHER & EDMONDS

1-3 Grand Avenue, Leadenhall Market, London EC3V 1LR
Tel: 020 7626 5816 or 020 7623 5946
Open: Mon-Fri 6.30am-4pm
Closed: Sat, Sun, Bank holidays
Tube: Monument, Bank **Bus:** 8, 25, 26, 35, 47, 48, 49, 242
Mainline station: Fenchurch Street **Payment:** cash, cheques, Amex, Delta, JCB, MasterCard, Switch, Visa
Bespoke delivery, takes orders

One of the original established butchers in the Arcade (now not so very grand, but charming

SEA SALT £250
(WITH ADDED SEAWEED)
FROM FRANCE
50p per pack

Previous page

The Spice Shop

Notting Hill – *see page 102*

Borough Market

– see page 155

GUSTIBUS

Spitalfields Organic Market

– see page 67

nonetheless) the aptly named Butcher & Edmonds has been sought out by media and film-makers intent on capturing the olde worlde delights of its sawdust-coated terracotta tiles and cream and maroon-washed stone walls. 'JR' (actor Larry Hagman), they chuckle, claimed 'never to have seen beef like it' - certainly not in Texas. The three-week hung Scotch beef is much in demand by City Livery companies and directors' dining rooms, though game in season is perhaps their major seller. Christmas brings bronze turkeys from Huntingdon while eggs come 'direct from a chap in Woolwich'; in other words, trusted suppliers are a mainstay of the business. Arrive early or phone through an order to ensure supply.

Chocolate

CHARBONNEL ET WALKER

20 Royal Exchange, London EC3B 3LP
Tel: 020 7283 5843

Main shop: see Mayfair, page 41

Delicatessen

the deli bar

117 Charterhouse Street, London EC1M 6AA
Tel: 020 7253 2070
Fax: 020 7253 4947
Open: Mon,Tue 9am-8pm, Wed-Fri 9am-11pm, Sat 9am-5pm
Closed: Sun **Tube:** Farringdon, Barbican **Bus:** 4, 56 **Mainline station:** Farringdon **Payment:** cash, cheques, Amex, Delta, MasterCard, Switch, Visa

Bespoke deliveries within EC1, London-wide hamper service

This trendy, goods- and people-packed little deli owes both its long opening hours and much of its buzzy atmosphere to the existence of the eponymous bar, where the same range of top-notch foods and wines are served. Owner Mike Foskett turned his attention from nightclubs to this 'Enoteca-style' operation following a few years' sojourn in Italy; judging by the careful, if abundant, selection of goods on offer, this endowed him with a palate for the finest Mediterranean produce. Most of the foods and wines are Italian: apart from the fresh filled pastas flown in from Milan (pumpkin ravioli, asparagus panzerotti), there are fine vegetable and fruit preserves from Delizie di Calabria and Conserve della Nonna, Sardinian honeys, a full range of flours from Sala Cereali and an array of enticingly wrapped sweetmeats. A fine Spanish range includes tuna from Ortiz, sardines by Ramòn Peña and Navarrico vegetables. Celebrity spotters look out for artist John Hoyland and writer/broadcaster Michael Dobbs, both regular customers.

Cheese shop

INTERNATIONAL CHEESE CENTRE

3B West Mall,
Liverpool Street Station,
London EC2M 7PY
Tel: 020 7628 6637 or 7628 2343
Open: Mon-Wed 7.15am-8pm, Thu-Fri 7.15am-8.30pm, Sat 10.30am-7.30pm **Closed:** Sun, Bank holidays **Tube:** Liverpool Street **Bus:**11, 23, 42, 100, 133, 141, 172, 214, 271 **Mainline station:** Liverpool Street
Payment: cash, cheques, Amex, Delta, MasterCard, Switch, Visa
Bespoke delivery, mail-order (international), product list, takes orders

Though the original Goodge Street shop is no more, The International Cheese Centre now has a presence at three mainline stations, a wise move that has ensured its survival and allowed for interesting developments. Designed, according to the proprietor, as 'a mini Harrods like it used to be' the Liverpool Street shop is certainly packed with fine groceries and a huge selection (the list features some 400) of cheeses from round the world. The shop is open to browsers and very unintimidating; tasting (on request) is positively encouraged. Whilst it is perfectly possible to buy a small wedge of cheese for lunch - or, indeed, a generously filled sandwich - where the shop scores well is as a last-minute dinner-party stop. You'll need to buy your greenery elsewhere, but here are savoury nibbles, oils, dressings, pickles and chutneys aplenty (extra virgin, tarragon and cep-flavoured oils, 15- and even 40- year old balsamic vinegars, truffle sauces, Muriel's British Pickles, Piazza & Co. Sicilian preserved vegetables). Sweetmeats, too - anything from chocolate Olivers to elegant Panettoni. The fine wine selection includes £200 bottles, plus vintage port, or you could round off the evening with Delamain cognac or an 1893 Armagnac.

Branch: see Pimlico, page 46
see Marylebone, page 39

Fishmonger

★ H.S. LINWOOD & SONS

6-7 Grand Avenue,
Leadenhall Market, London
EC3V 1LR
Tel: 020 7929 0554
Fax: 020 7929 2194
Open: Mon-Fri 6am-3.30pm
Closed: Sat, Sun, Bank holidays
Tube: Monument, Bank **Bus:** 8, 25, 26, 35, 47, 48,149, 242
Mainline station: Fenchurch Street **Payment:** cash, cheques, Amex, Diners, MasterCard, Switch, Visa
Delivery to Central London, takes orders

A venerable fishmonger of over a hundred years' standing; and, indeed, the only fishmonger left at Leadenhall. Survival is no doubt assisted by the Royal Warrant to HM Queen Elizabeth II, though the quality of the seafood speaks for itself.

I know how to shop for food. I know the rules: never shop for food when you are hungry or depressed, and (courtesy of Miss Piggy) never eat more than you can lift. 

Nigel Slater

Smoked salmon is a mainstay and various grades - 'quality assured', 'best' and 'trimmings' are on offer. Fresh scallops, too, range from tiny queenies to huge, succulent 'jumbos'. This is a rare source of fresh, raw prawns and other hard-to-come-by items such as salt cod and sachets of squid ink. A cooked seafood stand offers the likes of cured herring, shelled whelks, cockles, mussels and crayfish tails. You may well find bargains among the superbly fresh fish on display; if not, the sight of an enormous stuffed turtle, or the maroon and gold décor on dark wood of this listed building are a pleasure in themselves.

Chocolate

MAXWELL & KENNEDY

The Mall, West Concourse, Liverpool Street Station, London EC2A 2NA
Tel: 020 7638 2847
Open: Mon-Fri 8am-8pm, Sat 10am-6pm, Sun 11am-5pm
Closed: occasional Bank holidays
Tube: Liverpool Street **Bus:** 11, 23, 42, 100, 133, 141, 172, 214, 271 **Mainline station:** Liverpool Street **Payment:** cash, cheques, Amex, Delta, MasterCard, Switch, Visa
Bespoke deliveries within central London, mail-order

This very enticing shop, spanning two units of the busy Liverpool Street Station shopping mall, is designed to catch commuter gift and self-indulgence markets and, judging by the constant buzz, seems to be succeeding very well. The formula is one of classy, but unintimidating background (dark wood, gold lettering, but cheerfully coloured boxes and tinsel and giggly young staff). The young company is in fact Scottish in origin, but the sweets and chocolates have a distinctly English feel: there are violet and rose creams, Turkish delight, Cumbrian butter fudge, silver and gold dragees and jelly fruits; a good many truffles are pastel shaded and boldly flavoured with strawberry, vodka, Baileys or Malibu. Children's novelty animals are legion and diabetics are catered for, too, so you can be assured of finding an appropriate gift at a moment's notice. Since the company linkup, chocolates are now manufactured by

Charbonnel et Walker (see page 41), but recipes remain true to the Maxwell & Kennedy originals. There are numerous little shops throughout London; this is the largest.

Branches: too numerous to list here, please consult your local telephone directory

Butcher
Sausages

PORTERFORD

6 Bow Lane, London
EC4M 9EB
Tel: 020 7248 1396
Fax: 020 7236 5517
Open: Mon-Thu 6.30am-6.30pm, Fri 6am-7.30pm **Closed:** weekend, Bank holidays **Tube:** Mansion House **Bus:** 8, 11, 15, 17, 23, 25, 26, 172, 242, 521
Mainline station: Cannon Street
Payment: cash, cheques, Delta, Electron, MasterCard, Switch, Visa
Local deliveries

A dinner-party cook's dream of a butcher: long opening hours; swift, friendly and helpful service; and a large range of impressive cuts and preparations from well-sourced meat and poultry. The latter include boned, rolled and stuffed chicken, capon and duck. Saddle of lamb (the Gouda and spinach stuffed saddle is a visually impressive speciality) and simpler options for 'easy meals' are marinated lamb cutlets and pork noisettes. This is also a rare source of goose breast fillets, as well as the more usual duck, plus a great bargain: guinea fowl and pheasant legs at ridiculously low prices, thanks to a thriving restaurant trade in supremes. The restaurant business ensures supply of a full range of exotics (crocodile, kangaroo) as well as game in season, but purists will go for the free-range and organic Black Mountain Foods Welsh lamb, or magnificent rib of Scotch beef, almost invariably from a prize-winning carcase. Astonishingly for such tiny premises, there are 22 varieties of home-made sausage on offer, along with lamb offal and even biltong.

Clerkenwell

Italian
Delicatessen

★ G. GAZZANO & SONS

167-169 Farringdon Road,
London EC1R 3AL
Tel: 020 7837 1586
Open: Mon, Sat 8am-5pm, Tue-Fri 8am-6pm, Sun 10.30am-2pm **Closed:** Bank holidays **Tube:** Farringdon **Bus:** 19, 38, 63, 171a
Mainline station: Farringdon
Payment: cash, cheques, Delta, MasterCard, Switch, Visa
Takes orders

A long-established family business with cabinets and decor dating from the turn of the century, this neighbourhood Italian deli has devoted clientele covering the length and breadth of London. If travelling any distance, Christmas and Easter are the times to visit, as the Gazzanos' passion for Italian

> "The average Italian is a culinary geographer who knows that the best lemons are grown near Naples, the most fragrant herbs abound on the Italian Riviera, and that Veneto probably enjoys the widest variety of vegetables of any region. 
>
> Fred Plotkin, food writer

sweetmeats is given full rein. Colomba and panettone come in many shapes and flavours and include the excellent Tre Marie range; but you will also find tartufatas, nougats, *cavallucci, ricciardi* and *amaretti* in more guises than elsewhere, as well as fruits bottled in Moscato or Freisa. The range of fresh sausages and salume is impressive: Genovese, Napolitana, Lucanica, Finocchiona, wine-marinated Dolce di Carnia and the like, with *porchetta*, *speck*, *rostino* and *soppressata* amongst other preserved pork products. Both fresh and dried pastas (Molisana, Barilla, de Cecco) are here aplenty – 110 shapes at the last count. Visit in the Spring to secure seeds for unusual greenery: treviso, long red peppers, and a multitude of basils. Service is both helpful and friendly.

MYDDELTONS

Delicatessen

25a Lloyd Baker Street, London WC1X 9AT
Tel: 020 7278 9192
Fax: 020 7833 8858
Open: Mon-Fri 7am-7pm, Sat 7am-6pm **Closed:** Sun, Bank holidays **Tube:** Farringdon, Angel **Bus:** 19, 30, 38, 63, 73, 171a **Mainline station:** Farringdon **Payment:** cash, cheques
Takes orders

This little neighbourhood deli has established its usefulness over a number of years and is valued as much for its long opening hours as for its range of good quality food and wine. It appears to stock a little bit of everything: fruit and veg of course; free-range sausages, chickens and eggs; a small but very decent range of cheeses; breads from & Clarke's (see page 86) and cakes by Nadell Pâtisserie (see page 142); Crumpton's fruit cakes, handmade Belgian chocolates and Café de Paris coffee ground to order. Staples include preserves from Cottage Delight, organic jams by the All Natural Preserving Company, and fancy pastas such as frilly Tacconi and pink-striped Farfalline. Lunchtime sees a busy trade in cheese and charcuterie platters and gourmet sandwiches.

Branch: Pâtisserie Max, 61 Amwell Street, London EC1 R1UR
Tel: 020 7278 6181

French Bakery Pâtisserie

POUR L'AMOUR DU PAIN

15 Greville Street, London EC1 8SQ
Tel: 020 7242 2888
Open: Mon-Fri 7.30am-5.00pm
Closed: Sun
Tube: Farringdon **Bus:** 8, 17, 25, 45, 46, 171a, 242, 243, 501, 521
Mainline station: Farringdon
Payment: cash, cheques
Takes orders

Step inside this unassuming little shop tucked away from the main drag of Farringdon, and you might well imagine yourself in a small village bakery in France. Everything, from the yellow provençal-style wallpaper and check cloth, to the wrought iron bread stands, Trimco chill cabinets and the French accented service, fosters the happy illusion. The breads and pastries executed by master baker Jean Louis Bienvenu, who set up the shop in the summer of 1998, are decidedly provincial rather than parisian in style: weighty, generous and well priced rather than exquisite and expensive. The range encompasses the classics – *tarte tatin, millefeuilles, pain au chocolat*; the homely – flans, *chinois* with raisins (a French version of lardy cake); and the frankly pan-European – apple strudel, Danish. Filling savouries and sandwiches are the mainstay of the lunch trade: there is little left in the shop after 2pm. A small tea room has recently been opened at the back of the shop.

Bakery

ST JOHN BAKERY

26 St John Street, London EC1M 4AY
Tel: 020 7251 0848
Fax: 020 7251 4090
Open: Mon-Fri 9am- 'until the bread runs out', Sat 9am-12noon, 4pm-11pm **Closed:** Sun and Bank holidays **Tube:** Farringdon, Barbican **Bus:** 55, 153, 243, 505 **Mainline station:** Farringdon **Payment:** cash, cheque, Amex, Delta, MasterCard, Switch, Visa

A quiet little operation, this offshoot of the more famous restaurant exists largely to supply the St John eateries. Self-taught baker Manuel Manadé had an eye on retail sales since joining St John some four years ago, and a number of accolades – 'the best bread in London' enthused one famed cookery writer – have proven him right. You will find the bread sold at two or three select London shops, but will otherwise need to weave your way through a little passage into the bar area, where the adjoining bakery (a single electric bakers' oven) is on display. The range of breads is quite modest – some 8-12 lines – and is eclectically European in style, ranging from Irish soda bread to ciabattas, via French-style walnut and onion loaves. All are English flour based, and thus preserve a somewhat English character, despite the trademark well-developed, chewy crust (the light ciabatta is perhaps the sole exception). This is one bakery where the flavoured breads are more successful than the plain, thanks, no doubt, to restaurant contribution (zestily fresh pesto in the calzone, for example). Early birds may find restaurant pâtisserie on offer, too.

Sausages

SIMPLY SAUSAGES

341 London Central Markets, London EC1A 9NB
Tel/Fax: 020 7329 3227
Open: Mon-Fri 8am-6pm Sat 9am-1pm **Closed:** Sun and Bank holidays **Tube:** Farringdon **Bus:** 55, 243, 505 **Mainline station:** Farringdon **Payment:** cash, cheques

This shop offers an over-whelming variety of sausages, including seasonal varieties, all handmade to traditional recipes, only in natural skins, and with no artificial additives. Meat contents are high, and old favourites include beef-and-Guinness and duck-and-orange. There is also a vegetarian selection, with a Scarborough Fair sausage (full of fresh herbs) and Glamorgan (Caerphilly and leek) on offer.

Branch: see Soho, page 52

Italian Delicatessen

L. TERRONI & SONS

138-140 Clerkenwell Road, London EC1R 5DL
Tel: 020 7837 1712
Fax: 020 7365 0027
Open: Mon, Tue, Wed, Fri 9am-5.45pm, Thu 9am-2pm, Sat 9am-3pm, Sun 10.30am-2pm
Closed: Bank holidays **Tube:** Farringdon, Chancery Lane **Bus:** 55, 243, 505 **Mainline station:** Farringdon **Payment:** cash, cheques, MasterCard, Switch, Visa

The oldest Italian delicatessen in London (established 1878), this unusually spacious shop supplies just about anything and everything any true-born Italian, or Italophile, could ever want. Its strength lies not with painstakingly sourced artisan produce but rather an abundance of staples: four types of '00' flours, row upon row of pastas from Molisana and Rana, a vast range of Beretta salume, perhaps every style in the ubiquitous Mulino Branco, Grisbi and Loacker biscuit ranges, more types of *savoiardi* than one imagined existed. You will also find empty jars and cheap coffee sets mingling with prized oils and vinegars in elegant glassware. Fresh produce includes pastas, *salsiccie* and homemade sauces. You can pop in for salt cod, perfect pink garlic or simply basic fruit and veg; and maybe walk out with a couple of fine wines from a stunning range (Tignanello, Sassicaia and the best of Jermann, Maculan and Lungarotti). Christmas sees a floor-to-ceiling stack of panettoni and rather elegant hampers.

Shadwell

Butcher

HUSSEY'S

64 Wapping Lane, London E1 9RL
Tel: 020 7488 3686
Open: Mon-Sat 7am-6pm **Closed:** Sun, Bank holidays **Tube:** Wapping **Bus:** 100 **Mainline station:** Shadwell DLR **Payment:** cash, cheques, Delta, MasterCard, Switch, Visa
Bespoke deliveries locally

A gem of a butcher, located among a clutch of shops serving the local community, but with quality and range of produce to match any central London concern. Ian Hussey seems to have been born to the business, taking great pride in its longevity (the shop has been run by the family for nigh on fifty years) and its ability to provide a service way beyond the scope of any supermarket. Pigs' feet, tails, and just about every bit 'except the oink' were in evidence on our visit (all free-range), as was careful butchery of Scotch beef and lamb - Hussey's are associate members of the Guild of Scotch Quality Meat. All cooked meats - ham, salt beef, roast turkey - pies, and half a dozen varieties of sausage are home-produced, though black puddings – 'unbeatable' – come from MacSweens. There is game in season, plus eggs ('our eggs really are free-range' protests a notice) and a small selection of cheeses.

Shoreditch

Jewish Bakery

BEIGEL BAKE

159 Brick Lane, London E1 6SB
Tel: 020 7729 0616
Open: 24 hours, 7 days a week **Closed:** never **Tube:** Old Street **Bus:** 8, 67 **Mainline station:** Shoreditch **Payment:** cash, cheques
Takes orders for collection

More of an institution than a shop, yet remarkably easy to miss, except in the early hours of Saturday and Sunday morning, when its presence is betrayed by crowds of hungry nightclubbers. Given its location - tucked right at the north end of East London's Brick Lane - a visit is something of a pilgrimage, though you might well be rewarded not only by those famously chewy beigels but by the sight of Boy George or Billy Ocean tucking in. Other luminaries stay ensconced in their cars: Danny La Rue and Rod Stewart have been spotted by the amused proprictor, sending their drivers in to brave the milling munchers. You certainly don't need pop star salaries to indulge in a beigel, however: a smoked salmon and cream cheese classic weighs in at 95p while a perfect, plain buttered beigel will set you back just 20p. You can choose to have a platzel (no hole) instead, or indulge in gigantic cream eclairs, muffins or Eccles cakes washed down with spoon-supporting tea at the zinc bar. You can even buy your daily bloomer, cholah or black bread (weekends only) here, but it's those 8,000 beigels a day that keep the place buzzing.

Organic
Food Hall

FRESHLANDS
196 Old Street, London
EC1V 9FR
Tel. 020 7250 1708

Main shop: see Camden, page 109

Indian
Food Hall
Halal

TAJ STORES
112-114a Brick Lane, London
E1 6RL
Tel: 020 7377 0061
Fax: 020 7247 3844
Open: Mon-Sun 9am-9pm
Closed: never **Tube:** Liverpool Street, Aldgate East **Bus:** 67
Mainline station: Shoreditch, Liverpool Street **Payment:** cash, cheques, Delta, MasterCard, Switch, Visa

The elegant red and gold frontage, with a somewhat discordant display of coke tins, opens up to reveal a vast Bangladeshi/Indian cash-and-carry style store which also caters amply for personal customers. Thus you can stagger away with a well priced 20kg box of basic rice, or purchase a small packet of Watan super kernel basmati. Ghee, too, comes in small or gigantic tins, and this is certainly one of the best sources of bargain priced packs of spices whole or ground. A fast turnover of dry goods - spices, nuts, grains and flours - ensures an element of freshness. Meat is Halal; imported Indian ocean fish is, as ever, frozen, either whole, in 400g/800g blocks, or as steaks of terrifying dimensions - but at remarkably low prices. Otherwise goods run the gamut from basic cookery implements - plastic spoons to pots and pans - to rainbow coloured sugar-coated fennel seed and basil seed flavoured soft drinks.

Smithfield

Butcher
Free Range

MEAT CITY
507 Central Markets, Farringdon Road, London
EC1A 9NL
Tel: 020 77253 9606
Open: Mon-Fri 8.15am-6.15pm
Closed: Sat (open for collection by arrangement), Sun **Tube:** Farringdon, Chancery Lane **Bus:** 17, 45, 46, 63, 243 **Payment:** cash, cheques, Delta, MasterCard, Switch, Visa
Takes orders, bespoke delivery

Nigel Armstrong is a man with two missions: one is a Pentecostal ministry, the other is to purvey the finest naturally reared, free-range meat and poultry at affordable prices. Customers come here for 3-4 week hung Aberdeen Angus beef, 2-week matured Plantation pork, Group-grown veal, Royal Park venison and Golden Triangle turkey, all at prices 'affordable to everyone'. Nigel has eschewed joining the Q Guild to avoid the extra costs involved, and does not deal in organic meat for the same reason. After 17 years in the trade, he is confident of the supreme eating qualities of the meat he purveys. Frozen game and exotic meats (ostrich, kangaroo, bison) are available year round; it is, however, best to order anything you require and to phone before calling in: Nigel runs a one-man show and mornings are often spent on delivery rounds. Indeed there is often no meat on display as business relies on considerable reputation rather than passing trade.

Spitalfields

Bangladeshi
Grocer
Butcher
Halal

EASTERN GROCERS

53 Hanbury Street, London E1 5JP
Tel: 020 7377 1824
Open: Mon-Sun 9am-8.30pm
Closed: 25 Dec. **Tube:** Liverpool Street, Aldgate East **Bus:** 67
Mainline station: Liverpool Street, Shoreditch **Payment:** cash only

Despite the name, this is basically a major Bangladeshi store; indeed something of a cultural centre thanks partly to large-scale Halal meat supply, with a somewhat dour row of butchers in attendance. Less Anglo-friendly than the nearby Taj Stores (see page 65), this shop is nonetheless a good source of spices, pulses and grains, of pastry leaves and parathas, savoury snacks and puffed cereals, cakes, rusks and not least fish, both dried and frozen. The latter come uncompromisingly whole and generally huge. Names are often obscured or simply obscure to a Western shopper: ayer, boal, rohu, kaifu and the like, though you might also chance upon telapia or smelt. Dried fish include more familiar prawns and eel. Though it helps to know what you want, casual shoppers are more than welcome to browse.

Temple

L. BOOTH OF ST PAUL'S

Delicatessen
Greengrocer
Wild mushrooms

3 St Andrews Hill, London EC4V 5BY
Tel: 020 7236 5486
Fax: 020 7236 2963
Open: Mon-Fri 6.30am-4.30pm
Closed: weekend, Bank holidays
Tube: St Pauls **Bus:** 4, 11, 15, 17, 23, 26, 76, 172 **Mainline station:** Blackfriars **Payment:** cash, cheques, Amex, Delta, MasterCard, Switch, Visa

Spitalfields Organic Market

Brushfields Street

Open: Sun 9am-5pm **Tube:** Liverpool Street

Bus: 5, 8, 26, 35, 43, 47, 48, 78, 149, 242, 243a

Located in a building that once housed a wholesale fruit and vegetable market, Spitalfields takes its name from the hospital fields that once occupied the site. A general market operates from Monday to Friday, but in a fairly desultory way. It is at the weekend that the building really comes to life, and particularly on a Sunday, when the approach is organic. There are stalls selling organic fruit, vegetables, juices, breads, jams, relishes, pickles and eggs. Handmade, hand-woven, hand-dyed and hand-painted are the buzz-words at other stalls in the market, some of which offer extremely attractive goods. And if you're hungry, stalls and small restaurants around the edge of the building sell a variety of international foods such as crèpes, falafel, satay and Thai noodles.

“I used to go to Smithfield Market with Albert Roux, and stroking a plumb gigot, he would intone that it must have been a “very ’appy little lamb”. When our vaunted Food Standards Agency – still at its early white paper stage – understands that happy animals make better meat, and that animal welfare is a means of raising standards, some of that Frenchman's wisdom will have rubbed off.”

Rowley Leigh, from an article in *The Sunday Telegraph magazine*.

Bespoke deliveries within central London

A curious amalgam of a little shop - deli, greengrocer, wild mushroom specialist, wines and spirits - that relies less on passing trade (you're liable to miss it if you don't consult a map) than reputation. Indeed, the shop is something of an offshoot from restaurant supply – there's a wholesale arm at Borough Market (see page 155) – which means that those in the know can benefit from a prime collection of rather exquisite greengrocery: bunched carrots, borettane onions, grappes of shallots and smoked garlic, the tiniest of baby artichokes, black potatoes, quinces and, a real rarity, tomatillos. And then there are the wild mushrooms: fresh, frozen and dried, a year-round supply of *girolles, trompettes*, ceps, and others at perhaps the cheapest retail prices in London. Frozen tend to be brought in to order, so it pays to phone first. Preserved funghi include *cèpes à l'huile*, canned truffles and truffle pastes. Other items range from lunchtime trade groceries – British cheese and pasta salads to go – to gourmet exotica (lemongrass and lime leaf vinegar) and useful catering supplies such as cocktail cases. It's worth noting that Booth's mushroom stall at Borough Market is open for public trade every Saturday between 9am and 2pm.

R. TWINING & CO.

Tea

216 Strand, London
WC2R 1AP
Tel: 020 7353 3511
Fax: 020 7353 5336
Open: Mon-Fri 9.30am-4.45pm
Closed: weekend, Bank holidays
Tube: Aldwych, Temple **Bus:** 4, 11, 15, 23, 26, 76, 171a **Mainline station:** Charing Cross, Blackfriars **Payment:** cash, cheques, Amex, Delta, MasterCard, Switch, Visa
Mail-order

As much a museum as a shop, this narrow little Aladdin's cave of tea, coffee and related paraphernalia occupies the site of a coffee shop founded by Thomas Twining in 1706. Fine teas, a notch or two above the familiar basic range include: limited edition Keemun and Second Flush Darjeeling, plus 'export' teas such as the Prince of Wales, Queen Mary (reflecting Twining's Royal Appointment status) and a Vintage Darjeeling – this shop is the only UK source of this specialist collection, though all are available by mail order. There's a small range of coffees, too, all manner of brewing equipment, and even a selection of 'impulse buy' chocolates, from the entire Lindt range to

British specialities, such as Beech's violet creams.

Tower Hamlets

Jewish Delicatessen

★ ROGG'S

137 Cannon Street Road, London E1 2LX
Tel: 020 7488 3368
Open: Mon-Fri 9.30am-5.30pm, Sun 7am-2pm **Closed:** Sat **Tube:** Aldgate East **Bus:** 5, 15, 15b, 40
Mainline station: DLR Shadwell
Payment: cash, cheques
Food-to-go, orders taken

You will almost certainly have seen Barry Rogg and his shop featured on television, in weekend supplements and the world's glossiest magazines. It comes as something of a shock, then, to walk the unpromising roads of Tower Hamlets and find a shop much tinier and more ramshackle than pictures would have you believe. The range and quality of produce is no disappointment, however, any more than the ebullient character of the man himself. For over 50 years, Barry Rogg has maintained the fast-dying East European Jewish tradition of home-pickling herring and cucumbers in a variety of guises, cooking salt beef and pastrami, frying *gefilte* fish, and preparing chopped liver and herring. While buckets and trayfuls of these treasures occupy much of the shop, there is a great deal more: frankfurters and salume, *gaffelbidder* and *schmalz* herring, olives and gherkins, dried and fresh fruits, black bread, chollah and 'real' cheesecake – dense, creamy and almond-scented. A visit is liable to be punctuated with tasters of pickles, and colourful accounts of showbiz customers from a largely bygone era. Well worth visiting, if only to savour the atmosphere of the last remaining Jewish deli in London's East End.

STEPPING STONES FARM SHOP

Stepping Stones Farm, Stepney Way, London E1 3DG
Tel: 020 7790 8204

In the Area

The shop at Stepping Stones Farm is just a small part of this community enterprise and perhaps worth the trek (a 15 minutes walk from either station to the eastern, Stepney Green end of Stepney Way) only as part of a farm visit – the multitude of animals are immensely child-friendly, with some rather attractive breeds on display. That said, they have won a number of prizes for their considerable range of homemade jams, curds, jellies and marmalades, which vary seasonally, and an adventurous range of pickles and chutneys include Kashmiri garlic and sweet-pickled green tomato. The pullet, bantam and duck eggs are free-range and very fresh, and the staff are happy to put together little baskets of their produce. There are refreshments and plenty to keep children amused (not least three lolloping dogs) – both farm and shop are geared to bank holiday outings.

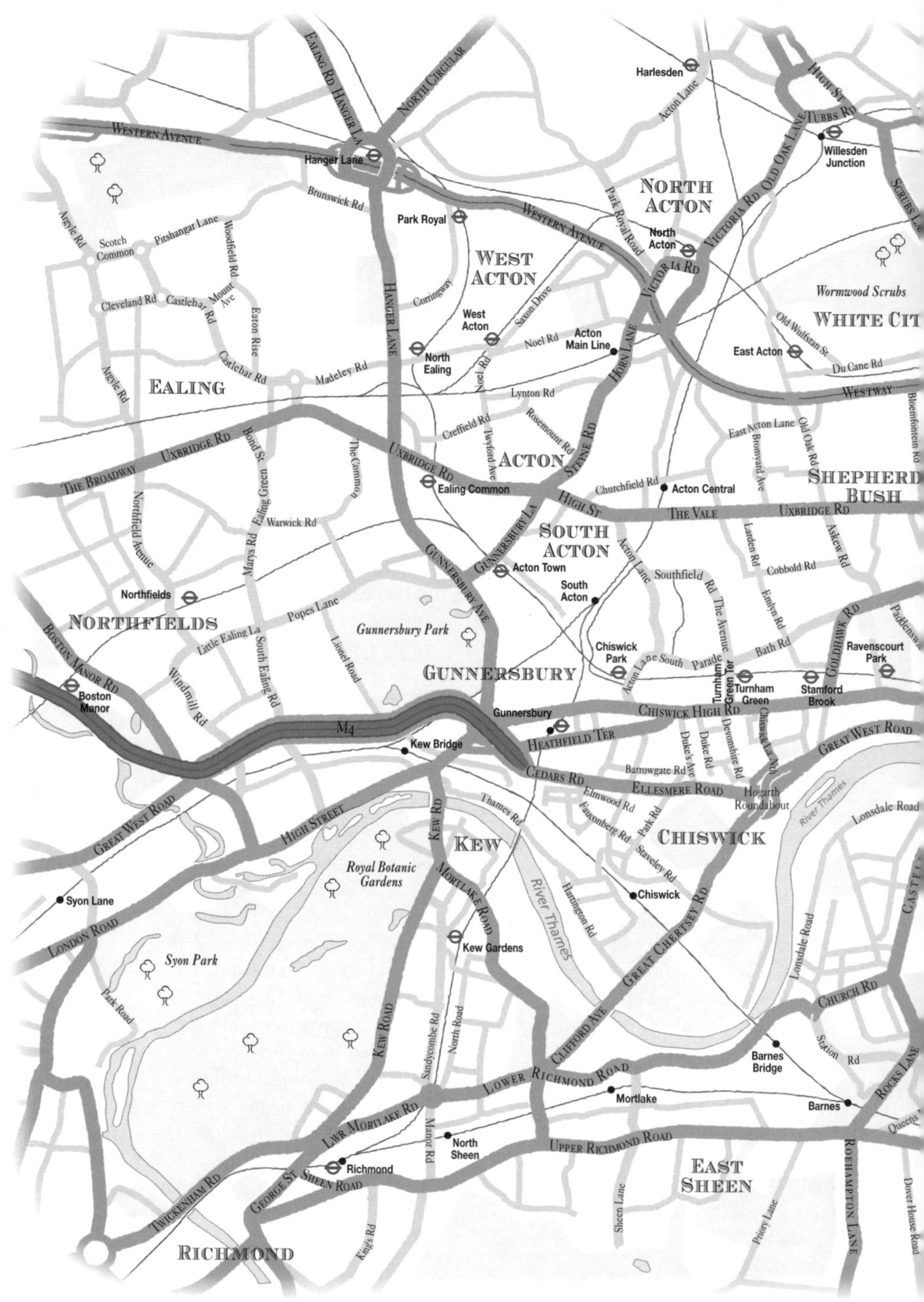
Ealing Rd
Hanger La
North Circular
Western Avenue
Hanger Lane
Harlesden
Acton Lane
High St
Tubbs Rd
Willesden Junction
Old Oak Lane
Scrubs La
Brunswick Rd
Park Royal
North Acton
Park Royal Road
Western Avenue
North Acton
Victoria Rd
West Acton
Wormwood Scrubs
Argyle Rd
Scotch Common
Pitshangar Lane
Woodfield Rd
Cleveland Rd
Castlebar Rd
Mount Ave
Eaton Rise
Coningway
Saxon Drive
White City
Old Wulfstan St
Hanger Lane
West Acton
Noel Rd
Acton Main Line
Horn Lane
East Acton
North Ealing
Du Cane Rd
Castlebar Rd
Madeley Rd
Noel Rd
Westway
Argyle Rd
Ealing
Lynton Rd
Rosemount Rd
Bloemfontein Rd
Creffield Rd
Twyford Ave
Steyne Rd
East Acton Lane
Bromyard Ave
Old Oak Rd
The Broadway
Uxbridge Rd
Bond St
The Common
Uxbridge Rd
Acton
Ealing Green
Ealing Common
Churchfield Rd
Acton Central
Shepherd's Bush
High St
The Vale
Uxbridge Rd
Northfield Avenue
Warwick Rd
Gunnersbury La
South Acton
Acton Lane
Larden Rd
Askew Rd
Marys Rd
Gunnersbury Ave
Acton Town
Southfield Rd
Cobbold Rd
Northfields
South Acton
Emlyn Rd
Popes Lane
The Avenue
Northfields
Gunnersbury Park
Little Ealing La
Lionel Road
Goldhawk Rd
Boston Manor Rd
South Ealing Rd
Chiswick Park
Acton Lane South
Parade
Bath Rd
Ravenscourt Park
Windmill Rd
Gunnersbury
Turnham Green Ter
Turnham Green
Stamford Brook
Boston Manor
Gunnersbury
Chiswick High Rd
Chiswick La Nth
M4
Heathfield Ter
Great West Road
Kew Bridge
Duke's Ave
Duke Rd
Devonshire Rd
Cedars Rd
Barrowgate Rd
Ellesmere Road
Hogarth Roundabout
River Thames
Great West Road
Thames Rd
Elmwood Rd
Lonsdale Road
High Street
Kew Rd
Park Rd
Fauconberg Rd
Kew
Chiswick
Royal Botanic Gardens
Mortlake Road
Staveley Rd
River Thames
Syon Lane
Harrington Rd
Chiswick
Great Chertsey Rd
Castelnau
London Road
Kew Gardens
Lonsdale Road
Syon Park
Church Rd
Park Road
Kew Road
Sandycombe Rd
North Road
Clifford Ave
Station Rd
Barnes Bridge
Rocks Lane
Lower Richmond Road
Mortlake
Barnes
Lwr Mortlake Rd
Manor Rd
North Sheen
Upper Richmond Road
Queens
Richmond
Sheen Road
George St
East Sheen
Twickenham Rd
Sheen Lane
Priory Lane
Roehampton Lane
Dover House Road
King's Rd
Richmond

West

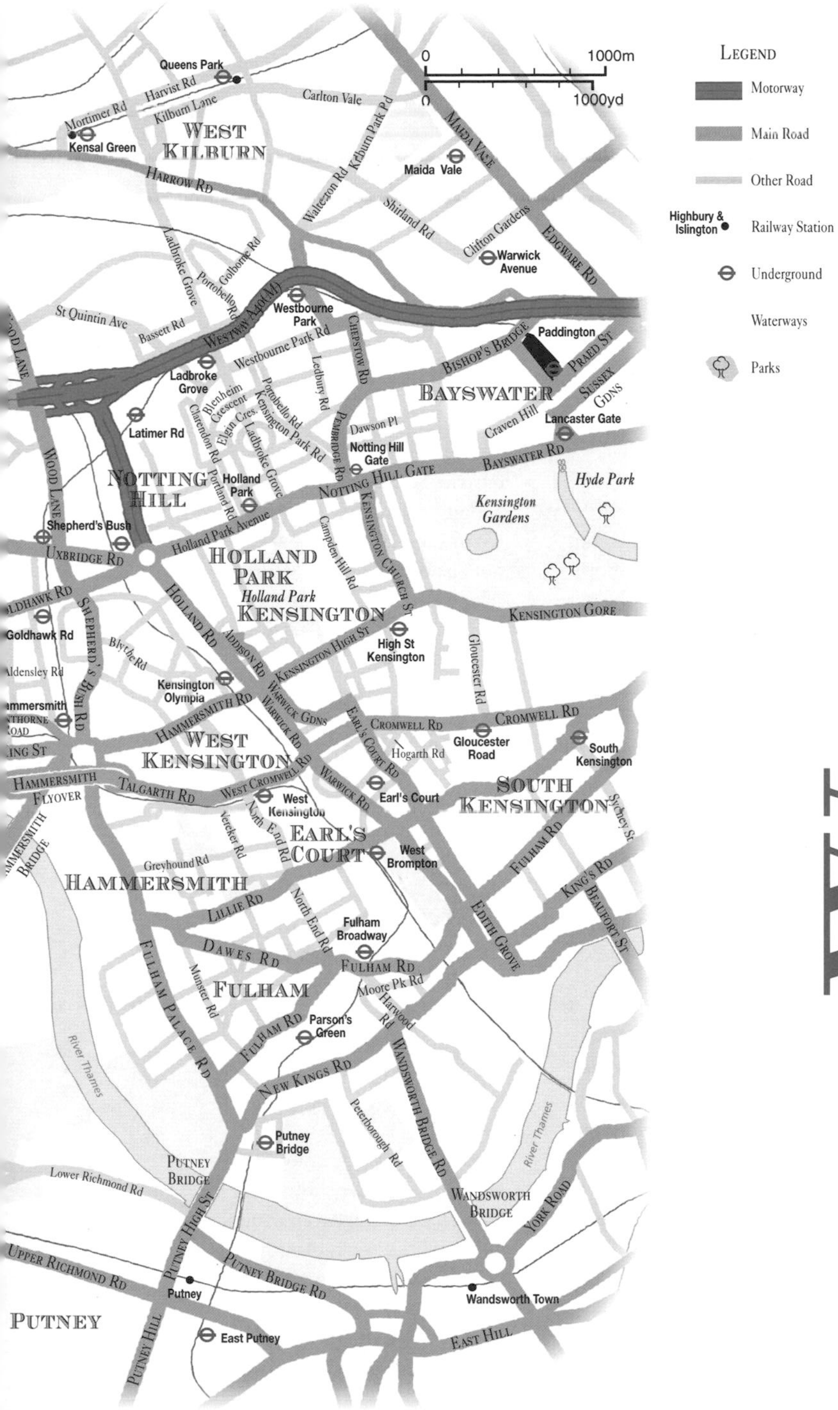

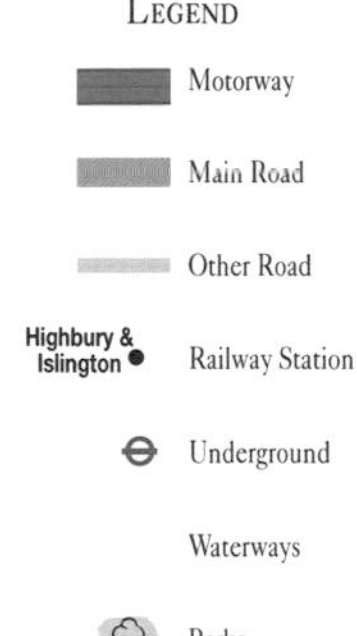

0
1000m
0
1000yd
Legend
Motorway
Main Road
Other Road
Highbury & Islington
Railway Station
Underground
Waterways
Parks
Queens Park
Harvist Rd
Kilburn Lane
Mortimer Rd
Kensal Green
West Kilburn
Carlton Vale
Kilburn Park Rd
Maida Vale
Harrow Rd
Walterton Rd
Shirland Rd
Clifton Gardens
Warwick Avenue
Edgware Rd
Ladbroke Grove
Golborne Rd
Portobello Rd
St Quintin Ave
Bassett Rd
Westway A40(M)
Westbourne Park
Westbourne Park Rd
Chepstow Rd
Bishop's Bridge
Paddington
Praed St
Sussex Gdns
Bayswater
Ledbury Rd
Latimer Rd
Blenheim Crescent
Elgin Cres.
Clarendon Rd
Portobello Rd
Kensington Park Rd
Pembridge Rd
Dawson Pl
Craven Hill
Lancaster Gate
Bayswater Rd
Notting Hill Gate
Hyde Park
Wood Lane
Notting Hill
Holland Park
Portland Rd
Kensington Gardens
Kensington Church St
Campden Hill Rd
Shepherd's Bush
Uxbridge Rd
Holland Park Avenue
Holland Park
Kensington
Kensington Gore
Goldhawk Rd
Shepherd's Bush Rd
Holland Rd
Addison Rd
Kensington High St
High St Kensington
Gloucester Rd
Blythe Rd
Aldensley Rd
Kensington Olympia
Hammersmith
Hammersmith Rd
Warwick Gdns
Warwick Rd
Earl's Court Rd
Cromwell Rd
Gloucester Road
South Kensington
Hogarth Rd
West Kensington
Talgarth Rd
West Cromwell Rd
Hammersmith Flyover
Hammersmith Bridge
Earl's Court
South Kensington
Sydney St
North End Rd
Vereker Rd
Earl's Court
West Brompton
Fulham Rd
Greyhound Rd
Hammersmith
King's Rd
Lillie Rd
Beaufort St
Fulham Broadway
Edith Grove
Dawes Rd
Fulham Rd
Munster Rd
Fulham
Moore Pk Rd
Harwood Rd
Fulham Palace Rd
Fulham Rd
Parson's Green
River Thames
New Kings Rd
Wandsworth Bridge Rd
Peterborough Rd
Putney Bridge
Putney Bridge
Lower Richmond Rd
Wandsworth Bridge
York Road
Putney High St
Upper Richmond Rd
Putney Bridge Rd
Putney
Wandsworth Town
Putney
East Putney
East Hill
Putney Hill

Chiswick

Cypriot
Greek
Delicatessen
Grocer
Greengrocer

★ T. ADAMOU & SONS

124-126 Chiswick High Road, London W4 1PU
Tel: 020 8994 0752
Open: Mon-Fri 8.30am-7pm, Sun and Bank holidays 9.30am-2pm **Closed:** 25, 26 Dec **Tube:** Turnham Green **Bus:** H91, 27, 237, 267 **Mainline station:** Chiswick **Payment:** cash, cheques

Originally hailing from northern Cyprus, Theodosios Adamou opened his eponymous shop in 1959 (he is credited as the man who brought the aubergine to Chiswick) and though the business is now run on a day-to-day basis by his sons, Adam and Ionas (Nagy), this patriarch still keeps a weather eye on it. Either sides of the main door are stacked with fresh fruit and vegetables. Inside to the right there is always a good selection of fresh herbs and salad leaves (dill, rocket, mint, purslane, spinach, curly endive, depending on the season) and more specialist vegetables such as leaf celery and kolokassi for Greek cooking. Greek breads are available daily, while on Tuesdays, Ukrainian rye bread comes in from a specialist bakery in Bradford. Alongside the huge array of dried and tinned ingredients, herbs and spices for continental and Asian cookery, Greek Cypriot specialities include cheese (several styles of feta, soft and hard anari for salads or cooking; kefalotiri); salted smoked herrings (eaten cut in slices as an accompaniment to drinks or alongside stewed black-eyed beans); thick, fresh sheep's yogurt from Cyprus; bastourma and loukanika sausages; vine leaves in brine; marinated olives; traditional pastries (including baklava and kadaifi; dried blonde figs from Kymi (in season) and packets of nuts galore. There is also a selection of ground Greek coffee, and olive oils from Kalamata and Crete.

Fishmonger

COVENT GARDEN FISHMONGERS

37 Turnham Green Terrace, Chiswick W4 1RG
Tel: 020 8995 9273
Fax: 020 8742 3899
Open: Tue, Wed 4.30am-5.30pm, Fri 4.30am-5.45pm, Sat 4.30am-5pm **Closed:** Mon, Sun and Bank holidays **Tube:** Turnham Green **Bus:** E3, H91, 27, 237, 267**Mainline station:** Chiswick **Payment:** cash, cheques

A family-owned fishmonger for over 20 years, the shop is run by Phil Diamond, who, in another guise, works as PR for the National Federation of Fishmongers.

He stocks an impressive range of fresh fish and seafood including black bream

Luigi's Delicatessen

Chelsea – *see page 23*

HOT DOGS
TUCK INTO THE BIG TASTE
HILL

Portobello Road Market

Notting Hill – *see page 99*

Brixton Market – *see page 157*

Sri Thai

Shepherd's Bush – *see page 105*

(imported from France), king and queen scallops, crab, large squid, sparkling fresh mackerel, swordfish steaks, loin of tuna and red mullet. In the shellfish range he usually has palourde clams and sometimes surf clams, among others. 'But', says Diamond, to survive these days, fishmongers 'have to forget being fishmongers and become entrepreneurs'. Accordingly, he is widening his range to include fish-related products – fresh seaweed, some cooked fish and marinated seafoods including boiled octopus, anchovies flavoured with chillies, rollmop and herring. However, he has stopped making fresh sushi since the supermarkets got in on the act, producing what he considers to be inferior quality sushi at much lower prices.

GROVE PARK DELI

Delicatessen

22 Fauconberg Road, London W4 3JY
Tel/Fax: 020 8995 8219
Open: Mon-Fri 8am-6.30pm, Sat 8am-4pm, Sun 9am-2pm **Closed:** Bank holidays **Tube:** Gunnersbury **Bus:** E3, 237, 267, 391 **Payment:** cash, cheques, Delta, MasterCard, Switch, Visa
Catering, food-to-go

A chance meeting between two food-loving Aussies – both have cooked professionally – led to the founding of this useful and much appreciated deli. It stocks many unusual items such as Australian olive oils and Tasmanian honey, and there are a legion of home-made goodies on offer, from take-away *pissaladiere* at lunchtime, to soups and stuffed chicken breasts to take home for supper. It sells fine breads from independent bakeries as well as its own–made focaccia, and a small range of cheeses.

"Two or three weeks into the English season, we cannot move for asparagus, and its price tumbles. This is the time to go crazy with the stuff, to make soups, risotto and pasta, to serve it with fish, chicken or in a navarin of lamb."

Rowley Leigh, Chef

Greengrocer

★ M & C

35 Turnham Green Terrace, London, W4 1RG
Tel: 020 8995 0140
Fax: 020 8747 0274
Open: Mon-Sat 6am-6pm **Closed:** Sun and Bank holidays **Tube:** Turnham Green **Bus:** E3, H91, 237, 267 **Mainline station:** Chiswick **Payment:** cash, cheques
Bespoke delivery

Formerly Macken & Collins and now solely owned by the enthusiastic Andrew ('we're known for our queer gear') Georghiou, this smallish shop packs in an impressive range of top-quality fruit and veg, much of which is unique to them. Suppliers to the River Café amongst other leading restaurants, their private customers include leading food writers Nigella Lawson, Joscelyn Dimbleby, Carole Handslip and Lindsey Bareham, as well as the local people. At the time of our visit, among the autumn goodies we spotted was an impressive range of fresh wild mushrooms – including morels – and squash, globe and Jerusalem artichokes, four different types of garlic, fresh horseradish, an impressive range of salad leaves, cavolo nero, Swiss chard, cime di rapa (Italian turnip greens), fresh borlotti beans, eight different varieties of potatoes, oriental greens and several varieties of plum and cherry tomatoes – including Sicilian cherry tomatoes on the vine. In the fruit department, a good range of English apples, pears and soft fruits in season are stocked, as well as a wide variety of exotics. They also have a growing range of organic produce. Andrew and his friendly team are happy to order in produce that they don't usually stock at customers' request.

Butcher

MACKEN BROS.

44 Turnham Green Terrace, London, W4 1QP
Tel: 020 8994 2646
Open: Mon-Fri 7am-6pm, Sat 7am-5.30pm **Closed:** Sun and Bank holidays **Tube:** Turnham Green **Bus:** E3, H91, 27, 237, 267 **Mainline station:** Chiswick
Payment: cash, cheques

This butchers stocks high-quality Scotch beef, fine English lamb, free-range poultry, additive-free, free-range pork, chicken and lamb, fresh duck legs and breasts and a range of homemade sausages. Also available are MacSweens haggis, boned and stuffed quail, flavoured meats for the grill or barbecue, French tame and wild rabbit, hare, venison – including saddle – wild boar haunches and saddles as well as portions at weekends, diced venison, English veal and fresh game in season. At Christmas, they stock Bramble Farm, free-range organic turkeys and Julie Goodman's free-range geese. Wider range available at weekends.

French
Bakery
Pâtisserie

MAISON BLANC

26-28 Turnham Green Terrace,
London W4 1QP
Tel: 020 8995 7220

Main shop: see St John's Wood, page 127

Delicatessen
Grocer

★ MORTIMER & BENNETT

33 Turnham Green Terrace,
London W4 1RG
Tel: 020 8995 4145
Fax: 020 8742 3068
Open: Mon-Fri 8.30am-6.30pm, Sat 8.30am-5.30pm **Closed:** Sun and Bank holidays **Tube:** Turnham Green **Bus:** E3, H91, 27, 37, 267, 391 **Payment:** cash, cheques, Delta, MasterCard, Switch, Visa
Free local delivery, mail-order

Dan Mortimer and Diane Bennett have run this fabulous delicatessen for over 10 years now. Packed to the gunwhales with exceptional and often unusual produce from France, Italy, Spain, Portugal and other continental countries as well as the UK, they sell cheese, charcuterie, hams, preserves, breads, cakes, desserts and much more besides. Seasonal specialities include Christmas puddings from Ireland, *stollen* and *lubkuchen* from Germany, mini Cheddar truckles from Mull, plus baby Stiltons, Lancashires and Cheshires. Wild smoked salmon comes from Ireland and Scotland. This high-class emporium (surely one of the best delis in London staffed by true enthusiasts) has become a selling point amongst the local estate agents and a meeting place for locals who pop in for the regular weekend tastings where they can also meet the producers of the goodies they taste. This is where the independent shops have an edge on the supermarkets, says Diane, whose passion is cheese. They buy direct from Neal's Yard Dairy (see page 30), and also support small farmers both in the UK and on the Continent. She will sell 3 whole Vacherins (luxury winter cheeses from France) on a Saturday, having matured them behind the scenes until they are at their peak (which supermarkets with their fast stock turnover cannot do).

Among the more unusual items, look out for Saba (a sweet and fruity grape must, a relative of balsamic vinegar), herby pancetta from Greve in Tuscany, smoked goose wing and goose salame from Udine. Breads come from specialist Italian and German bakers, as well as from & Clarke's (see page 86).

Chocolate

★ THEOBROMA CACAO

43 Turnham Green Terrace,
London W4 1RG
Tel: 020 8996 0431
Open: Mon-Sat 9.30am-6pm, Sun 9.30am-5pm **Closed:** Bank holidays **Tube:** Turnham Green **Bus:** E3, 27, H91, 237, 267, 391 **Payment:** cash, cheques, Delta, Switch, Visa

With its slate floor, pale woodwork and designer

lighting, this smart, modern shop sells a wide range of handmade truffles and chocolates (varying in cocoa content from 34-90%). Run by Phil Neal and his business partner, Cal Brown, it opened in December 1999 after extensive researches in Europe, looking at the style of chocolate shops over there. In the window is an ikon of chocolate art – a large chocolate leaf moulded from the 100-year old cacao tree at Kew (the name of the shop derives from the Latin name for the chocolate tree and is supposed to mean 'food of the gods').

Experienced pastry chef (ex Royal Lancaster Hotel, Claridges, Aspinalls) and self-taught chocolatier Neal works with 15 different blends of Valrhona chocolate to make a wide variety of flavoured delicacies using about 30 different flavours. There are around 4,000 chocolates on sale at any one time – quite a feat since Neal makes them all himself in the downstairs kitchen. The service is very personal and he will make anything on request, even very small orders. The chocolates will last up to six months if kept in a cool place (not the fridge, which will make it sweat). Neal also sells Italian amaretti, French nougat, *marrons glacés* and *pruneaux d'Agen*. There are plans to open further premises in the near future.

Ealing

AU GOURMET GREC

Polish
Greek
Grocer
Delicatessen

124 Northfield Avenue, London, W13 9RT
Tel: 020 8579 2722
Open: Tue, Thu, Fri 9.30am-6pm, Wed 9.30am-1.30pm, Sat 9am-5pm **Closed:** Sun **Tube:** Northfields **Bus:** E2, E3 **Mainline station:** West Ealing **Payment:** cash, cheques

A cornucopia of a shop filled with goods reflecting the backgrounds of the Greek husband and Polish wife owners, with a devoted local clientele. On offer are smoked meats, sausages and hams from Poland, Greece, Italy and Germany. There are weekly deliveries of smoked sprats, and a good selection of herrings, marinated olives, marinated mushrooms, and several cheeses. They also sell a marvellous selection of Polish and Greek sweets. On the pre-packed food line they have a wide range of dried mushrooms, barleys and flours.

RICHARDSON'S FINE FOOD

Butcher
Fishmonger

88 Northfield Avenue, London W13 9RR
Tel: 020 8567 1064
Fax: 020 8932 0074
Open: Mon-Thu 8am-5.30pm, Fri 8am-6pm, Sat 8am-4.30pm
Tube: Northfields **Bus:** E2 ,E3
Mainline station: West Ealing
Payment: cash, cheques, Delta, MasterCard, Switch
Food-to-go

This attractive, award-winning butcher, very popular amongst the local residents, has a wonderful range of fresh meat and sausages; the latter won them gold medals from the North West London Butchers' Association. Pies can be made to order, and cooked dishes include *boeuf bourguignon* and chicken breasts marinated in green Thai curry or lemon. There is a good selection of pâtés, cheeses and game in season, along with rabbit and venison, and even marinated haggis. Smoked fish is available, and fresh fish can be supplied upon request.

Branch: 110 South Ealing Road, London W5 4QJ
Tel: 020 8567 4405

7 Packhorse Road, Gerrards Cross, Bucks. SL9 7QA
Tel: 01753 886636

Butcher
Organic

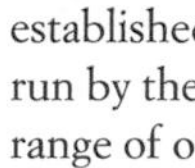

THOROGOODS

113 Northfield Avenue, London W13 9QR
Tel: 020 8567 0339
Fax: 020 8566 3033
Open: Tue-Sat 8am- 5pm **Tube:** Northfields **Bus:** E2, E3
Mainline station: West Ealing
Payment: cash, cheques
Free local delivery, mail-order

This very friendly neighbourhood butcher, established 38 years ago and run by the owner, has a wide range of organic meat and free-range poultry. Its speciality products include lamb cushions, chicken cushions and marinated legs of lamb. There is also a choice of frozen boned stuffed ducks, with a selection of stuffings. Their sausages are also popular.

Earl's Court

Filipino
Thai
Grocer
Greengrocer

MANILA SUPERMARKET

11-12 Hogarth Place, London SW5 0QT
Tel: 020 7373 8305
Open: Mon-Sun 9am-9pm **Tube:** Earls Court **Bus:** 74, 328, C1, C3
Payment: cash, cheques, Amex, Delta, MasterCard, Switch, Visa.

This exotic shop, which specialises in Filipino foods, has a fresh fruit and vegetables delivery every Monday and Friday from Thailand and the Philippines. It also stocks a full range of Filipino cooking essentials, from dim sum, spicy pork sausages, spring rolls, prawns and fish to frozen *papaitan*, a local delicacy consisting of tripe, heart and liver, and packets of pigs blood for making Filipino-style black pudding. They also have a wide selection of frozen leaves - pepper, jute, bitter melon and sweet potato - and packets of frozen grated *cassava*. There is a wonderful range of shrimp pastes, jars of salted anchovies, dried shrimp and *ikian bilis*, packets of dried chillies, sweet and sour sauces, chilli pickles, spiced vinegars, and a wide selection of noodles. The staff are charming and helpful.

Fulham

Fishmonger

BOX'S OF FULHAM
110 Wandsworth Bridge Road, London SW6 2TF
Tel: 020 7736 5766 (24 hours)
Fax: 020 7736 4509
Open: Mon-Sat 8.30am-5.30pm
Closed: Sun **Tube:** Fulham Broadway **Bus:** 14, 22, 28, 195
Payment: cash, cheques, Amex, Delta, MasterCard, Switch, Visa
Free delivery within a 3-4 mile radius of the shop in the Fulham and Chelsea areas.

Managed with enormous enthusiasm by Gino Massi for the past 7 years, Box's sell a range of high-quality fresh fish and seafood, including swordfish (from France), tuna loins, monkfish, sea bass (farmed and wild), halibut and squid (sourced from Grimsby, Newlyn and Devon). They also sell prime salmon for sushi. Fresh wild salmon and sea trout are available from early April to September. Downstairs, when the weather is not too hot, they smoke their own salmon and haddock (using charcoal sawdust from old whisky barrels) and are happy to smoke customers' own fish, to order. Like Panzer's in St John's Wood (see page 128), with salmon they separate out the oily cuts from the dry, depending on the customer's preference (the closer you get to the skin, the oilier it is, according to Gino). Gravad lax is made to order. Iranian beluga and sevruga caviar is also for sale, while seasonal delicacies include carp

North End Road Market

Open: Mon-Sat 9am-6pm **Closed:** Sun **Tube:** Fulham Broadway **Bus:** 14, 22, 28, 195

Apparently Fulham, now built up and comparatively 'gentrified', once boasted many market gardens, which perhaps explains the presence of the mainly fruit and vegetable market which occupies one side of North End Road, south of Lillie Road. Some 50-60 stalls stretch along the pavement, off the busy road, and many are beautifully arranged, with superior produce and good-value prices. There is a good fish stall as well, and a few stalls offering various types of household goods.

WORTH A DETOUR

Harvey Jones Painted Kitchen Shop, 57 New King's Road, SW6 4SE
Tel: 020 7731 3302

and live eels at Christmas (for their Jewish and Italian clientele, respectively). The range of seafood includes giant prawns, lobster, crab and a variety of oysters in season. For foodies in search of the unusual, gulls' eggs are available on rare occasions.

Fishmonger

★ COPE'S

700 Fulham Road, London SW6 5SA
Tel: 020 7371 7300
Open: Mon 10am-8pm, Tue-Fri 8.30am-8pm, Sat 9am-6pm **Closed:** Sun **Tube:** Fulham Broadway, Parsons Green **Bus:** 14 **Payment:** cash, cheques, Delta, MasterCard, Switch, Visa

Wholesale suppliers of quality fish and seafood to, among others, The Food Ferry, Harvey Nichols and surrounding restaurants, Cope's also operates both as a traditional fishmonger and a seafood lunch bar (you can nip in for some crab sandwiches or a plate of oysters to order). This modern, efficient, family-run shop sells fish and related products such as home-smoked, undyed cod and haddock and smoked cod's roe (all smoked at the Bromley branch). Related items such as taramasalata and fishcakes are made on the premises, alongside sushi lunchboxes. Fish-related products such as sauces, soups and sea salt are also available. Cope's buys more than half their fish from Cornwall, and their window display of gleaming fresh fish and shellfish is impressive. At the time of going to press there are plans for opening another shop in the Clapham area.

Branch: 6 Widmore Road, Bromley, Kent BR1 1RY
Tel: 020 8460 3343

Delicatessen
Grocer

ELIZABETH KING

34 New Kings Road, London SW6 4ST
Tel: 020 7736 2826
Fax: 020 7736 7056
Open: Mon-Fri 9am-8.30pm, Sat 9am-6pm, Sun 10am-3.30pm **Closed:** Bank holidays and associated Sun **Tube:** Parsons Green **Bus:** 2 **Payment:** cash, cheques, Amex, Delta, Master Card, Switch, Visa

A handy grocer and delicatessen in the heart of Fulham, packed with fresh fruit and vegetables, bowls of olives and artichoke hearts, dried and fresh pasta, a good range of rice, oils, and vinegars. The local French population has influenced the supplies, and there is a good selection of *saucissons, madeleines* and muscatel raisins, Meaux mustard, jars of *salmis de pintade, poulet basquaise* and *coq-au-vin*, along with products from Gascony, such as *graisse d'oie.* Other European cuisines are also represented with German-style sliced rye bread, Dutch fruit loaf, English cakes such as Yorkshire brack and a good selection of British cheeses (including the unpasturised Wigmore sheep cheese, Yarg, Wigmore, Cashel Blue and Ticklemore goat), all in good condition. Holiday specialities include Italian panettone and German *pfeffernüsse*, biscuits and *stollen* at Christmas, and Ackerman's Easter eggs (see page 129). There is also a good selection of salad ingredients.

Portuguese delicatessen

LISBOA DELICATESSEN

6, World's End Place, London SW10 0HE
Tel: 020 7376 3639

Main shop: see Notting Hill, page 97

Delicatessen

MOORE PARK DELICATESSEN

85 Moore Park Road, London SW6 2DA
Tel: 020 7736 2087
Open: Mon-Fri 10am-7pm, Sat 10am-2pm **Closed:** Sun and Bank holidays **Tube:** Fulham Broadway **Bus:** 11, 14, 22, 211
Payment: cash, cheques
Office catering, food-to-go

Situated in a quiet side street, yards from Chelsea football ground, this smart, cream-painted shop was established just under ten years ago by ex-model and local resident, Victoria Knyvett-Hoff. Specialising in English products (including cheeses, clotted cream fudge and toffee, Cumberland sausage, Cartmel Village sticky toffee pudding) and Italian

produce (they have an extensive range of Carluccio products) as well as other continental delicacies such as Portuguese Elvas figs from Conservas Rainhas Santa, Iranian and Russian caviar, French (yes!) caviar from Aquitaine, and organic olive oil from Catalonia. A favourite with, among others, Lloyd Grossman, this deli is best known, perhaps, for its personalised game pies (made to order only) and its freezer-to-oven supper dishes ("perfect for cheating dinner party hosts", says Victoria). They also make gourmet sandwiches and soup-of-the-day, which people reportedly travel great distances to buy at lunchtime. There is also a good deli counter with prepared salads, pasta sauces, smoked salmon, salume etc.

Butcher

★ RANDALLS

113 Wandsworth Bridge Road, London SW6 2TE
Tel. 020 7736 3426
Open: Mon-Fri 8.30am-5.30pm,

Sat 7am-4pm **Tube:** Fulham Broadway **Bus:** 14, 22, 28, 195 **Payment:** cash, cheques, Amex, Delta, MasterCard, Switch, Visa

Owned by Brian Randall, who knows many of his customers on a first-name basis, this well-run shop has been around for well over a decade selling high-quality meat and delicatessen goods. It is hard to leave here without buying much more than you originally came in for and if you want the meat to be boned or cut for you in a special way, this is accomplished with good grace and at high speed by skilled hands!

Around 20 per cent of the meat and poultry is organic with the majority of the rest free-range. They source their beef from Highgrove and Inverary (Aberdeen Angus or cross) with the lamb also from Highgrove or the West Country. Dinner party presentation cuts of lamb such as crown roast or guard of honour are always available, as are the marinated chicken pieces, the homemade sausages, venison and wild boar. They also stock a wide variety of game in season, as well as MacSween's haggis, and they make their own burgers from high-quality ground beef. The cheese counter at the back is well-stocked with British and continental fare and there is a delicious range of home-made preserves and biscuits to go with them. Kelly Bronze turkeys are available at Christmas and Kelly chickens are also for sale. Expect plenty of good-humoured banter from the cheerful staff. A favourite with TV chef, Jamie Oliver.

MAGPIES
152 Wandsworth Bridge Road, London
SW6 2UH
Tel: 020 736 3738

In the Area — A fascinating antique and bric-à-brac shop with an interesting line in antique kitchenalia.

Hammersmith

BUSHWACKER WHOLEFOODS

Wholefood
Organic

132 King Street, London
W6 OQU
Tel: 020 8748 2061
Open: Mon, Wed-Sat 10am-6pm, Tue 11am-6pm **Closed:** Sun and Bank holidays **Tube:** Hammersmith, Ravenscourt Park **Bus:** 27, 190, 267, 391, H91 **Payment:** cash, cheques, Delta, MasterCard, Switch, Visa
Food-to-go

This is a large wholefood shop, stocking a large range of organic and natural food. There is a good range of food-to-go, and a selection of vegetarian cheeses and organic fruit and vegetables. Apples and apple juice are delivered direct from Crones Orchard, Norfolk, and honey comes directly from aviaries.

Butcher
Organic
Game dealer

STENTON FAMILY BUTCHERS

55 Aldensley Road,
London W6 9PL
Tel: 020 8748 6121
Open: Tue, Wed, Fri 8am-6.30pm, Sat 8am-5pm, Thu 8am-1pm **Closed:** Monday **Tube:** Hammersmith, Ravenscourt Park **Bus:** 190, 267, 271, 391
Payment: cash, cheques

A good local butcher, run by owner Mr Stenton, who specialises in organic meat, including Welsh Black Beef, Gloucester Old Spot and Blue pork - a cross between wild boar and traditional pork - and welfare reared veal. He is also a licenced game dealer and one of the rare London butchers who will also dress customers' game. He sells a good line in Orkney Pâtés, and the full range of the Rannoch Smokery.

> "I think of myself as a demi-organic. I'm very in favour of it, but I'm not a zealot. Food isn't good just because it's organic. It has to taste good too."
>
> Sophie Grigson

Delicatessen

SUTHERLANDS

140 Shepherds Bush Road,
London W6 7PB
Tel: 020 7603 5717
Fax: 020 7603 1499
Open: Mon-Fri 8.30am-7.30pm, Sat 8.30-5pm, Sun 8.30am-3pm
Tube: Hammersmith **Bus:** 72, 295, 220, 283, 72 **Payment:** cash, cheques, Amex, Delta, MasterCard, Switch, Visa
Catering

Trading successfully even in the long shadow of the local Tesco, this increasingly well-stocked deli is something of an oasis in the foodie doldrums between Hammersmith and Holland Park. First-time food retailer John Sutherland opened up a few years ago using his redundancy money from British Airways, and in the years since, this charming Scotsman has gradually built up and broadened his stock range. The double front windows are brimful of freshly baked breads (focaccia, rye, soda, pugliese, sourdough, ciabatta etc) on one side and cakes, croissants, pâtisserie and savoury pastries on the other. The delicatessen counter sells pâtés (even wild boar liver pâté sometimes), rillettes, salads, cheeses, hams, salume and dips, while at the groaning table opposite you can help yourself to the huge bowls of olives and marinated vegetables. The fridges at the back hold Neal's Yard Dairy produce (see page 30), fresh herbs, Martin Pitt free range eggs, and excellent French cakes and tartes. At Christmas, there are truckles of Neal's Yard Dairy cheeses (see page 30), Ackerman's chocolates (see page 129), *marrons glacés*, superior panettone and other seasonal goodies. Sutherlands stock a good range of teas, including herbal and fruit teas, as well as selected French wines and spirits. They do a busy lunchtime sandwich and soup trade, and there are a couple of tables out front and a tiny café at the back - ideal for breakfast or lunch.

Holland Park

French Pâtisserie

CHAMBERY

108 Holland Park Avenue, London W11 4UA
Tel: 020 7221 3598
Fax: 020 7221 4328
Open: Mon-Sun 8am-8pm
Closed: 25 Dec. & 1 Jan. **Tube:** Holland Park **Bus:** 94 **Payment:** cash, cheques, MasterCard, Visa, Switch
Cakes made to order, catalogue, catering, delivery

In 1996, Frenchman Jean-Claude Chaufour left Tom's Deli (see page 104), which he had co-founded with Tom Conran, to purchase this friendly pâtisserie from the Cullen grocery chain. Pride of place goes to the rich French classic gateau, *Opéra*, a dark chocolate layered biscuit cake soaked in coffee, chocolate and praline mousse, and Harlequin, made of layers of white chocolate interleaved with sponge and milk chocolate. Both have a 60% cocoa content. Increasingly popular are Chafour's Madeira loaves. The range has recently expanded from chocolate, lemon and vanilla to chocolate orange, double chocolate, coffee-and-almond, and coconut-and-carrot. An assortment of Belgian chocolates, imported from the century-old manufacturer, Neuhaus, provide welcome gifts, while individual portions of cappucino cakes, vanilla and cassis mousse, Montblanc - a white chocolate mousse with chestnut spread - delicious fruit tartlets or *crême brulées* can be enjoyed on the premises with a cup of coffee. Designer cakes that can be ordered for special occasions have of late also become increasingly popular.

Cheese shop
Delicatessen

JEROBOAMS

96 Holland Park Avenue, London W11 3RB
Tel: 020 7727 9359
Fax: 020 7792 3672
Open: Mon-Fri 9am-7.30pm, Sat 8.30am-7pm, Sun 10am-4pm
Tube: Holland Park, Notting Hill Gate **Bus:** 94 **Payment:** cash, cheques, Amex, MasterCard, Switch, Visa
Catalogue, mail-order

There are a number of Jeroboams shops throughout the capital, but most sell only wines. Two however also sell food. These specialise in the finest cheeses from the UK, Ireland and continental Europe, and supervise the maturing themselves. Some 160 varieties, some very unusual, are stocked. On the occasion of our visit, a sheep's cheese from the Azores was on offer. The staff are highly knowledgeable and friendly. Hampers and gift boxes, available all year round, are especially popular at Christmas, and as well as cheeses include biscuits, chutneys, smoked salmon, and many other delicacies. They also stock a range of other goodies such as French preserved food in jars (including guinea fowl in red wine and goose confit), oils, charcuterie, good fresh bread, fine wines and champagnes.

Branch: see Belgravia, page 20

Butcher
Organic
Game dealer

★ C. LIDGATE

110 Holland Park Avenue, London W11 4UA
Tel: 020 7727 8243
Fax: 020 7229 7160
Open: Mon-Fri 7am-6pm, Sat 7am-5pm **Closed:** Sun and Bank holidays **Tube:** Holland Park **Bus:** 49, 94, 295 **Payment:** cash, cheques, Amex, Delta, MasterCard, Switch, Visa
Bespoke delivery, delivery, mail-order

David Lidgate is the fourth generation of his family to run this butchery business, established by his great-grandfather in 1850, and justly renowned as a top-rate butcher, as a series of awards proudly displayed on the walls attest. No growth promoters, hormones or antibiotics are used in the rearing of the meat, much of which is organic or organically fed, and animal welfare is a priority. Among organic meats on offer are beef and lamb from Prince Charles' farm at Highgrove, Gloucester Old Spot pork from Gatcombe Park, the home of the Princess Royal, and pure-bred Aberdeen Angus beef from the Queen Mother's estate at Castle May. A wide range of sausages, hams, pâtés and quiches are made on the premises. The pies are also homemade and worth a special mention: the words 'National

> "I go to Lidgate not just for the quality of the meat, which is unparallelled, but also for the service by which I mean the advice, information and expertise on offer. I am addicted to this shop."
>
> Nigella Lawson

Pic Champion' are fully justified - they are made daily with fresh vegetables, home-made butter-based pastry and good cuts of meat. Excellent cheeses are always available. In the autumn and at Christmas you can order game birds and bronze turkeys. Their chicken comes from a variety of sources: free-range birds come from Suffolk Farms, and organic ones come from Kelly's. Nigella Lawson's favourite butcher.

French Bakery Pâtisserie

MAISON BLANC

102 Holland Park Avenue, London W11 4UA
Tel: 020 7221 2494

Main shop: see St John's Wood, page 127

Greengrocer

★ MICHANICOU

2 Clarendon Road, London W11 3AA
Tel: 020 7727 5191
Fax: 020 7243 5719
Open: Mon-Fri 9am-6.30pm, Sat 9am-5.30pm **Closed:** Sun and Bank holidays **Tube:** Holland Park **Bus:** 94 **Payment:** cash, cheques
Delivery

An independent greengrocer is a rare phenomenon, but that's not the only reason this small shop deserves to be patronised. Don't be phased by its chaotic appearance - displayed on the floor-to-ceiling shelves are a huge array of exotic fruits and vegetables.

In addition to the basics, you can find a large range of squashes - acorn, spaghetti, blue and yellow onion - as well as pumpkins, sweet potatoes, Japanese mustard cress, yellow Dutch courgettes, French Jerusalem artichokes, cardoons, oxheart tomatoes, Kenyan jalapeño chillies, lemon grass, strings of smoked garlic, as well as several varieties of wild mushrooms and white truffles. The two Greek Cypriot owners pride themselves on stocking produce from all corners of the globe, and the fruit selection doesn't disappoint either. Quinces from Turkey, golden kiwis from New Zealand, Colombian gooseberries, Israeli strawberries, African guavas, pomegranates, kumquats, custard apples, persimmons, sharon fruit, Thai mangosteens - a sort of sherbety lychee, and the unusual sapodillo or chico from India - with a texture like kiwi and a taste of brown sugar. There is also an assortment of dried berries and nuts and boxes of Italian free-range eggs - popular for their startling deep orange yolks.

Italian Delicatessen

SPECK

2 Holland Park Terrace, Portland Road, London W11 4ND
Tel/Fax: 020 7229 7005
Open: Mon-Fri 9am-8.30pm, Sat 8.30am-7pm **Closed:** Sun, Easter, Bank holidays, fortnight in August **Tube:** Holland Park **Bus:** 94 **Payment:** cash, cheques, Amex, MasterCard, Switch, Visa
Catering, food-to-go

Passers-by never fail to be entertained by the theatrical display of fresh pasta made daily in the window of this chic Italian deli. Famous locals John Cleese and Patsy Kensit cannot resist their tortelloni filled with fresh spinach or porcini mushrooms, ricotta and parmesan, or the ready-to-bake cannelloni and lasagna. Other delicious home-made specialities in the chilled cabinet are soups; napoletana, tomato-and-aubergine or cream-and-mushroom pasta sauces, and desserts such as chocolate mousse with amaretti or *panna cotta*. The excellent traiteur counter is stocked with delicacies such as *risotto al pesto, involtini* of speck (smoked ham cured in the Dolomites wrapped round thin French bean parcels), marinated artichokes and basil or rocket pesto. There is also a wide variety of Italian cheeses, cold meats and salume, which the charming and helpful staff will allow you to taste. For Christmas or special occasions, treat yourself to an elaborate box of panettone or pandoro. Also interesting are the luxury dried pastas and a distinctive range of extra virgin olive oils and balsamic vinegars.

Kensington

Cheese shop

★ BARSTOW & BARR

32/34 Earl's Court Road, London W8 6EJ
Tel/Fax: 020 7937 8004
Open: Mon-Fri 10am-6.30pm, Sat 9am-6pm, Sun 11.30am-4.30pm **Closed:** Bank holidays **Tube:** High Street Kensington **Bus:** C1, 9, 9a, 10, 27, 28, 49, 328 **Payment:** cash, cheques, Delta, MasterCard, Switch, Visa
Catalogue, mail-order, wholesale

A small and bright shop with a branch in Islington, Barstow & Barr is among London's best cheesemongers. It stocks over 120 carefully chosen British, Irish, French and Italian cheeses, often award-winners, and many of them bought directly from the farms and matured on site to achieve the best condition possible. Among the rarer English cheeses are Chewton cheddar-style cheese, and Richard III Wensleydale. The French collection includes a prize-winning brie de Meaux Claris, Epoisse and in season, excellent Coulommiers. All cheeses can be tasted and felt, and advice is willingly forthcoming. Euphorium breads (see page 137), olives, jams, pickles and organic vegetables are also on offer.

Branch: see Islington, page 137

Bakery
Pâtisserie
Delicatessen

★ & CLARKE'S

122 Kensington Church Street, London W8 4BH
Tel: 020 7229 2190
Fax: 020 7229 4564
Open: Mon-Fri 8am-8pm, Sat 9am-4pm **Closed:** Sun and Bank holidays **Tube:** Notting Hill Gate **Bus:** 27, 28, 31, 52, 70, 94, 328 **Payment:** cash, cheques,

Amex, Delta, MasterCard, Switch, Visa **Mail-order**

A treasure trove of a shop, this small establishment, attached to Sally Clarke's award-winning restaurant next door, offers many foods actually produced in the restaurant kitchen. Its speciality however, are the 35 types of bread, baked daily, on offer. There is the justly famous rosemary and raisin bread, an oatmeal honeypot bread, fig and fennel, as well as a wide selection of rye, sourdough, French and Italian breads. Cakes - their rich chocolate cake is especially delicious - and their own-brand shortbreads are also made on the premises. The hand-rolled bitter chocolate truffles are to die for, as are the granola, spiced nuts and buttery oat biscuits. Freshly baked pizza and focaccia are available to take away or eat in. There is also a wide selection of fruits, vegetables, butters, Neal's Yard Dairy cheeses (see page 30), preserves, olives and olive oils, and a small café space at the back.

HAMLINS OF KENSINGTON

3 Abingdon Road, London W8 6AH **Tel:** 020 7376 2191 **Fax:** 020 7937 6121 **Open:** Mon-Fri 9am-4pm **Closed:** Sat, Sun and Bank holidays **Tube:** Olympia, High Street Kensington **Bus:** 9, 10, 27, 28, 31, 49 **Payment:** cash, cheques, Delta, MasterCard, Switch, Visa **Catering, delivery, food-to-go**

Two eccentric Irish chefs make all the food in the downstairs kitchen for Hamlins' extensive catering and delicatessen outlet. Robert Mcareavey used to work at the Shakespeare Globe restaurant and Mark Howard was a sous-chef at Harrod's, a culinary pedigree that guarantees the quality and home-cooked taste of the food on offer. The menu in the deli upstairs changes daily, with prices that are hard to beat. At lunchtime, the hot soup might be a simple but tasty leek-and-potato, a popular carrot-and-coriander or a more exotic lobster-and-lemongrass. Starters include chicken satay with peanut & sesame seed dip, serrano ham bruschetta with manchego cheese-and-truffle honey and chicken-and-asparagus terrine. For mains, there is a wide range of homemade quiches as well as pies, pizzas, arancini rice balls, a selection of waldorf, pasta, bean, rice and raw salads, massive fish cakes made with four types of fish, and a couple of chicken dishes. Accompanying breads comprise baguettes, ciabatta, granary and a delicious walnut. Puds on offer vary from pecan pie and treacle tart to lemon-and-sultana cheesecake. At Christmas, expect to find Christmas cake and mince pies.

Middle Eastern
Organic
Butcher
Delicatessen

MILLER OF KENSINGTON

14 Stratford Road, London W8 6QD
Tel: 020 7937 1777
Fax: 020 7376 2320
Open: Mon & Sat 8am-1.30pm, Tue-Fri 8am-6pm **Closed:** Sun and Bank holidays **Tube:** Olympia, High Street Kensington **Bus:** 9, 10, 27, 28, 31, 49 **Payment:** cash, cheques, Delta, MasterCard, Switch, Visa
Catering, local delivery

Owner Mohamed el Banna learned all about the butcher's trade from his former boss, John Miller, whose shop he bought some 15 years ago. The main counter displays exclusively organic meat, chicken, quails and veal. Purchases can be vacuum packed on request, considerably extending their fridge life. A festive speciality is the famous Victorian Royal Roast, a goose stuffed with duck, in turn stuffed with pheasant, then chicken, partridge and quail, all boned. Miller's is one of the few butchers in London to boast its own cold store, where meat is hung for a minimum of two weeks. Mohamed is a member of the Soil Association and possesses a hygiene certificate, awarded by the Meat Training Council. His Egyptian origins are reflected in some of the Middle Eastern specialities on offer, such as trays of baklava, cow's milk feta cheese and an Egyptian hard cheese made from buffalo milk, similar to Pecorino. Marinated olives in large bowls, foie gras and bresaola stand next to quail eggs, haggis, smoked duck breast, smoked Scotch salmon and organic free range eggs. Tins of Egyptian *ful medames* beans, jars of French soup and duck gizzard confit, Italian pasta and pasta sauces, chutneys, and a selection of cold-pressed extra virgin olive oils adorn the shelves.

Iranian
Pâtisserie
Grocer
Greengrocer
Delicatessen

★ REZA PÂTISSERIE

345 High Street Kensington, London W8 6NW
Tel: 020 7602 3674/603 0924
Fax: 020 7610 4221
Open: Mon-Sun 9am-8.30pm
Closed: Christmas **Tube:** Kensington Olympia, West

Yasar Halim Pâtisserie

Harringay – *see page 136*

Carluccio's

Covent Garden – *see page 29*

C. Lidgate

Holland Park – *see page 84*

& Clarke's

Kensington – *see page 86*

Maison Blanc

St John's Wood branch – *see page 127*

Kensington **Bus:** 9, 10, 27, 28, 49 **Payment:** cash, cheques

Rather like the next-door-but-one Super Bahar, Reza carries a little bit of everything Iranian, from pickles to ice cream (no more Halal meat, however). It even advertises Iranian Caviar with greater prominence than its pastries, and indeed one largeish tin of Beluga would cost more than the entire counter display of pâtisserie. But the seductive scent of rosewater and roast pistachios is what entices one in, and the dual displays of roast nuts and melon seeds on the one side, and a myriad of sweet pastries on the other, draw the eye irresistibly. There are at least 30 varieties of pastry on offer at any one time, all superbly fresh (baked on the premises) and disconcertingly un-named – partly because the selection changes all the time, and largely because non-Iranians would find most names meaningless. But service is more than helpful, offering either a simple division between familiar baklavas and generic 'cookies' or discriminating more finely on request, stopping to explain, perhaps, the role of saffron-scented crystal sugar in treating stomach upsets. Best bet is to ask for a selection box; half a kilo in weight costs surprisingly little and all are superb, the plainest looking pastries sometimes offering the most excitement in the mouth.

"I go to the local Indian and Chinese shops and am never happier than when I'm squeezing the produce in a Middle Eastern grocer. 

Nigel Slater

★ SUPER BAHAR

Iranian
Grocer
Greengrocer

349a Kensington High Street, London W8 6NW
Tel: 020 7603 5083
Open: Mon-Sun 9am-8.30pm
Closed: Bank holidays **Tube:** Kensington Olympia, West Kensington **Bus:** 9, 10, 27, 28, 49 **Payment:** cash, cheques

Located usefully almost next door to the Reza Pâtisserie, with whom there is linked ownership but also healthy rivalry. Super Bahar describes itself as purveying Middle Eastern/Oriental/Continental food but is in truth an Iranian grocery and greengrocery par excellence, indeed something of an Iranian cultural centre: one wall is lined with native videos, cassettes, cookbooks and even backgammon sets, and Iranian music plays uncompromisingly in the not-so-background. Here you will find freeze-dried herbs and elusive spice mixtures:

zatar, sumak, sour grape, lime and yoghourt powders. Sourness is a common denominator: sour grape juice, pomegranate and morello cherry syrups, dried sour apricots, dried barberries and barberry paste, lemon-salted pistachios. Other staples include roast chickpea flour, pickled garlic cloves and scented waters. Glowing red saffron, too, available in any size from small sachets to beautifully scripted caskets. But this is, most famously, London's prime over-the-counter source of wholesale-priced Iranian caviar, of which there is an improbably well stocked chill counter display. As no credit cards are accepted, you will need to fill your pockets with wads of notes (purchases in the £500 league are a common sight). But you can equally well purchase a few pistachio-stuffed dates or simply browse at will.

Notting Hill

Bakery

THE BREADSTALL

172 Portobello Road, London W11 2EB
Tel: 020 7221 3122
Open: Mon-Fri 8am-6pm, Sat 8am-7pm, Sun 9am-5pm **Closed:** 25, 26 Dec. & 1 Jan. **Tube:** Notting Hill, Ladbroke Grove
Bus: 23, 52, 70 **Payment:** cash, cheques
Cakes and pastries made to order

Albert Vince did so well selling specialty bread from his stall on Portobello Road market, that when the former Dewhurst butchery behind him became vacant, he promptly moved inside. Despite the shop's tatty interior, the bread is good and freshly baked daily by French and Italian chefs in their south London bakery. Hence the choice of ciabatta, Tuscan sourdough, campaillou, foccaccia - either rosemary-and-seasalt or olive, and scrumptious walnut and raisin bread. The bagels, small black rye, and 1000-seed Bavarian bread come from the Beigel Bake in the East End (see page 64). The selection of viennoiserie includes *pain aux raisins*, butter croissants, pain au chocolat and French fruit folds. There are muffins and apple crumble slices, large butter almond and pecan tarts, scones, flapjacks and chocolate stick crunch bars, as well as packets of homemade Farmhouse biscuits and cookies. Their moist Madeira cakes come in assorted varieties including carrot and apple-and-toffee.

Branches: see stalls at Berwick Street Market, page 48, and Northcote Road Market, page 173

Fishmonger

★ CHALMERS & GRAY

67 Notting Hill Gate, London W11 3JS
Tel: 020 7221 6177
Fax: 020 7727 3907
Open: Mon-Fri 8am-6pm, Sat 8am-5pm **Closed:** Sun and Bank holidays **Tube:** Notting Hill Gate **Bus:** 12, 27, 28, 31, 52, 70, 94, 302, 328 **Payment:** cash, cheques, Delta, MasterCard, Switch, Visa
Free delivery

This excellent fishmonger presents its fresh fish and shellfish - brought in from the major Scottish and English ports daily - beautifully arranged and iced on a huge marble slab, looking rather like an impressionist painting. You will find fresh tuna, seabass, salmon and sole lying next to oysters, crab, lobster and langoustines boiled on the premises. In addition, they also stock caviar, smoked salmon, smoked cod's roe, and free-range chickens. Owner John Gray is more than happy to order special items, such as carp or pike, which are not normally stocked.

Belgian Pâtisserie Bakery

DE BAERE

101 Notting Hill Gate, London W11 3ZL
Tel: 020 7792 8080
Fax: 020 7243 0888
Open: Mon-Sat 8.30am-6.30pm, Sun 9am-3pm **Closed:** 25, 26 Dec. & 1 Jan. **Tube:** Notting Hill Gate **Bus:** 12, 94, 28, 31, 52
Payment: cash, cheques, Electron, MasterCard, Solo, Switch, Visa
Cakes made to order.

Confectioner Rik de Baere's excellent Belgian specialities are gâteaux with weird names, such as Guess, the World Champion Cake in 1994 and 1995 (bitter chocolate mousse, orange crème brulée, crisp biscuit), Ministry of C (vanilla and chocolate mousse and almond chocolate sponge) or Princess (a chocolate pyramid with orange mousse on a crisp biscuit base). Most will serve 5-6 people. Marginally less fattening is the Croute au Citron with a meringue topping or an apple, pear or apricot sponge. Those with a plainer preference can choose the loaf-shaped butter cake, plain, lemon or chocolate. There is also a mouthwatering range of pastries, such as *millefeuille*, October (crème pâtissière filling) or Manjari (chocolate exterior with vanilla mousse). You can sample them upstairs in the cosy café. De Baere also sells a variety of croissants, like almond or pistachio-and-chocolate tortillons and plain or sesame sprinkled baguettes - all made at the company's own bakery in west London, as well as savoury quiches, pastries and filled rolls.

Branch: see Knightsbridge, page 33, see South Kensington, page 53, see Mayfair, page 41

Spanish
Delicatessen
Grocer

P. DE LA FUENTE

288 Portobello Road, London W10 5TE
Tel/Fax: 020 8960 5687
Open: Mon-Sat 9am-6pm
Closed: Sun and Bank holidays
Tube: Ladbroke Grove **Bus:** 7, 23, 28, 52, 70, 295 **Payment:** cash, cheques, Amex, Delta, MasterCard, Switch, Visa

Located near the flyover, P. de la Fuente has been a Spanish grocery store since 1972. Typical Spanish staples such as extra virgin olive oils are stacked neatly alongside cider, wine and sherry vinegars, tins of tripe with chickpeas and *fabada*, a peasant stew from Asturias. There is a huge selection of black and green tinned olives in a variety of sizes, plain, pitted or stuffed with anchovies, pimientos, lemon, chilli or cheese. Saffron strands come in boxes or in a tiny, handblown glass bottle with cork stopper. Alternatively, you can buy it in a packet already ground. Cans of smoked paprika are also available. At Christmas, Spanish sweetmeats, such as torrón (Spanish nougat) with almonds and nuts make their appearance. The delicatessen counter at the rear of this small shop offers a choice of salume, chorizos, cured cold meats, morcilla, cured serrano ham and Spanish bacalao (dried salt cod). The cheeses include a variety of cabras and manchegos at various stages of maturation. Sample also the

loose olives and soaked dried beans displayed in large bowls. Stacked against the wall, towers of terracotta pots tempt you to buy, take home and cook.

Delicatessen

FELICITOUS

19 Kensington Park Road, London W11 2EU
Tel: 020 7243 4050
Fax: 020 7243 4052
Open: Mon-Fri 9am-9pm, Sat 9am-7pm, Sun 10am-5pm
Closed: 25, 26 Dec., 1 Jan. **Tube:** Notting Hill Gate, Ladbroke Grove **Bus:** 7, 23, 27, 28, 31, 52, 70, 328 **Payment:** cash, cheques, Amex, Electron, MasterCard, Solo, Visa
Catering, delivery, food-to-go

Lady Felicity Osborne has turned her attention from designer fabrics (Osborne & Little) to designer food, with her attractive and airy deli offering enticing gourmet groceries and fine wines. Despite stiff competition from nearby Mr Christian's (see page 98), Felicitous holds its own. Award-winning de Gustibus organic breads (see page 38), only available on Saturdays, sell out in the first half-hour of the day. Among the preserves, Mrs Huddleston's homemade conserves, Escoffier's handmade Sweet Pepper Chutney in a square kilner jar and a pottery honey jar of Mel de Montanya stand out. Own-brand products include extra virgin olive oil; muesli; low-fat, gluten-free granola; gold chocolate dragées and cocoa-dusted almonds. Felicitous is big on chocolate. Don't miss award-winning Valhrona handmade chocolate truffles or marinated and glazed citrus slices hand-dipped in chocolate. The deli counter offers a range of cheeses, salume, cooked and dried hams, pastrami, quail Scotch eggs, sundried tomatoes and big bowls of marinated and stuffed olives. Daily traiteur dishes cooked on the premises by a former chef from Kensington Place include turnip-and-chive soup with organic bread, saffron risotto, cornfritters and Tuscan tortellini. Downstairs, among many herbs, spices, baskets and hampers is a fascinating variety of pasta.

Spanish
Delicatessen
Grocer

★ R. GARCIA & SONS

248-250 Portobello Road, London W11 1LL **Tel/Fax:** 020 7221 6119 **Open:** Tue-Sat 8.30am-6pm **Closed:** Sun, Mon and Bank holidays **Tube:** Notting Hill Gate, Ladbroke Grove **Bus:** 7, 23, 28, 52, 70, 295 **Payment:** cash, cheques, Amex, Delta, MasterCard, Switch, Visa

This delighful tienda has been in the Garcia family for three generations now, and has long been a place of pilgrimage for Spanish food lovers. The shelves are crammed full of Spanish and Mediterranean produce - tins of olives, artichoke, eggplant and palm hearts, sardines, mussels, snails and squid, not to mention dried pulses and beans, chick peas and a large selection of pasta. The cold cabinet sports dried salt cod and marinated anchovies, among the staples, but it is really the delicatessen counter, spanning the width of the shop at the rear, which pulls the crowds. Here, giant serrano hams sway from the ceiling, while below, customers can choose from a large range of salamis, chorizos, cured cold meats and dried hams. Sweet acorn-fed ham is a speciality. The cheeses are equally absorbing; there are cabras and manchegos at all stages of maturation, plus smoked Idiazal from the Basque region, made with sheep's milk. Try also the many varieties of marinated olives, dry, fleshy or stuffed. The huge variety of typically Spanish sweetmeats includes torrón (Spanish nougat) with almonds and nuts, boxes of polvoron biscuits and the divine *alfajores almendras* (with almonds, honey and cinnamon). Worth noting, too, is the vast range of European extra virgin olive oils. Among its celebrity customers is Tom Conran, a compliment indeed from a fellow deli-owner!

Fishmonger

GOLDBORNE FISHERIES

75 Golborne Road, London W10 5NP
Tel. 020 8960 3100
Fax: 020 8968 5455
Open: Mon 10am-4pm, Tue-Sat 8.30am-6pm **Closed:** Sun and Bank holidays **Tube:** Ladbroke Grove, Westbourne Park **Bus:** 7, 23, 28, 31, 52, 70, 295, 302
Payment: cash, cheques

Mauritian owner George Ng has introduced the exotic fish of his native shores to multi-cultural Golborne Road. Impressively, George bypasses Billingsgate and sources his supply directly from abroad. Crayfish comes from Cuba and Mozambique, while capitaine blanc is flown over from Mauritius. Rarer fish such as rascasse - intrinsic to *bouillabaisse* - weaver and parrot fish are also regularly on offer. Jamie Oliver and Anthony Worrall Thompson are among the celebrity chefs who can be spotted browsing among the langoustines, lobster tails, tiger prawns and yellow grupa. Astutely, George caters for his cosmopolitan clientele: conger eel, octopus and black sabre fish are favoured by the Portuguese, squid and hake by the Spanish and the exotics such as snapper, king fish and dolphin fish are preferred by the Afro-Caribbean community. For Brits with more traditional tastes, there are whole salmon and tuna sliced to order, monkfish, mussels, oysters, scallops, live spider crabs and top quality cod, the last two supplied directly by fishermen in Plymouth.

Bakery
Organic
Special Diet

THE GRAIN SHOP

269a Portobello Road, London W11 1LR
Tel/Fax: 020 7229 5571
Open: Mon-Fri 9.30am-6pm, Sat 9am-6pm **Closed:** 25, 26 Dec. & 1 Jan. **Tube:** Notting Hill Gate, Ladbroke Grove **Bus:** 7, 23, 28, 52, 70, 295 **Payment:** cash, cheques

People come to this small shop from miles around to buy their bread, which caters for special diets and like all the food on offer, is baked on the premises. Using only organic flour, there are yeast-free, wheat-free and sugar-free loaves. Favourites are the large sourdough, rice bread – organic wholemeal flour peppered with brown rice and sunflower seed bread – so moist it has the texture and flavour of nutty cake. There's also olive-and-rosemary, honey-sweetened corn bread and rye sourdough (wheat and yeast-free). Teatime treats include vegan sugar-free date-and-lemon slices, vegan wheat-free sesame and gluten-free flapjacks. At Christmas, you can buy vegan sugar-free mince pies or sugar, wheat and gluten-free Christmas cakes.

BOOKS FOR COOKS

4 Blenheim Crescent, London W11 1NN
Tel: 020 7221 1992

This tiny shop is the place to go to be inspired to try something creative with all the delicious ingredients picked up in the nearby shops and market. It is crammed full of books covering every conceivable culinary area of the globe. You are guaranteed to find recipes to tempt your taste buds, or ideas on how to change your diet, and if you can't, the very helpful staff are on hand to guide you. Recipes from the books stocked in the shop are often being demonstrated in the little kitchen at the back and if you want to improve your culinary abilities, workshops are available for around £20.

The limited but carefully chosen groceries include some exotic herb teas, a variety of honeys - try the Miel des Pyrenées from sea lavender, dandelion or thyme. Also unusual is the Biona organic red rice from the Camargue, and hemp seed.

Branch: see Battersea, page 172

Butcher
Game dealer
Organic

★ KINGSLAND MASTER BUTCHERS

140 Portobello Road, London W11 2DZ
Tel: 020 7727 6067
Fax: 020 7727 0706
Open: Mon-Thu 7.30am-6pm, Fri & Sat 6.30am-6pm **Closed:** Sun and Bank holidays **Tube:** Notting Hill Gate, Ladbroke Grove **Bus:** 23, 52, 70 **Payment:** cash, cheques, Amex, Delta, MasterCard, Switch, Visa
Delivery

Truly a family business - brothers Philip and Haydn Field and both their sons work here, while Mrs Field makes the pies - Kingsland styles itself as an Edwardian butcher with old-fashioned values of friendly, personal service. It offers a wide choice of free range, organic and speciality meats: pork is supplied from rare breeds such as Gloucester Old Spot, Middle White and British Saddleback, while beef is from Longhorn and Ayrshire grass-fed cattle. Indeed they are London's only accredited Rare Breeds Survival Trust retail outlet. The sausages are handmade, and come in interesting combinations such as apricot-and-garlic, Merguez, or wild boar-and-apple. In the summer, you can find marinated meats for casseroles or kebabs. Dressed cuts such as crown roast or saddle of lamb are prepared on request. Game in season might range from English partridge, teal, woodcock and widgeon to guiñea fowl, grouse, mallard, pigeon and even peacock. Exotica available to order include crocodile and locusts. The cold counter offers assorted salume, cold meats, free-range and quail eggs, pâtés and cheeses, as well as Ann Field's excellent homemade pies. Lining the shelves are Mrs

Bridges' chutneys, mustards, lime-and-lemon curds, marmalades and conserves, a variety of country-style stuffings, and jars of sauces such as cranberry with port and pickle.

Halal
Moroccan
Grocer
Greengrocer
Delicatessen

★ LE MAROC

94 Golborne Road, London W10 5PS
Tel. 020 8968 9783
Open: Mon-Sat 9am-7pm
Closed: Sun and Bank holidays
Tube: Ladbroke Grove, Westbourne Park **Bus:** 7, 23, 28, 31, 52, 70, 295, 302 **Payment:** cash, cheques

Step inside this shop and you are suddenly transported to Morocco. A colourful display of glazed earthenware tagine pots, couscous steamers, teapots, and ornate wall plates greet the eye. It's the food, though, which draws the local, very cosmopolitan, clientele. The halal meat counter sells homemade kofte, spicy merguez sausages, Moroccan salami and marinaded cubes of meat and chicken with spices and herbs, as well as lamb chops, legs and shoulders. From the cold cabinet, try the different kinds of feta. Occupying central stage are huge wooden bowls of olives, ranging from small, pitted white olives for tagine to fleshy, Greek Kalamata. Alongside is a big pot of ghee, whole preserved lemons, dried fruits and delicious shabaki, (fennel and spice pastry twirls soaked in honey and dipped in sesame seeds, only available during Ramadan). Open wooden boxes offer loose fine and medium couscous, three grades of semolina, pulses, beans, grains, dried raisins, sultanas and apricots. The shelves are filled with a fine selection of teas, including loose gunpowder, tins of halva, black and green olives, extra virgin olive oils, honey, packets of almonds and Tunisian dates on the vine. A stall outside sells pitta, unleavened bread, as well as fresh fruit and vegetables, including chillies and big bunches of mint.

Moroccan
Delicatessen
Grocer
Greengrocer

LE MARRAKECH

64 Golborne Road, London W10 5PS
Tel: 020 8964 8307
Fax: 020 8964 8316
Open: Mon-Sat 9am-7.30pm
Closed: Sun and Bank holidays
Tube: Westbourne Park, Ladbroke Grove **Bus:** 7, 23, 28, 31, 52, 295 **Payment:** cash, cheques
Catalogue, catering

Mohammed ben Ariba comes from Marrakech, so everything here has a Moroccan slant. There is a wide variety of olives and pickles, including the pungent preserved lemons and, occasionally, home-made harissa, and a plethora of Arab ingredients from couscous to *ful medames* beans in tins. He also sells tagines and couscousières and other decorative dishes, essential for that authentic look. The shop will happily cater for private parties.

North African Pâtisserie

L'ETOILE DE SOUS

79 Golborne Road, London W10 5NL
Tel. 020 8960 9769
Open: Mon-Sat 8am-6pm
Closed: Sun and Bank holidays
Tube: Ladbroke Grove, Westbourne Park **Bus:** 7, 23, 28, 31, 52, 70, 295, 302 **Payment:** cash, cheques

This irresistible North African and French pâtisserie boasts a huge variety of pastries made on the premises. Moroccan and Tunisian specialities consist of nutty fruited rusks, coconut macaroons, shortcrust crescents, squares, boats and oblongs with either clove-and-date, almond or hazelnut-and-rosewater fillings, all dusted in icing sugar, piled high on huge baking trays in the window. There is a wonderful assortment of *millefeuille* baklava soaked in honey, stuffed with pistachios or almonds. During Ramadan, be sure not to miss out on the cinnamon and fennel spiced honey and sesame twirls or crisp honeyed pastries. Customers can sample the sweetmeats at the stand-up coffee counter, and those with a less sweet tooth can opt for Danish pastries, almond croissants, chocolate dipped squares of candied fruit and nuts or Portuguese *pasteis de nata*. A range of individual and whole cream cakes is also on offer. Breads include sesame sprinkled long white loaves, also available in crescents, and flat brown or white loaves scored with a cross. Another North African speciality is a large, flat unleavened bread, doughy in texture, which can accompany savoury dishes or be spread with cheese or jam.

> "Moroccan food is what George Lucas would have made if he'd been a cook instead of merely a film director."
>
> AA Gill, food critic, *The Sunday Times*

Portuguese Delicatessen

★ LISBOA DELICATESSEN

54 Golborne Road, London W10 5NR
Tel: 020 8969 1052
Fax: 020 8964 1976
Open: Mon-Sat 9.30am-7.30pm, Sun & Bank holidays 10am-1pm **Closed:** 25, 26 Dec. & 1 Jan. **Tube:** Ladbroke Grove, Westbourne Park **Bus:** 7, 23, 28, 31, 52, 70, 295, 302 **Payment:** cash, cheques

London's largest, best and most friendly Portuguese deli, just across the street from its pâtisserie sister, is 'just like having Portugal at home,' say its customers. The shelves are crammed full with all sorts of diverse groceries, ranging from virgin and extra virgin olive oils, beans, pulses, pasta, rice, rusks, baby foods, powdered *pudim* mixes, dried figs, nuts, raisins, jams - including tomato and quince and crystallised fruit to tins of sardines, mussels, anchovies, baby eels and pickled vegetables. Herbs and spices include hot piri-piri sauce. Huge sides of bacalhau - dried salt cod - are piled high, ready for cutting to order, along with pigs' trotters, noses and ears, typically used to make a *feijoada* or bean stew. The deli counter stocks cured meats and salamis, morcela blood sausage, smoked pork ribs, mild Portuguese chorizo, presunto dried ham as well as an impressive variety of cheeses – cabra, manchego, creamy queijo alavao and pungent, nutty queijo azores. There are also loose black, green, Kalamata and garlic herbed olives. Christmas treats include packets of muscatel raisins, sugar or chocolate coated almonds and honey-and-spice corn cookies.

Branches: see Fulham, page 80
see Camden, page 110

Portuguese Pâtisserie

LISBOA PÂTISSERIE

57 Golborne Road, London
W10 5NR
Tel. 020 8968 5242
Fax: 020 8964 1976
Open: Mon-Sun 8am-8pm
Closed: 25, 26 Dec. & 1 Jan. and Bank holidays **Tube:** Ladbroke Grove, Westbourne Park **Bus:** 7, 23, 28, 31, 52, 70, 295, 302
Payment: cash, cheques
Catering delivery

Lisboa is always crowded. Some come to buy the typically Portuguese pastries and cakes, all homemade, but most stay to sample them over a cup of really excellent Sical coffee. Customers adore the *pasteis de nata*, a rich cream and egg custard inside a flaky pastry case, baked until the top catches. Equally irresistible is the cinnamon spiced *travesseiro* or pillow cake, filled with pumpkin and *queijada de Sintra*, an orangey cream cheese cake.

MR CHRISTIAN'S

Delicatessen Bakery

11 Elgin Crescent, London
W11 2JA
Tel: 020 7229 0501
Fax: 020 7727 6980
Open: Mon-Fri 6am-7pm, Sat 5.30am-6pm, Sun 7am-4pm
Closed: 25, 26 Dec & 1 Jan, Notting Hill carnival in August
Tube: Notting Hill Gate, Ladbroke Grove **Bus:** 23, 52, 70
Payment: cash, cheques, Amex, Delta, MasterCard, Switch, Visa
Catering, food-to-go

Mr Christian's takes its name from the famous New Zealand author and television broadcaster Glynn Christian, who established it 26 years ago. This deli has become a Notting

Portobello Road market

Open: Mon-Wed 8am-6pm, Thu 9am-1pm, Fri, Sat 7am-7pm **Closed:** Sun **Tube:** Notting Hill Gate, Ladbroke Grove **Bus:** 23, 52, 70

Make a day of it at what is perhaps the most eclectic London market of them all. (In fact you really need two days to see and absorb everything.) At the Notting Hill Gate end, antique stalls, shops and indoor markets sell an amazing variety of goods, from cigarette cards and old tins and boxes, to silver jugs and grandfather clocks. At the more northerly, seedier end, there are many supposed second-hand stalls – but a lot of the stock, mainly clothes, looks more fourth or fifth hand. In between there are craft and bric-à-brac markets – many young designers showing objets, clothes and jewellery – and the food market. The food stalls stretch roughly from Colville Terrace to Lancaster Road, lining one side of the road. They operate to a lesser extent during the week, supplying fairly ordinary, but surprisingly cheap, fruit and vegetables to the locals, but come into their own on a Saturday, when the place is packed (particularly since the international success of the film Notting Hill). That's when the fast food sellers appear, offering Thai noodles and Jamaican patties, the latter a reminder of the Afro-Caribbean flavour of the area, exemplified by the Notting Hill Carnival, held here yearly at the end of August. There are good fish, bread and meat stalls, and you can also find glorious cut flowers. On Thursdays under the Westway, from eleven to six, there is a small organic market, with good vegetables, bread, meat, dried fruit and nuts. Don't miss The Spice Shop and Books for Cooks, just round the corner in Blenheim Crescent.

Hill institution, renowned for the efficient and friendly service of long-time owners Greg and Tricia Scott and their staff. Shelves and tables groan with marvellous breads boasting unusual combinations, such as & Clarke's (see page 86) fig-and-fennel, rosemary-and-raisin or olive-and-sun-dried tomato breads. The latest addition, which invariably sells out, is a caramelised garlic French farmhouse loaf from Baker & Spice (see page 33). Equally irresistible are their almond croissants and own-made flapjacks and chocolate brownies. On Saturdays, so many passers-by queue up at their stall outside, it's hard to squeeze by. The cabinets of the shop are abundantly stocked with huge bowls of olives, 25 types of salume, homemade pâtés and pesto - try rocket or walnut - and some 90 varieties of carefully chosen cheeses from Britain and Europe. Extra boxes of chocolate and truffles are ordered for holiday seasons, while at Christmas, Italian panettone and pandoro sway from the ceiling. Don't leave without seeking out their extensive own-brand lime, lemon and banoffee curds, conserves, chutneys, relishes, mustards, jellies and pasta sauces.

OPORTO

Portuguese Pâtisserie

62A Golborne Road, London W10 5PS
Tel: 020 8968 8839
Open: Mon-Sun 8am-7pm, summer 8am-8pm **Closed:** 25, 26 Dec. & 1 Jan. and Bank holidays **Tube:** Ladbroke Grove, Westbourne Park **Bus:** 7, 23, 28, 31, 52, 70, 295, 302 **Payment:** cash, cheques

Across the road from Lisboa Pâtisserie, Oporto stocks a similar range of Portuguese cakes and pastries. Most of the typical *pasteis de nata, queijadas, bolos de feijao, bolos de arroz* and *bolos de coco* are made in their bakery in south London, but Maria, wife of the owner, Sebastian da Coste, is renowned for her homemade *pudim de caramelo* and a type of pineapple jelly flan. Equally delicious is the Jesuita, a flaky pastry cake with almonds, custard cream and cinnamon and a French-style apple tart, filled with generous slivers of apple and custard cream on a biscuit pastry base. In addition to savoury rolls of fish fillet, homemade roast pork and chicken escalopes you can try the more typical *rissois de camarao* (prawns in a white, creamy sauce encased in a pastry case) and the traditional *pasteis de bacalhau* (salt cod fishcakes).

Delicatessen

OUTPATIENTS

154 Notting Hill Gate, London W11 3QG
Tel: 020 7221 9777
Fax: 020 7243 2345
Open: Mon-Fri 10am-8pm, Sat 9am-7pm, Sun 11am-5pm
Closed: Bank holidays, 25 Dec, 2 Jan. **Tube:** Notting Hill Gate
Bus: 12, 94, 27, 28, 31, 52
Payment: cash, cheques, Amex, Delta, MasterCard, Switch, Visa
Catering, delivery, hampers made to order.

An offshoot of Damien Hirst and Matthew (son of Clement) Freud's high-profile restaurant, Pharmacy, next door, this innovative speciality food store, 'designed for people with a chronic addiction to quality', stocks an unusual product range. Sourced from small farms and estates round the world are rare condiments - Australian Wild Harvest sauces such as Macadamia Satay, bottled compotes of fruit, conserves and chutneys, estate-bottled olive oils, specialist vinegars, high-quality biscuits, pastas, pâtés de campagne and organic Scottish smoked salmon.They also have an amusing range of own-label goods, varying from Marcona salted Spanish almonds packaged in an ointment jar, to a more serious vintage eight-year-old balsamic vinegar made by Marino Tintori in Castelvetro, northern Italy and an extra virgin olive oil from Tuscany, equipped with stainless steel oil pourer tied round the neck. The deli counter boasts a daily selection of fresh food prepared by Pharmacy. Hampers containing exotic goodies such as Viadiù ginseng honey, figs marinated in spices and rum and vin santo are delivered anywhere in London. There is also a luxury Home Meal Replacement service. Each month, Pharmacy's head chef Michael McEnearney selects a range of starters, main courses and puds based on the current restaurant menu, which can either be collected or delivered to your door.

Wholefoods
Organic
Special diet

★ PORTOBELLO WHOLEFOODS

266 Portobello Road, London W10 5TY
Tel. 020 8968 9133
Fax: 020 8960 1840
Open: Mon-Sat 9.30am-6pm, Sun 11am-5pm **Closed:** 25, 26 Dec. & 1 Jan., Notting Hill carnival in August **Tube:** Notting Hill Gate, Ladbroke Grove **Bus:** 7, 23, 28, 52, 70 **Payment:** cash, cheques, Amex, Delta, MasterCard, Solo, Switch, Visa

The clue to Portobello Wholefoods' interesting, large range of vegetarian and health food products lies in its former ownership by Neal's Yard Bakery (see page 30), from where its bread still comes. Organic cheese-and-herb, sunflower and small organic 3-seed are best-sellers. Now independent, quality and diversity continue to be maintained, with shelves stacked with an impressive range of organic and wholefood goodies, including a good range for those on special diets (vegan, macrobiotic, detox, etc). Also on offer are pure fruit spreads and honey from around the world, plus culinary and medicinal herbs and spices. At Christmas, try the rich, gluten-free plum pudding, the GM-free Vegan Christmas cake or the Ultimate Organic Christmas Cake, also GM-free, soaked in organic brandy.

Herbs
Spices

★ THE SPICE SHOP

1 Blenheim Crescent, London W11 2EE
Tel: 020 7221 4448
Fax: 020 7229 1591
Open: Mon-Sat 9.30am-6.30pm, Sun 11am-5pm **Closed:** occasional Bank holidays **Tube:** Ladbroke Grove **Bus:** 7, 23, 52, 70 **Payment:** cash, cheques, Amex, Delta, MasterCard, Switch, Visa
Catalogue, mail-order

A small shop with an astounding range of products - some 2,000 owner Birgit Erath claims - from all over the world. Those you do not find on the shelves, she'll do her best to order for you. The herbs and spices are primarily organic, and come from India, China, Japan and South America. Advice is on hand for those having spice identification problems: 'Books for Cooks'(see page 95) is just opposite for those who need to know how the spice should be used. Most of the herbs and spices are for culinary use - there are over 20 different types of chillies, and a dozen paprikas - but many medicinal barks, roots and essential oils are also available, as well as beans, nuts, grains, pulses, dried fruit, rice and seeds.

> "A woman of taste does not drown herself even in the most expensive of scents, and a discriminating cook will not overwhelm a dish with flavouring."
>
> Constance Spry

Coffee
Tea

THE TEA AND COFFEE PLANT

170 Portobello Road, London W11 2EB
Tel/Fax: 020 7221 8137
Open: Tue-Sat 10.30am-6pm
Closed: Sun, Mon, Bank holidays
Tube: Ladbroke Grove **Bus:** 23, 52, 70 **Payment:** cash, cheques, MasterCard, Visa
Mail-order

Outside is a stall where you can

Shepherd's Bush Market

Open: Mon-Wed, Fri, Sat 9.30am-5pm, Thu 9.30am-2.30pm **Closed:** Sun **Tube:** Ladbroke Grove, Goldhawk Road **Bus:** 23, 52, 70

Come out at either Shepherd's Bush or Goldhawk Road tube stations, and one end of the market is there in front of you, stretching in a narrow arc alongside the railway viaduct, and into the arches beneath. Permanent shops occupy the arches, stalls the middle, and the other side of the narrow street is crammed with lock-up shacks. It is less a food market than a general household needs market, but with an international flavour that is enticing. There are stalls selling shoes, pots and pans, saris and household linens, hats fit for a Royal garden party, greetings cards, sweets, hair jewellery and wigs, candles and suitcases. A couple of conventional vegetable and fruit stalls at each end of the market offer good scoops and bags of selected produce for £1. The one in the middle of the market, though, displays probably the most varied Afro-Caribbean/Asian fruits and vegetables outside Brixton – including dasheen, chowchow (or chayote), fat, thin and long beans, okra and several types of sweet potato. There are a couple of good fishmongers, one of which, W.H.Roe, sells a huge variety of tropical fish, including yellow croakers, Trevally, jacks and pomfret. Butchers cater for the tastes of their customers too, with halal meat and chickens, various cuts of goat (one especially for curry), tripe, tongue and singed cows' feet. Eat some falafel from a popular stall, or a traditional British fry-up at one of the several cafés.

purchase a coffee or tea as you meander down the market. Inside is a small, bland room with a number of hessian bags against the walls, where the smell is wonderful, as is the choice. What makes this place stand out is that they roast and grind their own coffee right in front of you. A light roast produces a slightly acidic taste, medium is fairly floral while dark creates the familiar bitterness of a good espresso. On the right, as you enter, are the teas. They can be bought either as leaves or in tea bags, organic or otherwise. Apart from the more traditional teas from India, China and Japan, there are fruit teas and medicinal teas. On the left are the coffee beans which emanate from most of the South American countries, with a few from Africa.

Delicatessen
Bakery

TOM'S DELI

226 Westbourne Grove,
London W11 2RH
Tel: 020 7221 8818
Fax: 020 7221 7717
Open: Mon-Fri 8am-10pm, Sat 8am-6pm, Sun and Bank holidays 10am-4pm **Closed:** Notting Hill carnival in August
Tube: Bayswater, Notting Hill Gate **Bus:** 7, 23, 27, 28, 31, 52, 328 **Payment:** cash, cheques, Amex, Delta, Electron, MasterCard, Solo, Switch, Visa
Catering, delivery, food-to-go

On the left, as you enter this interesting shop owned by Sir Terence Conran's son Tom, a cold cabinet offers a selection of sweets such as home-made fruit crumble and bread and butter pudding. Opposite is a range of breads, croissants and sandwiches. Upstairs is a cosy café, frequented by the likes of comedian Dave Allen, super model Kate Moss and actor brothers Ralph and Joseph Fiennes. Downstairs is the deli, a haven of hidden delights which range from jars of foie gras with armagnac and port, Princesse d'Isenbourg Iranian caviar and an exclusive range of cold-pressed European olive, walnut and hazelnut oils, to Scottish smoked salmon, salume, chorizos, proscuitto San Daniele, blinis, quail eggs. Specially imported unpasteurised French cheeses include the rich, creamy explorateur and smokey vacherin, only in season from December to February. Neal's Yard Dairy (see page 30) supplies UK cheeses. The huge variety of appetising cooked food-to-go includes organic beef lasagne, *gnocchi di patate*, spicy tomato or mushroom pasta sauces, prepared salads, and several different pestos. A large table in the middle of the room displays big bowls of olives, marinated vegetables, pickles, seafood and antipasti. Among the varied groceries are jars of bottled French lobster, crab and salmon soups and large silos of loose coffee beans.

Food Hall
Organic

WILD OATS WHOLEFOODS

210 Westbourne Grove,
London W11 2RH
Tel: 020 7229 1063

Main Shop: see Freshlands, Camden, page 109

Le Pont de la Tour Foodstore

Bermondsey – *see page 152*

Villandry

Fitzrovia – *see page 32*

Taj Stores

Shoreditch – *see page 65*

Arigato's

Soho – *see page 50*

Lina Stores

Soho – *see page 50*

Shepherd's Bush

Middle Eastern
Halal
Grocer
Greengrocer

DAMAS GATE

81-85 Uxbridge Road, London W12 7NR
Tel: 020 8743 5116 or 020 8723 8428
Fax: 020 8749 0235
Open: Mon-Sun 9am-9pm **Tube:** Shepherd's Bush **Bus:** 207, 260, 283 **Payment:** cash, cheques, Amex, Delta, MasterCard, Switch, Visa.
Catering, food-to-go

This attractive delicatessen/supermarket is a treat to the eyes with its colourful display of exotic fruit and vegetables on the pavement outside the shop, and its wonderful array of Lebanese pastries inside. On offer is also a good range of breads, from pitta to large flat breads. There is a halal butcher counter with a fair selection of fresh meats; the cheese counter offers Middle Eastern cheeses, as well as Bulgarian feta. The deli counter has a breathtaking display of Middle Eastern food-to-go, very attractively packaged, from houmous and tabouleh, spring rolls, samosas, falafel, to *ful medames* and *mohallabia*. Staff are welcoming and more than willing to help.

Thai
Grocer
Greengrocer

SRI THAI

56 Shepherds Bush Road, London W 6 7PH
Tel/Fax: 020 7602 0621
Open: Mon-Sun 9am-7pm **Tube:** Hammersmith, Shepherd's Bush **Bus:** 72, 220, 295, 283
Payment: cash, cheques

This small grocery shop, started in 1986 by Sombal and Pascharin Thepprasits, specialises in Thai food and has a good range of fresh vegetables and herbs, flown in every Tuesday from Thailand. On the day of our visit they had 4 sizes of Thai aubergines, kai lan, chaom, a wonderful range of chillies and seasonal fresh fruit, including rambutan. The grocery side stocks ten different kinds of fresh curry pastes, along with a selection of tinned pastes, dried noodles of every variety, along with two types of rice, fragrant and glutinous, and a wide selection of flours including potato, rice, glutinous rice and tapioca and a delicious range of Thai dressings and sauces. Fresh noodles and egg noodles are available every Wednesday and sticky rice with banana and jam wrapped in banana leaf is made daily. There is also a large variety of frozen fish.

Turkish
Bakery
Pâtisserie
Greengrocer
Grocer

YASAR HALIM

182 Uxbridge Road, London W12 7GP
Tel: 020 8740 9477

Main shop: see Harringay, page 136

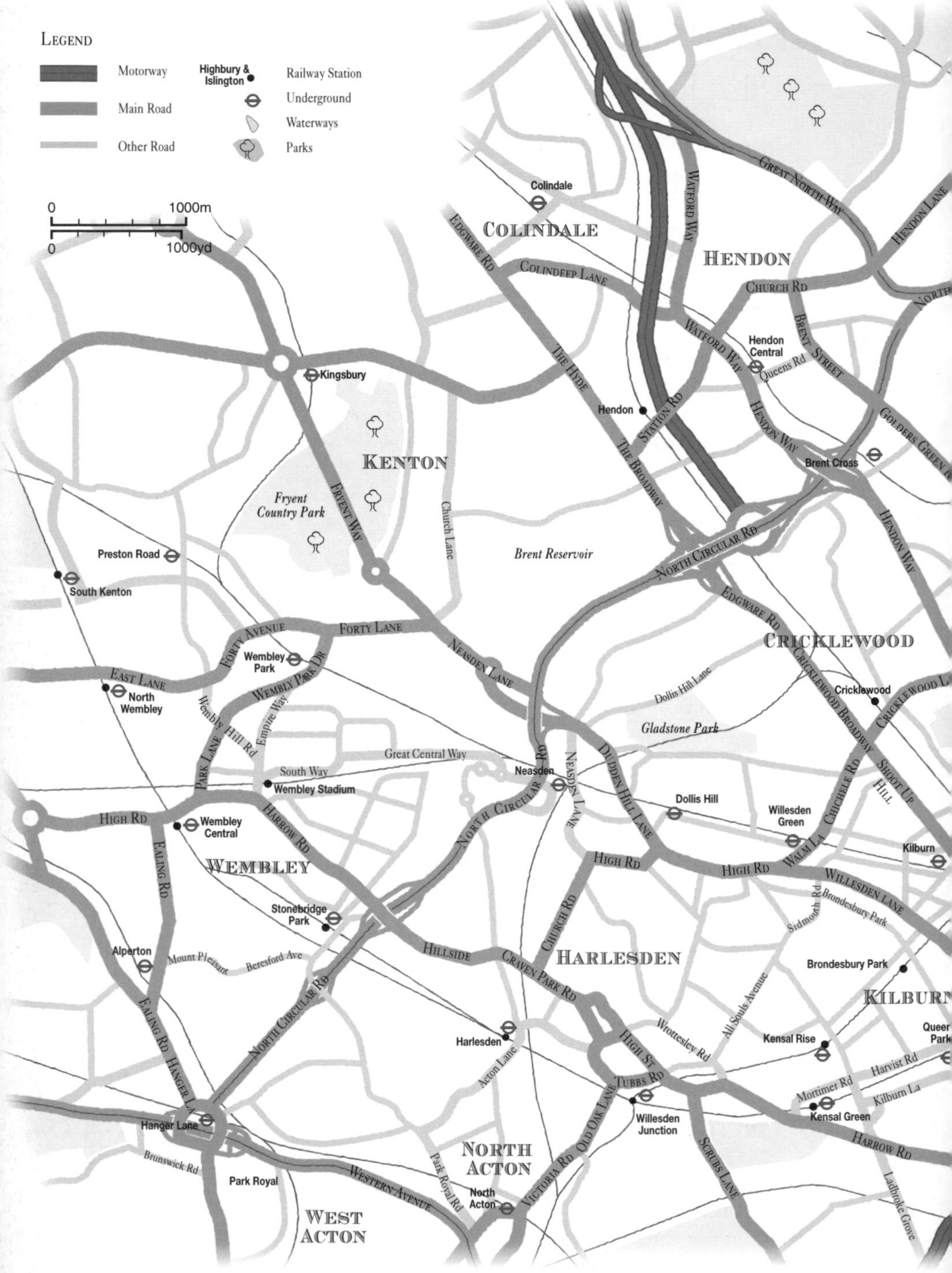

Legend
Motorway
Main Road
Other Road
Highbury & Islington
Railway Station
Underground
Waterways
Parks
0
1000m
0
1000yd
Colindale
COLINDALE
HENDON
Great North Way
Watford Way
Edgware Rd
Colindeep Lane
Church Rd
Hendon Central
Queens Rd
Brent Street
The Hyde
Hendon
Station Rd
Hendon Way
Golders Green
Brent Cross
The Broadway
Kingsbury
KENTON
Fryent Country Park
Fryent Way
Church Lane
Brent Reservoir
North Circular Rd
Preston Road
South Kenton
Forty Avenue
Forty Lane
Neasden Lane
CRICKLEWOOD
Cricklewood Broadway
Cricklewood
Wembley Park
Park Dr
East Lane
North Wembley
Wembley Hill Rd
Empire Way
Dollis Hill Lane
Gladstone Park
Great Central Way
Park Lane
South Way
Wembley Stadium
Neasden
Dudden Hill Lane
Shoot Up Hill
Chichele Rd
Dollis Hill
Willesden Green
High Rd
Wembley Central
Harrow Rd
Ealing Rd
WEMBLEY
Walm La
Kilburn
Willesden Lane
Brondesbury Park
Sidmouth Rd
Stonebridge Park
Church Rd
Hillside
Craven Park Rd
HARLESDEN
Alperton
Mount Pleasant
Beresford Ave
All Souls Avenue
Wrottesley Rd
Kensal Rise
Harlesden
Acton Lane
High St
Tubbs Rd
Harvist Rd
Mortimer Rd
Kilburn La
Kensal Green
Hanger Lane
Willesden Junction
Old Oak Lane
NORTH ACTON
Victoria Rd
Scrubs Lane
Harrow Rd
Brunswick Rd
Park Royal
Park Royal Rd
Western Avenue
North Acton
WEST ACTON
Ladbroke Grove

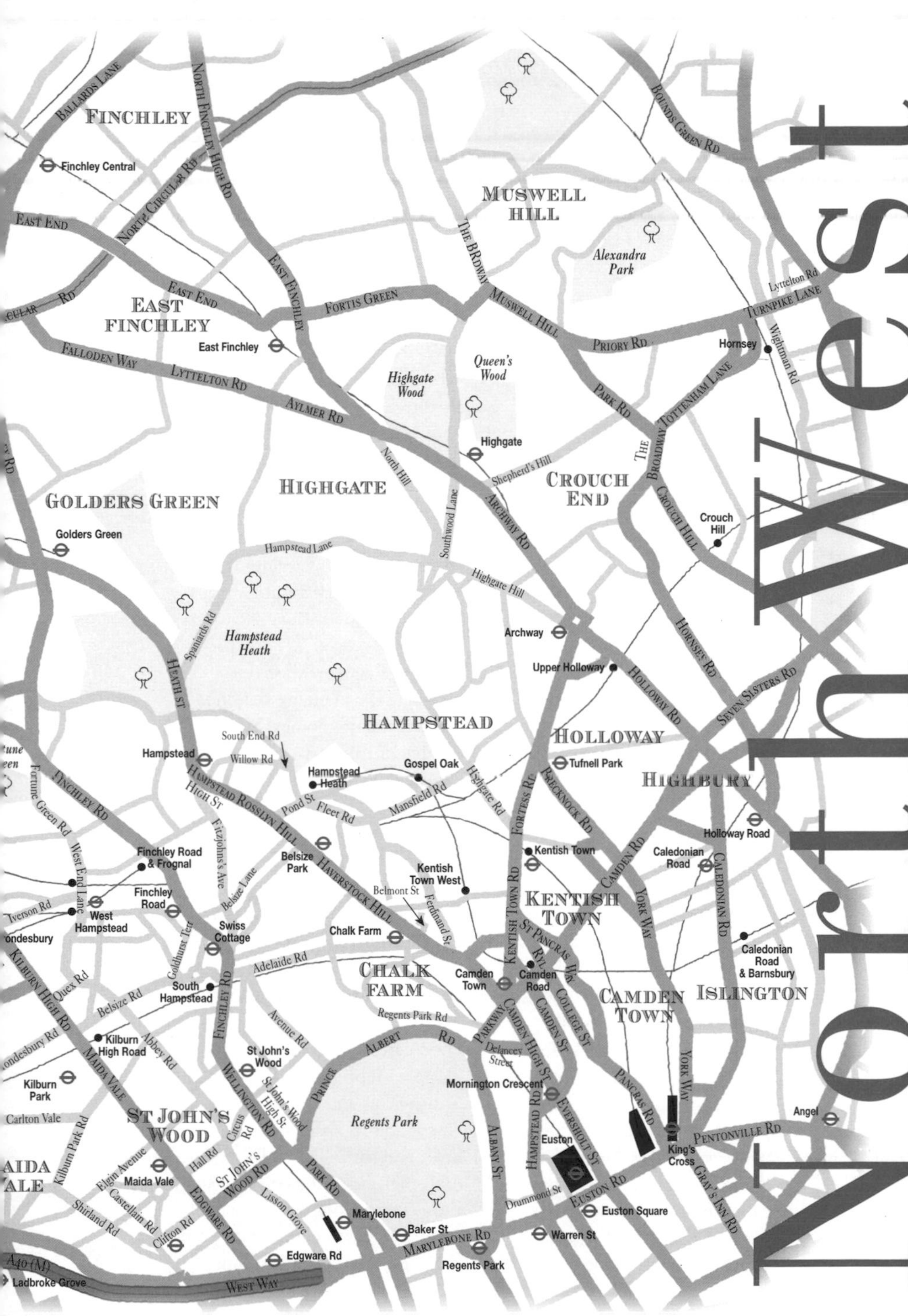
North West
Finchley
Ballards Lane
Finchley Central
North Finchley High Rd
North Circular Rd
East End
East End Rd
East Finchley
East Finchley
Falloden Way
Lyttelton Rd
Aylmer Rd
Fortis Green
Muswell Hill
The Brdway
Muswell Hill
Alexandra Park
Bounds Green Rd
Lyttelton Rd
Turnpike Lane
Wightman Rd
Hornsey
Priory Rd
Park Rd
Tottenham Lane
The Broadway
Queen's Wood
Highgate Wood
Highgate
North Hill
Shepherd's Hill
Crouch End
Crouch Hill
Crouch Hill
Highgate
Archway Rd
Southwood Lane
Golders Green
Golders Green
Hampstead Lane
Highgate Hill
Spaniards Rd
Hampstead Heath
Heath St
Archway
Upper Holloway
Holloway Rd
Hornsey Rd
Seven Sisters Rd
Hampstead
Holloway
South End Rd
Willow Rd
Hampstead
Hampstead Heath
Gospel Oak
Highgate Rd
Tufnell Park
Highbury
Fortune Green Rd
Finchley Rd
Hampstead High St
Rosslyn Hill
Pond St
Fleet Rd
Mansfield Rd
Fortess Rd
Brecknock Rd
Holloway Road
West End Lane
Finchley Road & Frognal
Fitzjohn's Ave
Belsize Park
Haverstock Hill
Kentish Town West
Kentish Town
Camden Rd
Caledonian Road
Caledonian Rd
Belsize Lane
Finchley Road
Belmont St
Ferdinand St
Kentish Town Rd
Kentish Town
York Way
Iverson Rd
West Hampstead
Goldhurst Terr
Swiss Cottage
Chalk Farm
St Pancras Way
Caledonian Road & Barnsbury
Kilburn High Rd
Quex Rd
Adelaide Rd
Chalk Farm
Camden Town
Camden Road
College St
Camden Town
Islington
Belsize Rd
South Hampstead
Finchley Rd
Avenue Rd
Regents Park Rd
Parkway
Camden High St
Camden St
Kilburn High Road
Abbey Rd
Albert Rd
Delancey Street
Pancras Rd
York Way
Maida Vale
St John's Wood
Wellington Rd
Prince
St John's Wood High St
Kilburn Park
Mornington Crescent
Carlton Vale
St John's Wood
Circus Rd
Regents Park
Hampstead Rd
Eversholt St
Angel
Kilburn Park Rd
Elgin Avenue
Hall Rd
St John's Wood Rd
Park Rd
Albany St
Euston
Pentonville Rd
King's Cross
Gray's Inn Rd
Maida Vale
Maida Vale
Castellain Rd
Edgware Rd
Lisson Grove
Drummond St
Euston Rd
Shirland Rd
Clifton Rd
Marylebone
Euston Square
Baker St
Marylebone Rd
Warren St
A40 (M)
Edgware Rd
Regents Park
Ladbroke Grove
West Way

Belsize Park

Delicatessen

BELSIZE VILLAGE DELICATESSEN

39 Belsize Lane, London NW3 5AS
Tel: 020 7794 4258
Open: Mon-Fri 8.30am-7pm, Sat 8.30am-6pm Sun 9am-2pm **Closed:** Bank holidays **Tube:** Swiss Cottage **Bus:** 13, 31, 46, 82, 113, 268 **Mainline station:** South Hampstead **Payment:** cash, cheques, Delta, MasterCard, Switch,Visa
Food-to-go

This small deli, tucked away in Belsize Village, is run by staff who used to work in Rosslyn Delicatessen (see page 118) some years ago. It is small and friendly and the selection is interesting and eclectic. The range of sausages available include *boudin blanc et noir*, Polish, Italian and French sausages, Portuguese chorizo and salume. Antipasti and salads include herrings, artichokes, aubergines in oil, olives, as well as lentil, couscous and bean salads. On the day we visited, among the prepared food-to-go were a Spanish omelette, salmon fishcakes, freshly cooked chicken with herbs and spices, vegetarian pasties, spinach-and-ricotta pancakes and chicken kievs. The cheese counter offers cheeses from France and Italy – in particular vacherin (in season), epoisses, chaource and explorateur. There is fresh pasta and cakes, such as chocolate fudge cake and poppy seed cake. A small range of breads includes beigels baked on the premises, and they also sell fresh coffee beans.

Delicatessen

THE DELICATESSEN SHOP

23 South End Road, London NW3 2PT
Tel: 020 7435 7315
Open: Mon-Fri 9.30am-7pm, Sat 9am-6pm **Closed:** Sun and Bank holidays **Tube:** Belsize Park **Bus:** 24, 168 **Mainline station:** Hampstead Heath **Payment:** cash, cheques, Delta, Mastercard (£10 minimum), Switch, Visa (£10 minimum)
Food-to-go

This long, narrow shop opposite the mainline station is packed full of goodies, in particular fresh pasta and sauces such as *funghetto*, clam and pesto. They also sell a good range of cheeses – their selection of sheep and goats' cheeses includes a ewe-only manchego and graviera goat's cheese from Crete, for example – and stock a selection of salume and Italian sausages. They sell some bread, cakes, chocolates and sweet biscuits, along with prepared dishes such as fishcakes and lentil burgers. The made-to-order sandwiches are a real treat. The staff are extremely helpful – on our visit the manager took time to tell an American customer how to make risotto for the first time.

Delicatessen

LE PROVENÇAL
167 Haverstock Hill, London NW3 4QT
Tel: 020 7586 2574
Open: Mon-Fri 9.30am-8pm, Sat 9.30am-7pm, Sun 9.30am-6pm
Closed: Bank holidays **Tube:** Belsize Park **Bus:** 168, C11, C12
Payment: cash, cheques, MasterCard, Switch (over £10), Visa

Established for 30 years, this deli stocks plenty of French and Italian produce, along with a growing range of British cheeses. Carluccio's products (see page 29) include sweet biscuits, white chocolate truffles and dried pasta, including the stunning black *tonnarelli di seppia* and huge pappardelle, along with jars of sauces to go with them. Other Italian makes are also stocked. Antipasti – including some large olives, aubergines in oil, sundried tomatoes and vegetables in jars – salads and dips are sold alongside a range of pies, brioches and filled breads. The cheeses are from Neal's Yard Dairy (see page 30) and other English, French and Italian suppliers. Breads are supplied by quality producers such as Baker & Spice (see page 33) and & Clarke's (see page 86). There is a good selection of jams, preserves, marmalades, chutneys and some excellent Italian wines.

Camden

Coffee

CAMDEN COFFEE STORES
11 Delancey Street, London NW1 7NL
Tel: 020 7387 4080
Open: Mon-Wed, Fri-Sat 9.30am-5.30pm, Thu 9.30am-2.30pm **Closed:** Sun and Bank holidays **Tube:** Camden Town, Mornington Crescent **Bus:** C2, 24, 27, 29, 31, 134, 135, 168, 214, 253, 274 **Payment:** cash only

A tiny and unprepossessing shop which perfumes the whole street (especially the basement Ladies in the nice little Greek restaurant next door) with the enticing aroma of roasting coffee beans. Hessian sacks of pale, unroasted beans line the walls; by the counter are washing-up bowls full of their glossy, dark brown, roasted equivalents – up to 8 different varieties. Roasting is done on the premises, and the beans can be roasted, ground and/or blended to individual specifications.

Food Hall
Organic

FRESHLANDS
49 Parkway, London NW1 7PN
Tel: 020 7428 7575
Fax: 020 7428 7676
Open: Mon-Sun 8am-9.30pm
Closed: Christmas Bank holiday
Tube: Camden Town **Bus:** C2, 24, 29, 31, 134,135, 168, 214, 253, 274 **Payment:** cash, cheques, Delta, MasterCard, Switch, Visa
Food-to -go

The new look of organic food selling – the glitzy superstore. Gone are the connotations of earnestness, lentils and open sandals: this 3,000-square-foot area, packed with produce, is a delight in which to browse. There's a fresh juice and snack bar near the huge front doors – where you can taste the health drink that is all the rage in the States, liquidised wheatgrass – and fresh fruit and vegetables are arranged in colourful mounds. The products on offer, some 2,000 lines, include organic meat and seafood, cheeses and dairy produce, authentic snow-dried tofu, vegetable patties, pure cane sugar, organic dog food, baby food and wines. There is also an extensive selection of vitamins and health foods, aromatherapy oils and various other natural remedies. Freshlands in Old Street (see page 65), the venerable parent of the Camden store, has been open now for over 20 years.

Branch: see Shoreditch, page 65; see Notting Hill, page 104

Inverness Street Market

Open: Mon-Sat 8am-5pm **Closed:** Sun **Tube:** Camden Town **Bus:** 24, 27, 29, 31, 134, 135, 168, 214, 253, 274

Amidst the crushing crowds en route to Camden Lock and Camden Market, particularly at the weekends, Inverness Street is like something from another era. An old-fashioned local fruit and vegetable market, now sadly much diminished in size, it sports from six to ten stalls which often sell fairly high-quality produce at a bargain price. At weekends there is a good cheese stall.

WORTH A DETOUR

- Camden Green Organic Produce Market, off Chalk Farm Road (weekends only)
- Richard Dare, 93 Regent's Park Road, NW1 8UR Tel: 020 7722 9428 , kitchen utensils
- Reject Pot Shop, 56 Chalk Farm Road, NW1 8R Tel: 020 7485 2326, cheap china

LISBOA DELICATESSEN

Portuguese Delicatessen

4, Plender Street, London NW1 OJT
Tel: 020 7387 1782

Main shop: see Notting Hill, page 97

Chalk Farm

AUSTRIAN SAUSAGE CENTRE

Sausages

10A Belmont Street, London NW1 8HH
Tel: 020 7267 5412
Fax: 020 7482 4965
Open: Mon-Fri 7am-5pm, Sat 7am-1pm **Closed:** Sun and Bank holidays **Tube:** Chalk Farm **Bus:** 24, 27, 31, 168 **Payment:** cash only

10A Belmont Street is also the address of Chalk Farm Studios, but persevere, and walk down an alley to the doorway covered in grey plastic strips. Inside it's all a bit basic, but this is a manufacturing outlet, not a ritzy shop. There's a cooler cabinet and little else, but it offers good-quality cooked meats and sausages – many of them to recipes from Austria and other points East – which are made on the premises and sold at factory prices.

British
Polish
Bakery

MOTA'S BAKERY
8 Ferdinand Street, London NW1 8ER
Tel: 020 7284 4644
Open: Mon-Fri 8am-5.30pm, Sat 9.30am-3pm **Closed:** Sun and Bank holidays **Tube:** Chalk Farm **Bus:** 24, 27, 31, 46, 168 **Payment:** cash, cheques
Catering, food-to-go

The sign outside this tiny corner shop advertises sandwiches, but there is more on offer, such as healthy-looking dishes on a hot plate, organic pizza or vegetarian chow mein. A few groceries, but the main interest is the bread, traditional English and Polish, including a four-seed wholemeal loaf which is packed with flavour.

Colindale

South-East
Asian
Food Hall

ORIENTAL CITY
399 Edgware Road, London NW9 0JJ
Tel: 020 8200 0009
Fax: 020 8200 0848
Open: Mon-Sat 10am-8pm, Sun 12 noon-6pm **Tube:** Colindale **Bus:** 32, 142 **Payment:** cash, cheques, MasterCard, Solo, Switch, Visa
Food-to-go

A huge food hall, containing plenty of Korean, Chinese, Thai and Indonesian specialities, although Japanese food predominates. Laid out in supermarket style, it makes shopping easier for non-Asians. As you go in you will find the fresh food section. Products are flown in from Asia twice a week. On the day of our visit, among the fresh fruit were Chinese pears and custard apples. In the vegetables section one could find white and green mooli, Oriental greens such as pak choy, choy sui, ong choy, kai choy as well as string beans, white aubergines, fresh turmeric and galangal from Thailand. The fish selection available was enormous, both fresh and frozen. Fresh fish included grey mullet, yellow croacker, sea bass, pomfret, squid, swordfish, scad and halibut. The meat counter had prepared meats for teriyaki which included thin slices of pork loin and belly, beef rib eye, duck tongues and feet. Various ready-to-go dishes included fish balls, fishcakes, dumplings, dim sum, etc. The shelves were groaning under the weight of jars of sauces, rice bags, flour bags and all sorts of spices.

Cricklewood

South-East Asian Food Hall

★ WING YIP

395 Edgware Road, London NW2 6LN
Tel: 020 8450 0422
Fax: 020 8452 1478
Open: Mon-Sat 9.30am-7pm, Sun 10.30am-5.30pm **Closed:** 25, 26 Dec. **Tube:** Brent Cross **Bus:** 32, 266 **Mainline station:** Cricklewood Broadway
Payment: cash, cheques, MasterCard, Visa

If the old adage – if you want a good Chinese meal, pick a restaurant with lots of Chinese eating in it – holds true, then it follows that if you want a good Oriental supermarket pick one where the natives shop. This is a huge, one-stop supermarket where you can get everything you need for Chinese, Japanese, Thai and other Oriental cooking, from the ingredients through to the wok and serving dishes. There is an impressive range of frozen fish and seafood, as well as a wet-fish counter, often selling live crabs. You will find a dazzling array of fresh Oriental fruit, vegetables, herbs and spices (including lots of Thai ingredients), along with packaged herbs, spices, rice and noodles.

Crouch End

DUNN'S

British Cakes

6 The Broadway, London N8 9SN
Tel: 020 8340 1614
Fax: 020 8348 7856
Open: Mon-Sat 7am-6pm
Closed: Sun and Bank holidays
Tube: Finsbury Park **Bus:** W7, W5, 41 **Mainline station:** Hornsey **Payment:** cash, cheques, Delta, MasterCard, Switch, Visa
Catalogue

This old-fashioned shop, with its enchanting window display of cakes for children decorated with Disney animals and film characters, is the place for traditional, old-fashioned English baked goods. Christopher Freeman, the fifth generation of his family to be a baker, produces a wonderful selection of bloomers, wholemeal and Granary breads, along with jam tarts, English cakes, biscuits and even hot-cross buns in September. He is particularly popular for his wedding and celebration cakes, justifiably so, as his Christmas cake took first place at the 1996 Baker's Fair. Freeman's talents also lie in charity fund-raising and every year he uses National Doughnut Week (usually held in February) to raise money for Save the Children.

Butcher
Game Dealer

★ FREEMAN'S BUTCHERS
9 Topsfield Parade, London
N8 8PR
Tel: 020 8340 3100
Open: Mon-Sat 8am-6pm
Closed: Sun and Bank holidays
Mainline station: Hornsey, Crouch Hill **Bus:** 41 **Payment:** cash, cheques
Bespoke delivery

All serious home cooks in this part of London cannot say enough good things about the service and produce sold here – as witnessed by the queues on Saturday mornings. Divided into 3 sections, the shop sells sausages (try the spinach-and-marjoram ones from a 1720 recipe, or the apple-and-venison recipe), ordinary meat and free-range and organic meats, including pork, lamb, chicken, beef and wild boar. Some of the meat products come from Black Mountain Foods in Wales, and you can also buy Martin Pitt free-range eggs and Childhay Manor ice cream. The shop is a licensed game dealer, selling pigeons and wild boar in season.

Euston

Indian
Pakistani
Confectioner

AMBALA SWEET CENTRE
112-114 Drummond Street, London NW1 2HN
Tel: 020 7387 3521
Open: every day 9am-9pm **Tube:** Euston, Euston Square **Bus:** 10, 18, 30, 68, 73, 188, 253
Payment: cash, cheques
Now an established enterprise with outlets all over the country, and even abroad, this recently renovated shop, spankingly clean and airy, is where it all started 35 years ago. In this Indian/Pakistani confectionery they sell sweetmeats, including *angir, imerti, barfi* and *gulab jamun*, made with lentils, cashews and condensed milk. Savoury snacks include samosas and various *pakora* (battered, salted vegetables). *Jalebis* are made on the premises, while most other goods are baked in a central kitchen near Stratford.

Branches: too numerous to list here; please consult your local telephone directory

Finchley

Japanese
Fishmonger
Grocer

★ ATARI-YA
595 High Road, London
N12 0DY
Tel: 020 8446 6669
Fax: 020 8446 6728
Open: Mon-Fri 10am-6.30pm, Sat-Sun 10am-7pm **Tube:** Woodside Park **Bus:** 82, 134, 260 **Payment:** cash, cheques

This small fishmonger has a predominantly Japanese clientele, so expect something out of the ordinary at rather steep prices. There is a large range to choose from such as bonito, turbot and yellow tail tuna and cuts especially for sushi. Some fish come whole; mackerel, pomfret and cutlass fish. For something a little more exotic, try kabayaki eel, octopus scallop or black tiger prawns. The freezer is stocked with squid, prawns, soba noodles and pork gyoza just like you get in Wagamama. There are some interesting packets on the shelves such as roasted seaweed and noodle sauces. Although everything is written in Japanese, there's always a small explanatory label in English and the man behind the fish counter is happy to explain what everything is.

Branch: 7 Station Parade, Noel Road, London W3 ODS
Tel: 020 8896 1552

Australian
Fishmonger

AUSTRALIAN SEAFOOD COMPANY

95 Ballards Lane, London N3 1XY
Tel: 020 8371 0308
Open: Tue-Thu 9am-8pm, Fri and Sat 9am-5pm, Sun 10am-3pm **Closed:** Bank holidays
Mainline station: Finchley Central
Bus: 38, 56, 73, 71a **Payment:** cash, cheques

An excellent shop specializing in fresh Australian seafood, but also importing some Australian game, including kangaroo, emu and salt water crocodile (the buffalo and the wild boar come from Dorset). Some of the fascinating fish, shellfish and crustaceans you will find here include Moses perch, yabbies, freshwater lobster (found only in Western Australia and flown in three times a week), small reef fish, blue manor and spanner crabs from Queensland and sea urchins. They also carry a selection of British seafood. To complement the fish, a range of sauces and oils – including Australian extra virgin olive oil – vinegars and mustards is also available. The staff are very helpful and the shop supplies top restaurants including Pharmacy and Livebait, and food stores such as Selfridges.

South African
Butcher
Game dealer

GRAHAM'S BUTCHERS

134 East End Road, London, N2 0RZ
Tel: 020 8883 6187
Open: Tue-Fri 8.30am-5.30pm, Sat 8am-4pm, Sun 9am-1pm
Closed: Mon **Tube:** East Finchley
Bus: 82, 134, 260 **Payment:** cash, cheques

Run by Graham and his wife, this small, friendly butcher sells free-range poultry and meat as well as its own range of sausages. These include tasty alternatives such as boerwors and beef-and-horseradish. There is some South African produce and biltong hangs from the ceiling as you enter the shop. Game such as pheasant is on offer, and Graham also stocks a small cheese section, the most notable varieties being organic Parmesan and Welsh goat's cheese.

Golders Green

Jewish
Bakery
Pâtisserie
Kosher
Parev

CARMELLI BAKERIES

126/128 Golders Green Road, London NW11 8HB
Tel: 020 8455 2074
Fax: 020 8455 2789

Open: Mon-Wed 7am-10pm, Thu 7am -Fri 2pm, Sun 7am-2am **Closed:** Sat, Jewish religious holidays **Tube:** Golders Green **Bus:** 13, 82, 260, 268 **Payment:** cash, cheques

This large, bustling Orthodox bakery sells a range of breads, including rye, granary and organic bread, although much of the shop is given over to cakes. Everything is made on site.The beigels have made this bakery famous and they are readily available given the shop's extensive opening hours. If a filled beigel doesn't appeal, there are take-away pizza slices, quiche, or potato burekas too. The cakes come in all sizes – large, such as apple ones with heavy lattice pastry, and small, ordinary sized cakes and pastries such as croissants. A particular speciality are the traditional wedding cakes. There is also a Parev section where the cakes and bread contain eggs but no dairy products.

Hampstead

Greengrocer

BRIAN LAY-JONES

36 Heath Street, London NW3 6TE
Tel: 020 7435 5084
Open: Mon-Sat 8am-6pm **Closed:** Sun and Bank holidays **Tube:** Hampstead **Bus:** 168, 268 **Payment:** cash, cheques

This traditional greengrocer has been around for 14 years selling a good range of fruit and vegetables to the residents of Hampstead, whilst managing to avoid the inflated prices of the area. Presentation is nice with an elegant display outside the shop. Not only is it a good place to find seasonal delicacies such as wild mushrooms or quinces, it's also great if you are looking for something exotic or out of season, such as summer berries in winter. If you live locally you can benefit from free delivery.

Italian Delicatessen

GIACOBAZZI'S DELICATESSEN

150 Fleet Road, London NW3 2QX
Tel: 020 7267 7222
Open: Mon-Fri 9.30am-7pm, Sat 9am-6pm **Closed:** Sun and Bank holidays plus last week in August and first two weeks of September **Tube:** Belsize Park **Bus:** 24, 46, 168, 268, C11, C12 **Mainline station:** Hampstead Heath **Payment:** cash, cheques, (£5 min) Amex, MasterCard, Switch, Visa
Food-to-go

Concentrating on Italian produce and homemade food only, this delicatessen has been established for nine years. As well as a varied range of cold meats, including San Daniele, Parma ham and bresaola, and cheeses – pecorino nero and sardo, both made with ewe's milk, mozzarella di buffala and taleggio – they also sell a selection of antipasti – chargrilled carrots, fennel and

"I've come round to realising that the way a potato is grown can be as important as the variety. Freshly-dug, organically grown potatoes are the best for flavour."

Lindsey Bareham, author of *In Praise of the Potato*.

SPUDS WE LIKE

A wide variety of potatoes are now available throughout the year and it's worth knowing their characteristics, so you make the appropriate choice for your cooking method

WAXY

Good for boiling and in salads.

- Arran Comet
- Cara
- Concorde
- Desiree
- Marfona (though some chefs say that this is 'the' spud for mashing)
- Nadine
- Pentland Javelin
- Ulster Prince
- Up-to-Date

FLOURY

Mash, bake, roast or deep fry

- Kerr's Pink
- King Edward
- Fianna
- Golden Wonder
- Maris Piper
- Morene

NEW POTATOES

Boil and toss in butter or use in salads (true new potatotes – the ones whose skins easily rub or scrape off - are only available from May-July and in October)

- Colmo
- Duke of York
- Dundrod
- Jersey Royal International kidney
- Maris Bard

SPECIALITY POTATOES

Boil and toss in butter or use in salads

- Anya
- Belle de Fontenay
- Charlotte
- Edzell Blue
- La Ratte
- Linzer Delicatess
- Pink Fir Apple
- Purple (sometimes Black) Congo
- Shetland Black

peppers, Italian and Greek olives, seafood salad – dried pasta and jars of pasta sauces. Prepared foods include stuffed tomatoes, baked radicchio, *pasta al forno* – lasagne, crespelli and canelloni are made in single or four-portion servings, although larger amounts can be ordered 48 hours in advance. Homemade pasta and sauces can also be bought separately. Cakes and desserts stocked include panettone and panforte, as well as homemade lemon polenta cake, cheesecake and delicious *panna cotta*.

Fishmonger

HAMPSTEAD SEAFOODS

78 Hampstead High Street, London NW3 1RE
Tel: 020 7435 3966
Open: Tue-Sat 7.30am-5pm
Closed: Mon, Sun **Tube:** Hampstead **Bus:** 168, 268
Payment: cash, cheques
Food-to-go

Situated off the main street, this small fishmonger is to be found at the end of an alley, alongside a fruit and veg stall. Although the range is small, the quality of the seafood on offer is excellent. Choose from prawns, big shrimps, or mussels, as well as big sea fish such as tuna, cod or even swordfish. If you are in a rush or don't feel confident cooking a seafood special, try their delicious cooked lobster. Prices are reasonable for the area and they deliver locally.

Delicatessen

JOY

511 Finchley Road, London NW3 7BB
Tel: 020 7435 7711
Fax: 020 7435 7007
Open: Mon-Fri 9.30am-7.30pm, Sat 9am-7pm **Closed:** Sun and Bank holidays **Tube:** Finchley Road **Bus:** 13, 82, 113 **Payment:** cash, cheques, Amex, MasterCard, Switch, Visa
Catering, delivery, food-to-go

This northerly sister to Realfood (see page 121) reflects adventurous food-seeker Kevin Gould's other role as 'caterer to the stars' (Nicole Kidman, Madonna and Tony Blair among them). Here the selection of groceries is smaller than at the Maida Vale shop, though you should still find much of interest, ranging from walnut vinegar to Carmona caperberries, spiced baby gherkins and Chalkidike wrinkled brown olives.
The emphasis is more on home-produced foods, whether condiments such as grape and fig chutney and preserved lemons; globe-spanning main dishes along the lines of *muttar paneer*, chicken korma, porcini, artichoke or fresh shrimp tortelloni, hefty pies and quiches; and desserts that major on huge, rustic fruit tarts and lighter, but challengingly proportioned, *millefeuilles*. Presentation reflects the ideals of quality, excitement and unfussiness that trademark Gould's catering. Finger-food dimension goods can be made to order, and weekdays see a fair range of aptly-packaged food-to-go. Welcome staples range from pastas and homemade sauces as found at Realfood, to fine ice-creams from Hill Station and Rocombe Farm.

Branch: see Realfood, Maida Vale page 121

French Bakery Pâtisserie

MAISON BLANC

62 Hampstead High Street, London NW3 1QH
Tel: 020 7431 8338

Main branch: see St John's Wood, page 127

French
Italian
Delicatessen

ROSSLYN DELICATESSEN
56 Rosslyn Hill, London
NW3 1ND
Tel: 020 7794 9210
Fax: 020 7794 6828
Open: Mon-Sat 8.30am-8.30pm, Sun 8.30am-8pm **Closed:** 25, 26 Dec., 1 Jan. **Tube:** Hampstead **Bus:** 46, 268 **Payment:** cash, cheques, Amex, Delta, MasterCard, Switch, Visa

This well-established French/Italian deli is reknowned for the range and quality of its food. It is well worth a visit, even if simply to marvel at the fascinating range of dried pasta which includes funghi-and-cuttlefish-flavoured farfalle and spaghettini with chilli. As with most Italian delis, it has a large range of pasta sauces and stocks quality olive oils from the usual Mediterranean countries. Don't assume that the freezer only contains ice-cream and sorbet; there is a good range of frozen fruit to choose from such as cranberries, blueberries and raspberries. There are some delicious grilled aubergine and artichoke hearts, but if you are looking for something a little different and not particularly Italian, barbeque sauces and tacos are tucked away at the back. The deli counter has home-cooked meats, chickens and pizza, as well as a good selection of mostly French cheeses with some lesser-known names such as Beaufort and Mimolette. The selection of salumi and hams is small but look out for the *foie gras entier* in season if you are after a mouthwatering treat.

Harlesden

Afro-
Caribbean
Food Hall

BLUE MOUNTAIN PEAK
3-9 Craven Park Road, London
NW10 4AB
Tel: 020965 3859
Open: Mon-Thu 7.30am-6pm, Fri, Sat 6.30am-6pm **Closed:** Sun and Bank holidays **Tube:** Harlesden **Bus:** 18, 206, 224, 226, 260, PR1 **Mainline station:** Willesden Junction **Payment:** cash, cheques
Delivery, wholesale

One of the largest Afro-Caribbean produce emporiums outside Brixton, its presence announced by great boxfuls of Puna Yam. Fruits and vegetables – Ugandan sweet potatoes and green bananas, chayote, mangoes, custard apples, tamarind and fresh red sorrel – are good value, as are row upon row of pulses and grains. Here you will find just about every hot sauce and chutney on the market, as well as plentiful supplies of Afro-Caribbean juices and concentrates: red sorrel, mauby syrup, bitters and herbal teas. The usual range of Afro-Caribbean breads is supplemented with roti and cassava-based bammy, there are patties and specially processed cheeses in the chill cabinet and preserved meats include dark mahogany West Indian smoked ham and garish red pickled pigs' feet, snouts and tails. The wholesale/cash-and-carry aspect ensures good value, and large quantity provision of all manner of staples.

Polish
Central
European
Grocer

T. MORAWSKI

157 High Street, London NW10 4TR
Tel: 020 8965 5340
Open: Mon-Sat 9am-5pm
Closed: Sun and Bank holidays
Tube: Willesden Junction **Bus:** 18, 206, 224, 226, 260, PR1
Mainline station: Willesden Junction **Payment:** cash, cheques

A useful little Polish/continental shop of the old order, well stocked with food beloved of the central European community but also frequented by those who have developed a taste for the rather good charcuterie, or the wide range of fruit syrups, preserves and sweetmeats. Expect to find innumerable brands of pickled gherkins and *sauerkraut*, each subtly different and with its own adherents. More rarified are jars of apple paprika, *aivar* (a red pepper sauce) and bean salads, also tinned carp, stocked alongside the anticipated herring fillets in soured cream or other sauces. There are packet soups with unusual combinations and strange names (but English is well spoken!); the now familiar *Krupczatka* (strong Canadian wheat) flour; *krakowska, sopocka, krajana and wiejska* sausages; and a striking variety of fruit and vegetable juices in distinctly un-British combinations – beetroot and apple, for instance. Good value bags of poppy seeds and dried mushrooms. There are plenty of black and other rye breads and sweetmeats include spiced biscuits and delicious chocolate-coated plums.

Kentish Town

B & M SEAFOODS/THE PURE MEAT COMPANY

Butcher
Fishmonger
Game Dealer
Delicatessen

258 Kentish Town Road, London NW5 2AA
Tel/Fax: 020 7485 0346
Open: Mon-Sat 9am-5.45pm
Closed: Sun and Bank holidays
Tube: Kentish Town **Bus:** C2, 134, 135, 214 **Payment:** cash, cheques, Amex, Delta, MasterCard, Solo, Switch, Visa
Local delivery

A unique combination of fishmonger, butcher, poulterer and game-dealer, and, just starting, delicatessen. The fish are stacked up in an icy and colourful design – they won the National Federation of Fishmongers' best fish display in 1998 – at the back of the shop, with chillers to the side containing organic beef, duck, chicken, pheasants, and homemade sausages. A speciality is smoked fish, such as halibut and marlin, and they also supply hickory-smoked turkey and chicken. The deli side is in its infancy as yet, but they highly recommend their Cornish cheese.

Wholefood
Organic

BUMBLEBEE NATURAL FOODS

30, 32, 33 Brecknock Road, London N7 0DD
Tel/Fax: 020 7607 1936
Open: Mon-Wed and Fri-Sat 9am-6.30pm, Thu 9am-7.30pm **Closed:** Sun and Bank holidays **Tube:** Kentish Town, Tufnell Park **Bus:** 10, 29, 253 **Payment:** cash, cheques, Delta, MasterCard, Switch, Visa
Bespoke delivery, food-to-go, vegetable box scheme

Not one, but three shops, selling what must be one of London's widest range of organic, natural and wholefoods. Numbers 30 and 32 offer home-baked goodies such as brownies, croissants and gluten-free breads, an extensive section of organic beers and wines, a good deli section with made-up foods to take away, and a vast selection of dried products. At number 33, across the road, you can find fresh fruits and vegetables, and herbs and spices, both fresh and dried.

Fishmonger
Poulterer

FISH AND FOWL

145 Highgate Road, London NW5 1LJ
Tel: 020 7284 4184
Fax: 020 7482 1500
Open: Fri 9.30am-5pm, Sat 9.30am-5.30pm **Closed:** Sun-Thu (but knock on the shutters and you could get served!), Bank holidays **Tube:** Kentish Town, Tufnell Park **Bus:** C2, 214, C11 **Payment:** cash, cheques, Delta, MasterCard, Visa
Catering

A restaurant seafood supplier – servicing such top restaurants as The Square, Chez Bruce, The Blueprint Café, l'Odéon and Orso, amongst many others – which is also open to the public two days a week. Because of that wholesale side, personal customers are assured of a unique freshness and interesting seasonality in both fish and poultry (imported Italian pigeons occasionally). As Adrian Rudolf used to work in a restaurant kitchen, customers can also get advice on how to cook what they buy.

Kilburn

Wholefood
Bakery
Greengrocer
Grocer
Organic

★ THE OLIVE TREE

84 Willesden Lane, London NW6 7TA
Tel: 020 7328 9078
Open: Mon, Tue, Thu-Sat 10am-6.30pm, Wed 1-6.30pm. **Closed:** Sun **Tube:** Kilburn , Kilburn Park **Bus:** 98 **Mainline station:** Brondesbury, Kilburn High Road **Parking:** outside the shop Mon-Fri 9.30am-4.30pm and all day Sat **Payment:** cash, cheques, Delta, MasterCard, Switch, Visa

Steve Hatt Fish & Game

Islington – *see page 143*

Super Bahar

Kensington – *see page 89*

Wembley Exotics

Wembley – *see page 130*

Fratelli Camisa

Fitzrovia – *see page 31*

The Olive Tree is a tiny cave of a shop, very easy to miss as you drive past. Inside, it is packed from floor to ceiling with every kind of organic food except fish and meat. The eye is immediately caught by a selection of pristine fruit and vegetables, mainly seasonal British but sometimes including unusual items such as mini avocados or custard apples. The owner, Costas Papantoniou, goes to New Covent Garden every weekday morning except Friday: 'It's the only way to guarantee the best.' On Fridays, instead of going to market, he receives a delivery of fresh organic fruit and veg from Chris Baur of Ripple Farm, near Canterbury, the most enterprising market gardener in southern England (he also supplies Bumblebee, see page 120, and Planet Organic, see page 19). Costas also makes a particular effort to stock good bread, some of which comes from Celtic Bakers and Neal's Yard Bakery (see page 30). Groceries include puffed spelt (gluten-free), flour and fresh yeast, nuts, honey, and olive oil - although no olives. Why, you ask, is the shop called The Olive Tree? 'Well' says Costa 'I am half Greek and olive oil is healthy - but also, I like the thought that if you rearrange the letters, the name becomes 'The I Love Tree'.'

Maida Vale

THE ORGANIC GROCER

Food Hall
Grocer
Delicatessen

17 Clifton Road, London
W9 1SY
Tel: 020 7286 1400
Fax: 020 7286 2717
Open: Mon-Sat 9am-8pm, Sun 10.30am-8pm **Closed:** Bank holidays **Tube:** Warwick Avenue **Bus:** 6 **Payment:** cash, cheques, Delta, MasterCard, Switch, Visa
Food-to-go

It hasn't taken this tiny shop long to build up a loyal following in the pleasant shopping district of Maida Vale. It makes a complementary addition to Realfood (see below) across the road. Don't let the name mislead, however, as not everything in the shop is organic- only about 80% of the cheeses can be labelled as such, for example. This mini supermarket also sells fresh fish delivered daily from Cornwall, dairy products, pasta, sweets, cereals and a variety of health foods. A juice bar serves fresh fruit and vegetable juices, and a resident chef prepares two fresh pasta sauces and take-away food daily, such as shepherd's pies, curries or soups.

REALFOOD

Delicatessen
Greengrocer
Organic

14 Clifton Road, London
W9 1SS
Tel: 020 7266 1162
Fax: 020 7266 1550
Open: Mon-Sat 8am-8pm, Sun 10am-6pm **Closed:** Bank holidays **Tube:** Warwick Avenue **Bus:** 6, 16, 46, 98 **Payment:** cash,

cheques, Amex, MasterCard, Switch, Visa
Bespoke delivery, catering, food-to-go, mail-order

Somewhat groundbreaking in terms of adventurous buying and insistence on sound provenance as well as palpable quality of produce when it first opened, Kevin Gould's fine food shop has recently undergone a dramatic facelift. A visit will confront you with an unprecedented array of tasting samples, ranging from caramelised Larguela almonds to Argan nut oil from Morocco, all lined up on a display/tasting counter that runs the whole length of the shop. A good many products in an eclectic range spanning Catalonian hazels, Seggiano honeys, paprika, hemp and rice oils, 'tradizionale' balsamic vinegars, Ferme St Christophe preserves, Senza Nome chocolate-coated fruits, to name but a few, carry entertaining and enthusiastic tasting notes reflecting Kevin's new-found role as newspaper and magazine journalist. Many products boast organic pedigree, and the majority are artisan produced. Breads include Neal's Yard Bakery (see page 30), & Clarke's (see page 86) and Matthew Jones; cheeses are a highly personal selection with the emphasis away from cow's milk: buffalo mozzarella tresses - the real thing; truffled pecorino, Pouligny and Selles-sur-Cher. Charcuterie

"Roberto Ferrari's mother was from Naples, and she'd sent him a huge plait of mozzarella. Overcoming my customary northern reserve, I agreed to try it. First a splash of soft olive oil and a grind of pepper, then straight in – no tomatoes, no basil, no avocado – just the sound of angels singing and the taste of milky clouds. This was Sophia Loren made into cheese."

Kevin Gould, owner of Joy and Realfood

includes Rannoch smoked chicken and Rougié foie gras, while pasta fresh and dried comes in 24 varieties, including glorious saffron tagliatelle. On our visit, the impressive array of fresh fruit and vegetables included speckled lettuce from the Veneto, organic fennel from Puglia, Syrian hand-pulled potatoes, Ligurian rocket and gigantic Sicilian citrons. Truly 'a temple to gastronomy' as Ms Lawson also said, and very friendly and accessible at that.

Branch: see Joy, Hampstead, page 117

Muswell Hill

Cheese shop

CHEESES

13 Fortis Green Road, London N10 3HP
Tel: 020 8746 2116
Open: Tue-Thu 10am-5pm, Fri. 10am-6pm, Sat. 9.30am-6pm. **Closed:** Mon and Sun **Tube:** Highgate **Bus:** 43, 102, 134, 234 **Mainline station:** Wood Green, Alexandra Palace **Payment:** cash, cheques, Delta, MasterCard, Switch, Visa
Hand-held deliveries

The shop is very small, with the window on a corner, which makes it invisible from the Muswell Hill Broadway end of the street. The present owner, Vanessa Wiley, worked here learning the business for nearly a decade before taking it over some six years ago. Like many others, she is an instinctive cheese-lover: she trained as a chef and had never thought of cheese until she went into the shop one day entirely by chance. She not only has a wide range of cheeses, but, much more important, the best – and at exactly the right stage of maturity. You will find Montgomery's Cheddar, Colston Bassett Stilton, Kirkham's Lancashire, James Aldridge's tornegus (washed-rind and deliciously potent), Mont d'Or gently oozing from under the rind, brie, Valençais, Selles-sur-Cher, and many more. If the cheese you want is not on display, ask: soft cheeses may be in the refrigerator. If you can, try to go during the week, rather than on Saturdays, as the queue is sometimes very long.

Coffee
Tea

W. MARTYN

135 Muswell Hill Broadway, London N10 3RS
Tel: 020 8883 5642
Open: Mon-Wed 9.30am-5.30pm, Thu 9.30am-1pm, Fri 9.30am-5.30pm, Sat 9am-5.30pm **Closed:** Sun, Bank holidays **Bus:** 43, 134 **Payment:** cash, cheques

The intoxicating aroma of freshly roasted coffee greets you as you walk through the door of this popular tea and coffee shop. Founded by the present owner's great-great grandfather in 1897, the shop still has a real turn-of-the-century feel with wooden shelves and old balance scales on the counter and photographs on the wall of the original shop. The wonderful aroma comes from the big range of coffees that are roasted on the premises. It also sells a selection of fine foods (jams and marmalades, teas, pickles and relishes, pâtés, marinades and vinegar), old-fashioned humbugs and fresh cakes from Dunn's (see page 112).

Italian Delicatessen

MAURO'S DELICATESSEN

229 Muswell Hill Broadway, London N10 1DE
Tel/Fax: 020 8883 2848
Open: Tue-Sat 10am-6pm, Sun 11am-4pm **Closed:** Mon **Tube:** Highgate **Bus:** 43, 102, 134, 144, 299, W7 **Mainline station:** Wood Green, Alexandra Palace
Payment: cash, cheques
Food-to-go

For some years now, lovers of robust Mediterranean flavours have flocked to Mauro's for ready-prepared Italian and other dishes. All courses of a dinner are available: antipasti include pâtés, tapenade, guacamole, charcoal-grilled vegetables, and salads such as mixed seafood, ham-and-salami with olives, and chick-pea with artichoke; you can follow this with any of half a dozen sorts of pasta, plain or coloured, plus a choice of sixteen pasta sauces. Other alternatives are various lasagnes, charcoal-grilled polenta with grilled vegetables and mozzarella, *pollo cacciatore*, *cassoulet*, or Beef Bordelaise. Puddings are limited (only *tiramisu* or chocolate mousse) but the shop sells a selection of Italian cheeses. You can also buy delicious ham roasted with fennel, very good spicy Italian sausages, various salume, olives, olive oils, and other Italian groceries. Apart from the cheeses, salume, and groceries, everything is prepared in the kitchens at the back. Parties are catered for (brochure available on request).

Fishmonger Poulterer

WALTER PURKIS & SONS

32 Muswell Hill Broadway, London N10 3RT
Tel:: 020 8883 4355
Open: Tue-Sat 8.30pm-5pm
Closed: Sun, Mon **Tube:** Highgate **Bus:** 43, 102, 134, 234
Mainline station: Wood Green, Alexandra Palace **Payment:** cash, cheques, Amex, Delta, MasterCard, Switch, Visa

Other shops come and go, but Walter Purkis has remained a focus for Muswell Hill shoppers for over a generation: the opening of a Marks & Spencer food-store just along the road has made no difference to his trade at all, he says. 'The supermarkets buy in bulk, and the best fish doesn't come in bulk. My customers know that.' He goes to Billingsgate every morning and buys as wide a selection of fish as you will find anywhere: cockles and mussels, crabs, scallops, oysters, sprats, mackerel, monkfish, red and grey mullet, halibut, sea bass, and wild salmon in season. At his second shop down the hill he has a smoke-house where he produces smoked trout, haddock, and tuna, his own kippers (dyed or undyed), and smokies, which he first tried at the suggestion of a customer a few years ago and has continued to sell ever since; on occasion, he also hot-smokes, notably halibut and mussels. (Hot-smoked halibut, in case you hadn't thought of it, is a more interesting alternative to smoked salmon for Christmas dinner.)

Branch: see 17 The Broadway, London N8 8DU
Tel: 020 8340 6281

St John's Wood

German
Bakery
Organic

BREAD SHOP

65 St John's Wood High Street, London NW8 7NL
Tel/Fax: 020 7586 5311
Open: Mon-Fri 7am-6.30pm, Sat 7am-6pm, Sun 8am-4pm
Closed: Bank holidays **Tube:** St John's Wood **Bus:** 13, 46, 82, 113 **Payment:** cash, cheques, Amex, Delta, MasterCard, Switch, Visa
Bespoke deliveries locally

A new and exciting addition to the London bread scene; other branches are sure to follow. Appalled by the lack of good bread in England ten years ago (and convinced that poor quality still predominates) Jonathan Cohen planned his perfect shop. Given Bread Shop's stunning modernity of design it is perhaps surprising to learn that easily observable standards of cleanliness were the prime principle. Certainly the cleanliness is palpable: all sales or display units rest on trolley wheels or are winchable, and part of the bakery section is open to view. But the feel is far from clinical: the self-service hopper pillars are decorated with swirls of colourful grains and pulses, shopping baskets are paper-lined willow. And the bread, all crunchy crusted and much of it multi-grained, looks entirely homely and wholesome. All the breads are 100% organic (and a small range of pastries largely so). While the baker is German and Germanic flours and styles predominate (*Saatenbrot, Kartoffelkruste, 7 Körner brot*) there is plenty to contrast with that essentially dense, moist, wholesome style: airy ciabattas, flaky, buttery croissants, the lightest, crunchiest of pretzels. Open two months at the time of inspection, but already attracting custom from afar.

Fishmonger

BROWN'S

37-39 Charlbert Street, London NW8 6JN
Tel: 020 7722 8237/6284
Fax: 020 7483 0502
Open: Tue-Sat 8am-5.30pm
Closed: Sun, Mon, Bank holidays **Tube:** St John's Wood **Bus:** 13, 46, 82, 113 **Payment:** cash, cheques, Amex, Delta,

MasterCard, Switch, Visa
Bespoke home deliveries locally

This excellent fishmonger wins the London Regional Championship almost every year. A visit will indicate that it could do so on its range alone: prime in-shore cod fillet, Cornish brill, Wild Irish salmon trout and Irish oysters sit alongside daurade royale from France and silver pomfret and king fish from Dubai. Smoked fish include eel, Manx and Loch Fyne kippers and whole sides of mild smoked salmon. Eel also come jellied, the tarama is homemade and the crab is dressed in exemplary fashion. Even the frozen fish represents a fascinating range: raw shrimp, Alaskan crab claws, soft shell crabs and octopus. Service is friendly and helpful.

Fishmonger

GRANT'S

69 Abbey Road, London NW8 0AE
Tel: 020 7624 9984
Fax: 020 7624 9953
Open: Tue-Sat 9am-5pm **Closed:** Sun, Mon, day following Bank holiday **Tube:** St Johns Wood **Bus:** 139, 189 **Mainline station:** Kilburn High Road **Payment:** cash, cheques, Amex, Delta, MasterCard, Switch, Visa
Bespoke deliveries

One not inconsiderable reason for visiting this out-on-a-limb little fish shop is the charming and knowledgeable service by Armando Lenia, six times British oyster-opening champion. Another is the freshness of the seafood, and the meticulous attention paid to dressing crabs and lobsters, and preparing seafood platters (order ahead for a party). Galway Bay oysters – of which Grant's are London's sole suppliers – can be delivered almost anywhere in London, thanks to the wholesale arm of the company (Red Bank Fish, contactable at the same number). In fact all the fish is very fresh, 'rotated every day', though there is also a small stock of frozen seafood (langoustines, prawns and so on), smoked fish including sprats and Loch Fyne salmon, salt cod, marinated anchovies and a range of good bottled soups (French Crustarmor and Irish chowders), plus the usual sauces and pickles.

Butcher

KENT & SONS

59 St John's Wood High Street, London NW8 7NL
Tel: 020 7722 2258
Fax: 020 7722 3075
Open: Mon-Sat 8am-5.45pm **Closed:** Sun and Bank holidays **Tube:** St John's Wood **Bus:** 13, 46, 82, 113 **Payment:** cash, cheques, Delta, MasterCard, Solo, Switch, Visa
Bespoke deliveries locally

Established for over 80 years, this Q-guild butcher's sizeable premises nonetheless have a modern, sparkling feel. The curved glass chill cabinet display reveals a wide range of convenient, kitchen-ready preparations: breaded veal escalopes, chicken and lamb kebabs, lemon and coriander satay, chicken fillets in yoghurt marinade, and burgers prepared with pride. Both these and the basics are of superlative quality: free-range and organic chickens are sourced from Welsh Black Mountain Foods, pork is from Plantation Pigs, beef is grass-fed Aberdeen Angus. Mince, too is Aberdeen Angus, unless 'pasture lamb', and there is both Dutch and English lamb's liver to be had. It is pleasing to find boiling fowl on sale. Hams and chickens are home-cooked and bought-in staples are of equal pedigree: Organic Earth pasta, for example. Response to an exacting local clientele is very helpful and friendly.

Chocolate

LEONIDAS

132 St John's Wood High Street, London NW8 7SG
Tel: 020 7722 1191
Open: Mon-Sat 9am-6pm
Closed: Sun, Bank Holidays
Tube: St John's Wood **Bus:** 13, 46, 82, 113 **Payment:** cash, cheques, Amex, Delta, MasterCard, Switch, Visa
Mail-order

This well established purveyor of Belgian pralines has a number of branches and concessions in London, but this is the largest and most exclusive. Somewhat forbidding glass cabinet displays – of china and crystal, both classic and modern in feel, as much as of chocolates – convey a curious amalgam of class and frivolous frill. There is nothing frivolous about the cool service, though assistants will meet the most exacting of demands. While this boutique in particular is decidedly geared to the gift market, the pralines themselves have their fans world-wide and there is nothing to stop you requesting a small bagful with no frills attached.

Branch: 15 Edgwarebury Lane, Edgware, Middlesex HA8 8LH
Tel: 020 8958 6720

French Bakery Pâtisserie

★ MAISON BLANC

37 St John's Wood High Street, London NW8 7NJ
Tel: 020 7586 1982
Fax. 020 7586 1087
Open: Mon-Sat 8am-6.30pm, Sun 9am-6pm **Tube:** St John's Wood **Bus:** 13, 46, 82, 113
Payment: cash, cheques, Delta, MasterCard, Switch, Visa

This popular 'boulangerie - pâtisserie-chocolaterie' is equally popular with local French residents as with those seeking to recreate their holiday memories. Maison Blanc pride themselves on producing fresh delicacies which elicit a genuine taste of France, rather than merely a hint. Everything is made on a daily basis, using French flour and traditional methods. The range of breads are baked in stone ovens and are free from fat and additives; baguettes and *flûtes de tradition* are the most popular, but other varieties, including *pain de campagne, pain au levain* and *pain aux olives,* are well worth tasting. They stock the traditional viennoiserie which one associates with France – *croissants, pain au chocolat* and *brioche* – as well as a variety of mouth-watering pâtisserie and savouries to eat in their tea-room or to take away. To celebrate Christmas try their traditional *Bûche de Noël,* followed by the *Galette du Roi* for the Epiphany.

Branches: see Chelsea, page 24, Chiswick page 75, Hampstead page 117, Holland Park page 85, Richmond page 181

Jewish
Delicatessen
Kosher
Parev

★ PANZER'S

13-19 Circus Road, London NW8 6PB
Tel: 020 7722 8596/8162
Fax: 020 7586 0209
Open: Mon-Fri 8am-7pm, Sat 8am-6pm, Sun 8am-2pm **Closed:** Bank holidays **Tube:** St John's Wood **Bus:** 13, 46, 82, 113
Payment: cash, cheques, Delta, MasterCard, Switch, Visa
Delivery, food-to-go, mail-order

At the time of our visit, Halloween, the pavement glowed with an almost fluorescent display of more pumpkins and squashes than one thought possible, amongst them Queensland Blue, Gem, Crown Prince, Dumpling and Giraumon Turban. Good vegetables, fruit, herbs and spices, mostly outside, included fresh wild mushrooms, persimmons, velvet-black figs, purple basil and plump pods of tamarind. Inside, alongside conventional groceries, are many lines which cater to the varied communities which have gravitated to St John's Wood. There are American packets and jars that you'll find nowhere else; one corner of the store specialises in Japanese foods (rice, dried seaweed and shiitake, miso, giant bottles of Kikkoman soy sauce). There are quite a few Carluccio products on offer – Castelluccio lentils, polenta and dried pasta – and a wall of shelves with fresh-baked breads of all kinds, including beigels in several flavours. It is on the charcuterie and fish counters that the Jewish flavour of the neighbourhood is most apparent. Whole sides of smoked salmon are there for the slicing, and you can choose to have it on the oily or dry side. There are also *latkes, gefilte* fish, herring, huge bowls of marinated olives, cooked and preserved meats galore, with a hanging display of a variety of packaged biltongs.

Spanish
Delicatessen

RIAS ALTAS

97 Frampton Street, London NW8 8NA
Tel: 020 7262 4340
Open: Mon-Sat 9.30am-8pm
Closed: Sun and Bank holidays
Tube: Warwick Avenue **Bus:** 6,

16, 98 **Payment:** cash, cheques, Delta, MasterCard, Switch, Visa

A very well stocked little shop, where all things Spanish – from *jamón serrano* to manchego – also include paella pans, earthenware cazuelas, even cosmetics. Canned foods abound: white asparagus, Albo seafoods and such classics as *fabada asturiana* and *callos con garbanzos*, plus huge tins of olives, oils and rice for paella. The fresh food counter carries stacks of chorizos and fresh cheeses such as tetilla. The Spanish sweet tooth is well catered for with shelves full of biscuits and cakes – *mantecadas, tortas de aceite* and so on – and sweetmeats: *roscos de vino, torrón*. Fresh pastries are Portuguese. Look out for fresh sandwiches filled with cheese or *jamón* (made to order) and their delicious homemade classic Spanish tortilla (lunchtime only). Sound breads and a basic range of wines complete the picture.

Swiss Cottage

Chocolate

★ ACKERMANS

9 Goldhurst Terrace, London NW6 3HX
Tel/Fax: 020 7624 2742
Open: Mon-Fri 9.30am-6pm, Sat 9.30am-5pm **Closed:** Sun (open Bank Holidays) **Tube:** Swiss Cottage, Finchley Road **Bus:** 13, 31, 82, 113, C11 **Mainline station:** South Hampstead, Frognal **Payment:** cash, cheques, Amex, Delta, MasterCard, Solo, Switch, Visa
International mail-order

Regarded by some as the finest English chocolatier, if only on account of their rather unique dark chocolate 'thins', Ackermans is yet another example of a European originator (German Jewish Werner Ackerman) establishing a British brand, and granted a Royal Appointment (HM the Queen Mother). Although lately linked up with the Charbonnel et Walker-Maxwell & Kennedy group, Ackermans shop preserves a rather reticent, family company feel. Service is charming and helpful; no eyebrows will be raised if you buy only a tiny sample in a plain cellophane bag. The mere aroma, however, is likely to inspire a larger purchase, and visitors would certainly do well to ensure supplies of those items that don't make the mail order list: 100s and 1000s, for example, or the fragile brandy-soaked cherries enrobed, stem and all, in dark chocolate. Ackermans counters are located in Selfridges (see page 43) and Fortnum & Mason (see page 44).

Chocolate

LESSITER'S

167a Finchley Road, London NW3 6LB
Tel: 020 7624 5925
Open: Mon-Sat 9.30am-6pm **Closed:** Sun **Tube:** Finchley Road, Swiss Cottage **Bus:** 13, 31, 82, 113, 268, C11 **Mainline station:** South Hampstead, Frognal **Payment:** cash, cheques, Delta,

MasterCard, Switch, Visa
Mail-order

This rather ramshackle shop has little truck with modernity, offering instead a warm welcome, a jumble of greeting cards and giftware, and a large selection of Lessiter's own chocolates, truffles and novelties. Were it not for the generally classy packaging, you might not realise that these are among the most highly regarded of British chocolates. Lessiter's describe themselves as 'Swiss Chocolatiers', reflecting family background and the use of Swiss couverture and liqueurs; but the majority of their chocolates (white chocolate dairy fudge, violet creams) have British appeal and all are manufactured in Hertfordshire, as they have been since the company was established in 1911. There are Lessiter's products concessions in major stores and a small range is sometimes carried in certain supermarkets. You'll need to come to the shop for the full range, though, including seasonally popular chocolate figures.

Wembley

Chinese Food Hall

LOON FUNG

1, Glacier Way, London
HA0 1HQ
Tel: 020 8810 8188

Main shop: see Chinatown, page 26

Indian Grocer

★ V.B. & SONS

147 Ealing Road, London
HAO 4BU
Tel: 020 8785 0387
Fax: 020 8902 8579
Open: Mon-Fri 9.30am-6.45pm, Sat 9am-6.45pm, Sun 11am-5pm **Closed:** Christmas **Tube:** Alperton **Bus:** 79, 83, 224, 297
Mainline station: Wembley Central **Payment:** cash, cheques, Amex, Delta, MasterCard, Switch, Visa

When you are planning to cook an Indian feast for a large number, this is the place to come to stock up on dried herbs, spices, rice, pulses and general Indian ingredients. But you really have to think big, because this is also where many Asian shop owners and restaurateurs shop, so most ingredients are sold in large quantities. Consequently there are good bargains to be had, and you'll find unusual snacks like bite-sized popadums and cassava chips, or packaged mixes to make Indian breads or sweets, such as *gulab jamon*. Look in the frozen-food cabinet for frozen parathas and ready-made meals, as well as some of the more exotic vegetables.

Indian Greengrocer

★ WEMBLEY EXOTICS

133-135 Ealing Road, London
HA0 4BP
Tel: 020 8900 2607
Fax: 020 8900 1669
Open: Mon-Sun 24 hours **Tube:** Alperton **Bus:** 79, 83, 224, 297

Mainline station: Wembley Central **Payment:** cash, cheques

Don't let the somewhat ordinary selection of everyday fresh fruit and stacks of garlic outside fool you – inside, this 24-hour greengrocer turns into a cornucopia of the most wonderful and exotic fruits from around the world. Depending on the season you'll be able to find small apple bananas, yellow and black passion fruits, jackfruits, mangosteens, rambutans and guava, as well as mangoes in just about every size and colour. When you are after out-of-the ordinary vegetables, this is the place for Thai yard-long beans, cassava, sweet potatoes, East African kontola drumsticks, lots of Kenyan imports and all types of aubergines, including round ones and pink ones. Locally made Indian pickles like carrot-and-lime and cauliflower are popular, as is the Kitchen Magic range of hotter pickles.

Willesden Green

Italian
Butcher
Delicatessen
Greengrocer

★ ENZO TARTARELLI

1 Sidmouth Parade, Sidmouth Road, London NW2 5HG
Tel: 020 8459 1952
Open: Mon-Sat 8am-7pm
Closed: Sun **Tube:** Willesden Green **Bus:** 52, 98, 260, 266, 302
Mainline station: Brondesbury Park **Payment:** cash, cheques

Enzo and his son Carlo are friendly, convivial and hardworking, having built this shop up from the butcher that it was 15 years ago to the 'butcher-deli-greengrocer' it is today. All the meat is organic apart from the veal. (It appears that customers prefer the 18-weeks-old veal to the darker, 30-weeks-old organic veal.) Suppliers are British although you can find French guinea fowl on offer. Pork sausages are homemade and come in two varieties - mild or chilli, and he also makes a chicken-raisin flavoured with mozzarella and rocket. There is a small range of pasta, either fresh or dried, as well as various brands of Italian risotto. Italian cakes (panettone, pandoro) and sweets (cantuccini, amaretti) are to be found, especially at Christmas. There is the usual range of deli sauces and antipasti but try Enzo's homemade pesto. Some of the fruit and veg is organic and there are some interesting varieties such as oak leaf lettuce. The cheeses are Italian and there is Parma ham and various salume on offer, including Enzo's own cooked ham on the bone. He also marinates chicken and pork ribs for the barbecue.

North Circular Rd
A406
Tottenham
Harringay
Stoke Newington
Highbury
Islington
Dalston
Hackney
Higham Hill
Walthamstow
Leyton
Stratfor
Bow
Stepney
Finsbury Park
Walthamstow Marshes
Hackney Marsh
Victoria Park
Northumberland Park
Bruce Grove
Turnpike Lane
Tottenham Hale
Hornsey
Seven Sisters
Blackhorse Road
Walthamstow Central
South Tottenham
Harringay
Harringay Green Lanes
Stamford Hill
Crouch Hill
Manor House
Finsbury Park
Stoke Newington
Clapton
Arsenal
Drayton Park
Holloway Road
Caledonian Road
Highbury & Islington
Caledonian Road & Barnsbury
Canonbury
Dalston Kingsland
Hackney Wick
King's Cross
Angel
Old Street
Bethnal Green
Stepney Green
Whitechapel
Bow Rd
Mile End

North East

Legend

- Motorway
- Main Road
- Other Road
- Highbury & Islington ● Railway Station
- Underground
- Waterways
- Parks

0 1000m

0 1000yd

Dalston

Turkish
Food Hall
Halal

TURKISH FOOD CENTRE
89 Ridley Road, London
E7 0LX
Tel: 020 7254 6754
Open: every day 8am-8pm
Mainline station: Dalston Kingsland **Bus:** 30, 56, **Payment:** cash, cheques

A supermarket-like shop, providing an extensive range of Turkish products. They only sell in-season produce, and the quality of both fruit and vegetables is high, though the selection changes frequently. There are usually great bunches of herbs (mint, coriander, dill) as well as long green chillies, plump tomatoes, peppers, aubergines, white courgettes, quinces and prickly pears. Sacks of pistachios, rice and dried pulses line the walls. The cheese counter offers excellent natural Greek yoghurts, fetas and halloumi, as well as other prepacked cheeses, and several types of marinated olives. The bakery produces fresh flat breads, sesame breads, plus an extensive selection of sweet pastries, such as *baklava* and *kadayif*, in different sizes. At the halal meat counter you can get lamb, goat and chicken.

Branches: see Harringay, page 136 and Tottenham, page 148

Ridley Road Market

Open: Mon-Sat 8.30am-6pm
Mainline station: Dalston Kingsland
Bus: 26, 30, 55, 56, 106

A traditional East End street market, best on Fridays and Saturdays, that has been kept alive and actually reinvigorated by the influx of immigrants over the years, among them West Indians, Africans, Turks and Asians. The narrow market, lining a street of lock-up shops, throbs to the varying ethnic rhythms emanating from music stalls, and the foods on offer are similarly varied (the beigel shop offers jerk chicken, chilli tuna and salt beef beigels!). Among everyday fruits and vegetables, sometimes offered in a bargain scoop - three mangoes for £1 - are colourful pyramids of Afro-Caribbean specialities, including jackfruits, soursops, yams, plantains, ready-made hot sauces, dried and smoked fish, and cooked snacks. Turkish herbs and other foodstuffs are on offer as well. Many of the lock-ups, as well as the stalls, reflect the cosmopolitan nature of the area and the market, selling unfamiliar parts of familiar animals, halal meat, seafood from warm waters (king fish, tilapia, flying fish, snappers and croakers), as well as clothes, beauty products, kitchenware and other household goods.

227-229 Lewisham High Street, London SE13 6LY
Tel. 020 8318 0436

Harringay

Turkish
Pâtisserie
Confectioner

ANTEPLILER

47 Grand Parade, Green Lanes, London N4 1AG
Tel: 020 8809 1003
Fax: 020 8809 1004
Open: every day 10am-9pm **Tube:** Turnpike Lane, Manor House **Bus:** 29, 141, 341 **Mainline station:** Harringay West **Payment:** cash, cheques

Antepliler is a Turkish confectioner offering an array of Turkish pastries made on the premises by a staff of six, including the owner Ahmet Ustunsumeli. The pastry is filo or konafa (a finely shredded dough which looks like tiny noodles); fillings are pistachio or pistachio and cream. Everything is coated with syrup, which means that it is incisively sweet, but Ahmet and his team have a very light touch so that it is also light, delicate, and surprisingly refreshing. Especially recommended are *sobiyet*, which are little crescents of very thin filo pastry filled with shredded pistachios and cream, *burma*, a filo pastry roll generously stuffed with chopped pistachios, and *kadayif*, a spectacular, crisp burnished tart about a yard across made of pistachios and konafa. Prices are by the 450 g/1lb and very reasonable.

Branch: see Newington Green, page 144

Greek
Bakery
Pâtisserie
Wedding
Cakes

BARNABY'S

8 Grand Parade, Green Lanes, London N4 1JX
Tel: 020 8802 0275
Open: Mon-Sat 8am-10pm, Sun 10am-8pm **Tube:** Turnpike Lane, Manor House **Bus:** 29, 141, 341 **Mainline station:** Harringay West **Payment:** cash, cheques

Barnaby's is Greek but owes its enormous popularity not only to its *baklava* and bread, but to its birthday cakes. The front part of the shop is given over to various Greek pastries such as *shiamali, shiamishi*, and *lokoumades*, plus other items such as buns stuffed with halloumi and *koubes* (minced lamb rolls); breads include sesame, tahini, and olive (you will often see assistants chopping olives by the kitchen door). At the back, British tastes are catered for with fruit tarts, cream slices, chocolate éclairs, and impressive celebration cakes: frozen ones can be bought directly, or fresh ones ordered, of any kind and decorated according to fancy (three to four weeks' notice is needed for a tiered wedding-cake). Prices are relatively modest.

Branch: 34 Green Lane, London N13 6 HT
Tel: 020 8889 4324

Turkish
Food Hall

TURKISH FOOD CENTRE
385-387 Green Lanes, London
N4 1EU
Tel: 020 8340 4547

Main shop: see Dalston, page 134

Turkish
Bakery
Pâtisserie
Grocer
Greengrocer

★ YASAR HALIM
493-495 Green Lanes, London,
N4 1AL
Tel: 020 8340 8090
Open: Mon-Sun 9am-10pm
Closed: Bank holidays **Tube:** Manor House, Turnpike Lane
Bus: 29, 141 **Mainline station:** Harringay Green Lanes **Payment:** cash, cheques

This food shop is set apart from the many others in this street by its popular bakery, well known for traditional wedding and birthday cakes. You'll also find a tempting selection of cakes, breads and large and small pastries, such as *louka* (honey balls); try the spinach and cheese pies made with pastry rather than filo and the homemade rice pudding. The grocery section sells everything you need for Turkish cooking, with seasonal specialities such as black-eyed beans, *colocassi*, and colourful sweet peppers.

Branch: see Shepherd's Bush, page 105

Highbury

Fishmonger

CECIL & CO.
393 Liverpool Road, London
N1 1NP
Tel: 020 7700 6757

Main shop: see James Knight of Mayfair, Mayfair, page 42

Butcher
Free Range
Organic

★ FRANK GODFREY
7 Highbury Park, London
N5 1QT
Tel/Fax: 020 7226 9904
Open: Mon-Fri 8am-6pm, Sat 9am-5pm **Closed:** Sun and Bank holidays **Tube:** Highbury & Islington **Bus:** 4, 19, 236
Payment: cash, cheques, Delta, MasterCard, Switch, Visa
Bespoke local deliveries

A well established Quality Guild butcher par excellence, and with a certain notoriety, resulting from a very public insistence on continuing to sell beef-on-the-bone during the period of the ban (albeit from the first government-certified BSE-free closed herd). All meat and poultry sold here is free-range and additive- and antibiotic-free. Some of it is organic, notably the Kelly chicken – declared by a certain celebrity TV chef, to be 'the best in Britain' – of which Godfrey's is one of very few suppliers. Good chickens are just one example of meticulous sourcing and knowledgeability: the Godfreys can tell you whether a particular bird is a 'label anglais', Freeman's or Kennel Farm free-range. Much of the beef and lamb is Orkney Island Gold, including beautifully prepared beef shin. While they concentrate on traditional excellence rather than innovation (beautifully

Le Marrakech

Notting Hill – *see page 96*

Milia's

Tottenham – *see page 148*

Panzer's

St John's Wood – *see page 128*

La Fromagerie

Highbury – *see page 137*

Planet Organic

Bayswater – *see page 19*

trimmed pork rib chops and lamb racks, for instance; and a full range of game that includes woodcock, wild rabbit and boar) they do offer a small selection of kitchen-ready marinated meats, and recently developed sausage lines have won a striking number of gold and silver medals at the Utrecht (meat Olympics) triennial competition.

Cheese shop

★ LA FROMAGERIE
30 Highbury Park, London
N5 2AA
Tel/Fax: 020 7359 7440
Open: Mon 10.30am-7.30pm, Tue-Sat 9.30am-7.30pm, Sun 10am-5pm **Closed:** All Bank holidays, except the first one in May **Tube:** Highbury and Islington, Arsenal **Bus:** 4, 19 **Mainline station:** Finsbury Park, Drayton Park **Payment:** cash, cheques, Amex, Delta, Electron, JCB, MasterCard, Solo, Switch, Visa
Catalogue, mail-order

When a national food magazine selected Patricia Michelson's shop as one of the UK's best specialist shops, it only confirmed what locals already knew. The range of more than 200 continental and UK farmhouse cheeses may be unequalled in London, and the mail-order catalogue reads like a guide to international cheese production. The selection isn't overwhelming, however, because you can taste before you buy in the traditional cheese room with its wooden shelves and straw mats. Try the Italian truffle cheese and French Pyrenéean sheep's cheese for a taste of something you don't get everywhere. Michelson also prides herself on the vast selection of artisan food products, and every surface is filled with discoveries from European markets. The big bowls of olives by the door, Poilâne sourdough bread from Paris, handmade Italian chocolates and Michelson's vivacious personality signal an enjoyable shopping experience the second you enter. Don't be surprised if you bump into one of the big-name TV chefs here - Nigel Slater is one of the regulars.

Islington

Cheese shop

BARSTOW & BARR
24 Liverpool Road, London
N1 0PU
Tel: 020 7359 4222

Main Shop: see Kensington, page 86

Bakery

EUPHORIUM BAKERY
203 Upper Street, London
N1 1RQ
Tel: 020 7704 6909
(bakery orders: 020 7704 6905)
Fax: 020 7704 6089
Open: Mon-Sat 8am-6pm, Sun 9am-3.30pm **Closed:** Bank holidays, Christmas period **Tube:** Highbury & Islington **Bus:** 4, 19, 30, 43 **Mainline station:**

Highbury & Islington **Payment:** cash, cheques, Amex, Delta, MasterCard, Switch, Visa
Bespoke local deliveries, catering

An excellent example of a restaurant off-shoot, though while the Euphorium bar and restaurant are minimalist and trendy, the breads and pastries of the bakery are firmly rooted in the French and British tradition. Some fifteen bread lines include as good a baguette as you will find anywhere, and equally crusty British cobs. Italian focaccia is rendered as authentic as possible by the use of '00' and semolina flours (for most breads and cakes the French pastry chef favours unbleached French flour and unsalted Dutch butter). Savouries – all pastry based – range from fashionable goats' cheese-and-pesto whirls to Cumberland sausage rolls and Cornish pasties. Sweet pastries include a full range of Viennoiserie; buttery fruit tarts; complex St Honoré and simple soured cream cheesecake; dark chocolate brownies and moist Bramley apple-and-ginger tea cakes. Cakes are available to order in any size, but usually 3 days' notice is needed. There are also beautifully packaged jams, chutneys and bottled liqueur fruits. All leftovers are given to the homeless at the end of each day.

JAMES ELLIOTT

Butcher
Free Range

96 Essex Road, London
N1 8LU
Tel: 020 7226 3658
Open: Mon-Fri 7am-5pm, Sat 6am-5pm **Closed:** Sun and Bank holidays **Tube:** Angel **Bus:** 38, 56, 73, 171a, 341 **Mainline station:** Essex Road **Payment:** cash, cheques
Bespoke deliveries locally

A very good butcher with a reassuringly generous, 'old-fashioned' window display crammed full of huge joints, whole carcasses and, in season, game birds in plumage. Part of the purpose is to show off prize-winning beef carcasses from Mathers of Aberdeen, or beautifully marbled and well hung beef rib joints. The excellent beef would be just one reason for shopping here: all meat is guaranteed free-range and traceable. They have dry-cured organic bacon, triple-smoked (over dry wood) gammon and home-cured salt brisket. A small range of homemade sausages includes, rather adventurously, wild boar-and-apple. Cheeses are chosen with great care: all are good farm-produced examples and include Lord of the Hundreds, Montgomery Cheddar and James Aldridge's Tornegus; an even more unusual find is Neal's Yard's Dairy (see page 30) outstanding *crème fraîche*. There are also plenty of good-quality pickles, chutneys and tapénades, as one would expect.

Delicatessen

★ LIMONCELLO

402 St John Street, London EC1V 4NJ
Tel/Fax: 020 7713 1678
Open: Mon-Fri 8.30am-7pm, Sat 9.30am-2.30pm **Closed:** Sun and Bank holidays **Tube:** Angel **Bus:** 19, 38, 153, 171a **Mainline station:** King's Cross **Payment:** cash, cheques, Amex, Delta, MasterCard, Switch, Visa
Catering service, food-to-go

Despite the Italian name (and yes, they do sell the eponymous liqueur, in pretty little bottles by Le Vale dei Mulini) and an Italian chef, a good deal of the produce at this popular little deli represents the best of British. Thus there are Neal's Yard Dairy cheeses (see page 30), Richard Woodall's bacon, Bay Tree chutneys and pickles, Cornish pasties from Cornwall, and Rocombe Dairy and Hill Station ice creams. But there are Italian cheeses too, fine pastas by Il Pastaiomalto and Benedetto Cavalieri and Infuso Natura jams. The traiteur items are Mediterranean-inspired: risotto, fishcakes, stuffed peppers, couscous, chunky roast vegetable salads and innovative items such as deep fried pumpkin with gorgonzola sauce. There are good things from further afield, too, such as the excellent Californian 'Consorzio' range of flavoured oils. Customised menus can be produced via the catering unit at Shoreditch (but discuss requirements at the shop).

Chapel Market

Chapel Street, London N1
Open: Tue, Wed, Fri, Sat 9am-3.30pm, Thu, Sun 9am-1pm **Tube:** Angel
Bus: 153, 274 **Mainline station:** Essex Road

Probably dating from the late nineteenth century, the market was such an integral part of the area that Chapel Street was formally renamed Chapel Market in the 1930s. It offers fruit and vegetables throughout the week, mainly concentrated at the Liverpool Road end, but takes over the entire length of the road at weekends, when you can find additional stalls offering herbs, fish, some Afro-Caribbean foodstuffs, greetings cards and Christmas decorations, cheap clothes and leather goods.

WORTH A DETOUR

↳Rhode Design, kitchens, 137-139 Essex Road
↳Gill Wing Cookshop, 190 Upper Street

Farmers' Markets

The first farmers' market in England opened in Bath in 1997, although the movement had been long established in America (a 1995 survey of 772 American farmers' markets suggested that more than 25,000 farmers sell only at farmers' markets). There are now, in early 2000, more than 120 such markets in England, three of them in London, masterminded by an American, Nina Planck, and with more planned. The idea is that farmers who are 'local' – in London that means within 100 miles of the M25 – can sell their own fresh produce direct to consumers. This produce includes fruits, vegetables, salads, juices, cheeses, herbs, meats, wines, eggs and breads, and much more, some of it organic (a speciality of both Islington and Notting Hill is organic chicken, which is also being supplied to London's best Italian restaurants). Farmers are not allowed to purchase and re-sell produce, so you can be sure they haven't made an early morning trip to New Covent Garden to re-stock.

The benefits are obvious. Family farms can be more viable and indeed often stay in business as a result of growing what customers want and selling it locally. Customers can have access to truly fresh and seasonal produce, and to the people that grow it. Many unusual crops can be grown as a result, instead of the monocropping encouraged by supermarkets, and many of the London markets can now supply things like striped beetroot, white courgettes, round carrots, pea shoots and Asian salad greens. Wasteful and environmentally unfriendly packaging, air-freighting, processing and chemical preservatives are reduced because 'food miles' – the distance many foods have to travel before they reach the customer - are done away with. Perhaps the nicest thing about farmers' markets is the social aspect they have come to represent. It's not only foodies who turn up, but pensioners and other locals, who all talk to suppliers and growers, and to their neighbours, at a set time each week. This has brought back to many neighbourhoods a sense of community which had been eroded and lost.

“A farmers’ market isn’t a new idea, but for lots of different reasons these age-old institutions went out of fashion. But, like all the best ideas, its time has come again. This market is good news for everybody.
It will provide fresh, reasonably local, seasonable food...
It will help raise farm incomes and give a much-needed boost to the farming economy... it will foster greater understanding between town and country by helping to reconnect people to the land.”

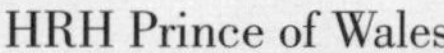
HRH Prince of Wales

★Islington Farmers’ Market
Sundays 10am-2pm
Essex Road, N1, opposite Islington Green
Tube: Angel

★Notting Hill Gate Farmers’ Market
Saturdays 9am-1pm
Behind Waterstones on Notting Hill Gate (at corner of Kensington Church Street)
Tube: Notting Hill Gate

★Swiss Cottage Farmers’ Market
Wednesdays 11am-4pm
Market Square, outside the Camden Library and Leisure Centre, off Avenue Road, NW3
Tube: Swiss Cottage

★London Farmers’ Markets Ltd.,
6 St Paul Street, London N1 7AB
Tel: 020 7704 9659
Fax: 020 7359 1938
e-mail: NinaPlanck@aol.com
Website: www.LondonFarmersMarkets.com

Italian Delicatessen

MONTE'S

23 Canonbury Lane, London N1 2AS
Tel/Fax: 020 7354 4335
Open: Mon-Fri 10am-7pm, Sat 9.30am-6pm **Closed:** Sun, except run up to Christmas, Bank holidays **Tube:** Highbury & Islington **Bus:** 4, 19, 30, 43 **Mainline station:** Highbury & Islington **Payment:** cash, cheques, Amex, Delta, MasterCard, Switch, Visa
Bespoke deliveries locally, food-to-go, hampers

A very 'modern-Islington' style of Italian deli, fresh and cool, with shiny steel shelving and shop-length chill display. Brushed steel bowls are filled with colourful gift items: chocolate 'caviar' and 'sardines', mini-panettone. Nothing of dull appearance would find house room here: nonetheless, the *fichi secchi, croccantini* and *teneri* in the most beautiful packaging are of the finest quality. The sheer perfection of the porcini is indeed an indication of their quality. Olive oils and vinegars represent a fine range, as do the carefully selected wines (Rocca Rubia, Copertino, Gavi di Gavi), all with useful tasting notes. There is an abundance of salume and a good collection of cheeses, including a variety of pecorini. Pride of place in the chill cabinet goes to Julia Monte's homemade pasta - such as herb-filled fresh ravioli - interesting sauces – rucola, rose harissa, siciliano – and traditional staples, including breaded chicken escalopes and stuffed peppers. Colourful Illy coffee sets and a dramatic display of elegant grappas complete the picture.

French Pâtisserie

NADELL PÂTISSERIE

Unit 4 & 5, Angel House, 9 White Lion Street, London N1 9HJ
Tel: 020 7833 2461
Fax: 020 7713 5036
Open: Mon-Fri 9am-5pm
Closed: Sat, Sun and Bank holidays **Tube:** Angel **Bus:** 4, 30, 38, 73, 214, 274 **Mainline station:** Kings Cross **Payment:** cash, cheques
Bespoke delivery

If you want to take a tip from French hostesses and let a professional prepare the dessert for your next special meal, this is one of the places to go to. Baker Michel Nadell and his team of artisan craftsmen prepare the exquisite-looking cakes and tarts that adorn all French pâtisseries to order. To help you make up your mind, send for their brochure with more than 20 photographs. Most of their business is wholesale, but personal shoppers can choose from a selection of chocolate gateaux, tarts and individual tarts. For a very special occasion, such as a wedding, try their *croque-en-bouche* decorated with sugar swans and flowers.

Italian Delicatessen

SAPONARA

23 Prebend Street, London N1 8PF
Tel/Fax: 020 7226 2771
Open: Mon-Fri 8am-7pm, Sat 9am-7pm **Closed:** Sun and Bank holidays **Tube:** Angel **Bus:** 38, 56, 73, 171a, 271 **Mainline station:** Essex Road **Payment:** cash, cheques, Switch
Bespoke deliveries locally

Marco Saponara has created a very enticing little shop-cum-café in a none-too-obvious location, set well back from Islington's main shopping drags of Essex Road and Upper Street. Carefully selected and home-prepared produce and a welcoming atmosphere ensure a constant buzz nonetheless. Marco's greatest source of pride, perhaps, is the fresh pasta he has flown over twice a week from Italy: tagliatelle and plump ravioli with interesting fillings are joined by generously-filled, tender crespelle. A good range of chef-made sauces, from lucanica to smoked salmon via the more usual arrabbiata and bolognese, are available to accompany the pasta, as is Marco's freshly pounded pesto. There is no shortage of good dried pasta either, including the all-too-rarely seen Spinosi. Salume includes *coppa di Parma, schiacciata piccante* and *salame al tartufo*; truffles are much in evidence in the cheese selection, too: three styles of truffled pecorino sit alongside (rather fine) fontina, buffalo mozzarella and other staples. A chilled cabinet contains entirely organic fruits and vegetables and there is organic coffee, too. The sweetmeats, from Maglio chocolates and luxuriously wrapped Tre Marie 'Collezione' panettoni to homemade tiramisu and pastries, are an indulgent delight.

Fishmonger

★ STEVE HATT

88-90 Essex Road, London N1 8LU
Tel/Fax: 020 7226 3963
Open: Mon-Sat 7am-5pm **Closed:** Sun, Mon, Bank holidays **Tube:** Angel **Bus:** 38, 56, 73, 171a, 341 **Mainline station:** Essex Road **Payment:** cash, cheques

Well established as one of London's best fishmongers, Steve Hatt is a fourth-generation incumbent and has obviously lived and breathed quality fish and seafood all his life. His driving force he describes as a 'relentless quest for quality', something so palpable that it attracts custom from far and wide. Celebrity clientele alone (even admitting that Islington is singularly blessed with the species) is too long to list. You can expect a wide range of fish, including the finest/priciest - wild sea bass, gilt-head bream – all as fresh as can be: tuna is sushi-class, lobsters live. Plenty of seafood choice, too: brown shrimps, raw prawns, Cornish crab every which way (including bags of white meat). Smoked fish include exotic swordfish and halibut, while haddock and mackerel are home-smoked. Festive specialities include anything from oscietra caviar to carp for Christmas and, indeed, a full range of poultry and game (the latter to order, rather than on display). All the usual adjuncts are there too: bottled 'fonds', squid ink, Perard fish soups. Something of an institution, the standards of which, one feels, will never slip.

Newington Green

Turkish Delicatessen

A HIGHER TASTE

47 Newington Green, London N16 9PX
Tel/Fax: 020 7359 2338
Open: Mon-Sat 7.30am-9pm, Sun 9am-6pm **Closed:** Bank holidays **Mainline station:** Canonbury **Bus:** 73, 171a
Payment: cash, cheques
Food-to-go

A new anglo-friendly name for the former Aziz Baba Deli Pastahanesi does not signify any other change: Turkish management remains the same, as does the local community café aspect and the vegetarian traiteur items, savouries and pastries, as well as good bread. Well-priced meze include idiosyncratically spelt humus, *tebule*, *cacik* and smoked aubergine; *böreks* (Turkish pasties) have traditional spinach, mushroom and feta fillings; breads include olive and tahini flavoured examples; and the large selection of freshly made pastries with exotic names such as *Seker Pare, Lor Tay Lisi and Fistik Ezmesi* (translations, e.g., pistachio and marzipan for the latter are proferred) are perhaps the real reason to visit. There is genuine Turkish delight, too.

Turkish Confectioner Pâtisserie

ANTEPLILER

33 Green Lanes, London N16 9BS
TeL: 020 7226 9409

Main shop: see Harringay, page 135

Italian Delicatessen

GALLO NERO DELICATESSEN

45 Newington Green Road, London N1 4QT
Tel: 020 7226 2002

Main shop: see Stoke Newington, page 147

Greek Bakery Pâtisserie

MANOR FARM BAKERY

108 Green Lanes, London N16 9EH
Tel: 020 7254 7907
Open: Mon-Sun 7am-8pm
Closed: Bank holidays **Mainline station:** Canonbury **Bus:** 141, 171a **Payment:** cash only

The name is perhaps a little misleading: there is nothing at all English about this traditional Turkish bakery, including most of the clientele; and the tube station of the same name is a considerable walk away. It's worth seeking out, however, for the quality and authenticity of the breads which include well-made basics (round 'hatted' crusty loaves and flat pittas), enriched dough breads and a small range of savoury and sweet pastries. As good a Turkish bakery as you will find anywhere in London.

Pentonville

Italian Delicatessen

OLGA STORES

30 Penton Street, London N1 9PS
Tel: 020 7837 5467
Open: Mon-Fri 9am-8pm, Sat 9am-7pm, Sun 10am-2pm
Closed: Bank holidays **Tube:** Angel **Bus:** 30, 73, 214 **Mainline station:** King's Cross **Payment:** cash, cheques, Delta, MasterCard, Switch, Visa

A small, friendly, Italian deli with useful opening hours. In fact, it stocks a vast array of Mediterranean produce. Though Christmas sees it packed to the gunnels with festive breads and cakes, sweetmeats are something of a year-round speciality, with both commercial and artisan-produced Sicilian pastries having a strong presence. Others include a wide range of *Jijonenca turròn*, Spanish fig cake and chocolate-coated figs, *torroncini* and Mulino Bianco biscuits. Of course you will find the basics in abundance: oils, balsamic vinegars, pasta - including, unusually, the prestigious Cipriani varieties - zampone and salume, tuna, anchovies, clams. Homemade lasagne, salsas, and ravioli stuffed with artichoke and wild mushrooms are popular. Fresh fruits and vegetables, and a decent range of wines, complete this one-stop shop facility.

South Woodford

Sausages
Organic

JOSHUA HILL'S

126 George Lane, London E18 1AD
Tel/Fax: 020 8989 3083
Open: Mon-Sat 8.30am-6pm
Closed: Sun and Bank holidays
Tube: South Woodford **Bus:** 179, 301, 549 **Payment:** cash, cheques, Amex, Delta, MasterCard, Switch, Visa
Local deliveries, mail-order

After just 4 years in South Woodford, Graham Hill has established a reputation for his 50 varieties of sausages that would be the envy of any central London location. Indeed, many a European businessman has been known to hop on the tube and secrete a cache of Hill's British bangers in his briefcase. To think of these paragons of excellence as British bangers is, perhaps, misleading. While it is no longer unusual to find that all meat used is free-range or organic, it is rare to come across an all-leg-meat pork sausage with no added fat. This means sacrificing a little succulence for density of texture and intensity of flavour, boosted by the use of roughly chopped fresh herbs (Hill never uses dried) and inventive additions of flavours such as Normandy shallots, Dutch East India spice mix, whole lemon, and hickory smoked pork. The majority of the sausages are also gluten-free, and a purist's touch ensures that all ingredients in the organic range are fully organic. Other meat-related products range from French venison terrine to Clonakilty black pudding. The shop also functions as a deli with beautifully displayed dips, sauces, anchovies, rollmops, pickles, olives and even sweetmeats and chocolates.

Stoke Newington

Delicatessen
Greengrocer
Grocer

★ THE COOLER

67 Stoke Newington Church Street, London N16 0AR
Tel: 020 7253 2070
Fax: 020 7253 4947
Open: Mon-Fri 9am-8.30pm, Sat 9am-8pm, Sun 10am-5pm
Closed: 'no chance' **Mainline station:** Stoke Newington **Bus:** 73 **Payment:** cash, cheques, Amex, Delta, MasterCard, Switch, Visa

This is the kind of Aladdin's cave of a store every area of London should have: long opening hours, child-friendly café attached, quality and flavour-led selection of just about anything one might wish for, much of it organic; even a smattering of local celebrities. Friendly rather than glossy (despite its name), The Cooler is so rumbustuously packed with goods you may have to hunt hard for what you're after – but this does allow for serendipitous discoveries. These include & Clarke's bread and biscuits (see page 86); 'Motte de beurre' (churned, unsalted French butter cut from a large tub); Coquetdale, Vacherin, Bath soft cheeses and *Cancaillotte* (a matured cheese spread) – many cheeses are imported from the Rungis market; olive oil from Nîmes, Armand Blott fish soups, *rouille*, piquant mussels and conserves; smoked goose breast, bacon from Woodalls, Burbush's Penrith pies and fresh organic meat from Craig Farm; Rainha Santa preserved fruits, Ackermans' chocolates, (see page 129), Irish Village Flours Children's Scone Mix; and a good range of organic fruits and vegetables. There are interesting juices and wines too. 'Shopping should be fun, not didactic', declares the manager - and here it certainly is.

Jewish
Orthodox
Fishmonger
Kosher

THE FISH CENTRE

8 Stamford Hill, London N16 6XZ
Tel: 020 8442 4412
Fax: 020 8442 4754
Open: Tue-Thu 8am-5pm, Fri

8am-1pm **Closed:** Sat, Sun, Mon, Jewish religious holidays **Mainline station:** Stoke Newington **Bus:** 67, 76, 106, 149, 243 **Payment:** cash, cheques **Bespoke deliveries locally**

This Orthodox Jewish-run fishmonger is a narrow slip of a place, with a small display of glisteningly fresh fish, and a considerably larger area packed full of white bags, ready-to-go. Shoppers enjoy the somewhat unusual experience of being served by fishmongers clad in black from head to toe; despite such sombre appearance, service is warm, humorous and helpful. Stock includes the basics: cod, haddock, pollock, and so on, plus plentiful supplies of fish with special appeal to the Jewish community: salmon, salmon trout, bream and carp. Traditional minced fish is apparently very popular with non-Jewish shoppers, too, on account of its evident quality, as is ready-to-cook rolled fish. A very popular shop despite its restricted opening hours.

Italian Delicatessen

GALLO NERO DELICATESSEN

73 Stoke Newington High Street, London N16 8EL
Tel: 020 7254 9770
Open: Mon-Fri 8.30am-6.15pm, Sat 8.30am-6pm **Closed:** Sun, Bank holidays **Mainline station:** Stoke Newington **Bus:** 67, 73, 76, 106, 149, 243 **Payment:** cash, cheques, Delta, MasterCard, Switch, Visa

The Gallo Nero delis (there is a second branch in Newington Green) have been established in the area for over 25 years and have a 'supply everything Italian' approach: olive oils to espresso pots to (Belgian!) chocolates. All the basics are there: de Cecco, Agnesi and Molisana pasta, a variety of risotto rice, good tins of tuna and anchovies. The Moris produce their own very popular pasta sauces and pesto, and the ham is home cooked. Homemade tiramisu panders nicely to the Italian sweet tooth, as do jars of rum babas and fruits in liqueur. Look hard to spot treasures such as beautifully soft fillets of baccala (salt cod) and precious (the £70 touch) bottles of traditional balsamic vinegar. A small range of wines completes the picture.

Branch: see Newington Green, page 144

Tottenham

Chinese Food Hall

LOON FUNG

111 Brantwood Road, London N17 ODX
Tel: 020 8365 1536

Main shop: see Chinatown, page 26

Greek Cypriot Food Hall

MILIA'S
200-202 St Ann's Road, London N15 5RP
Tel: 020 8802 7654
Open: Mon-Sat 9am-8pm
Closed: Sun **Tube:** Seven Sisters
Bus: 67 **Mainline station:** Seven Sisters **Payment:** cash, cheques, Switch, MasterCard, Visa
Catering, delivery, mail-order

This Greek Cypriot institution, with its friendly and helpful staff, is particularly good for bulk buying: there are bargain value cans of both olive and vegetable oils at the front of the shop. Finer grade oils can be found on the shelves. The rest of the stock is also very comprehensive, with lots of cheeses (flaoura Easter cheese, loose feta, small and large feta packets from Greece, halloumi and *kefalotyree* from Cyprus), honey, olives, Greek breads, many kinds of baklava and other sweets and pastries. The meat counter has speciality meats such as *bastourma, bast*, Loukanika sausages and *loundza*. On the day we visited, the fresh vegetables on offer included red raddishes, big bunches of celery with the leaves on, kollokassi, big mooli, aubergines, giant butter beans, bunches of rocket, and fresh figs from Cyprus. There were also the usual jars of olives, capers, peppers, pickled caper leaves, and tins of salted sardines and anchovies. They also had specialities such as *Trahanas* (used to thicken winter soups), and jars of walnuts in honey.

Green Street Market

Forest Gate, London E7
Open: Tue, Thu, Fri 8am-6pm **Tube:** Upton Park **Mainline station:** Forest Gate

A mecca for keenly priced Asian, African and Caribbean ingredients – and highly recommended by Indian chef, Cyrus Todiwala of Café Spice Namaste. At Green Street Supermarket you will find all sorts of Caribbean and Jamaican fresh fruit and veg, as well as myriad groceries. The large daily covered market halfway down the road feels very exotic indeed with its pulsating music and bustling, cheerful atmosphere. Visit B. B's Caribbean fismongers for catfish, croaker, and salt fish as well as more familiar creatures; or Toor Supermarket for huge bunches of fresh herbs and exotic African and Caribbean fruit and vegetables, as well as Indian and Bangladeshi beans of all shapes and sizes. Queues at friendly butchers are testament to the quality of the goat and mutton on sale.

Turkish Food Hall

TURKISH FOOD CENTRE
363 Fore Street, London N9 ONR
Tel: 020 8807 6766

542-544 Lordship Lane, London N22 5BY
Tel: 020 8365 8846

Main shop: see Dalston, page 134

Walthamstow Market

Walthamstow High Street
Open: Mon-Sat 8am-6pm **Mainline station:** St James St Walthamstow
Bus: 48

Claimed to be England's longest market, Walthamstow market occupies the length of the High Street all week, excluding Sunday, with over 500 pitches on the busiest day, Saturday. There are fruit and vegetable stalls galore, offering the usual variety and at quite reasonable prices, but you can find more exotic produce from Asia and the Caribbean, and there are also cheese, sausage and shellfish stalls. Otherwise the mix is of old clothes, new clothes, household goods, furniture and records. The atmosphere is bustling and very typically East End. If you're hungry, try a West Indian ready-made snack from a stall, or some pie and mash or eels and mash from old-fashioned pie shops actually in the market.

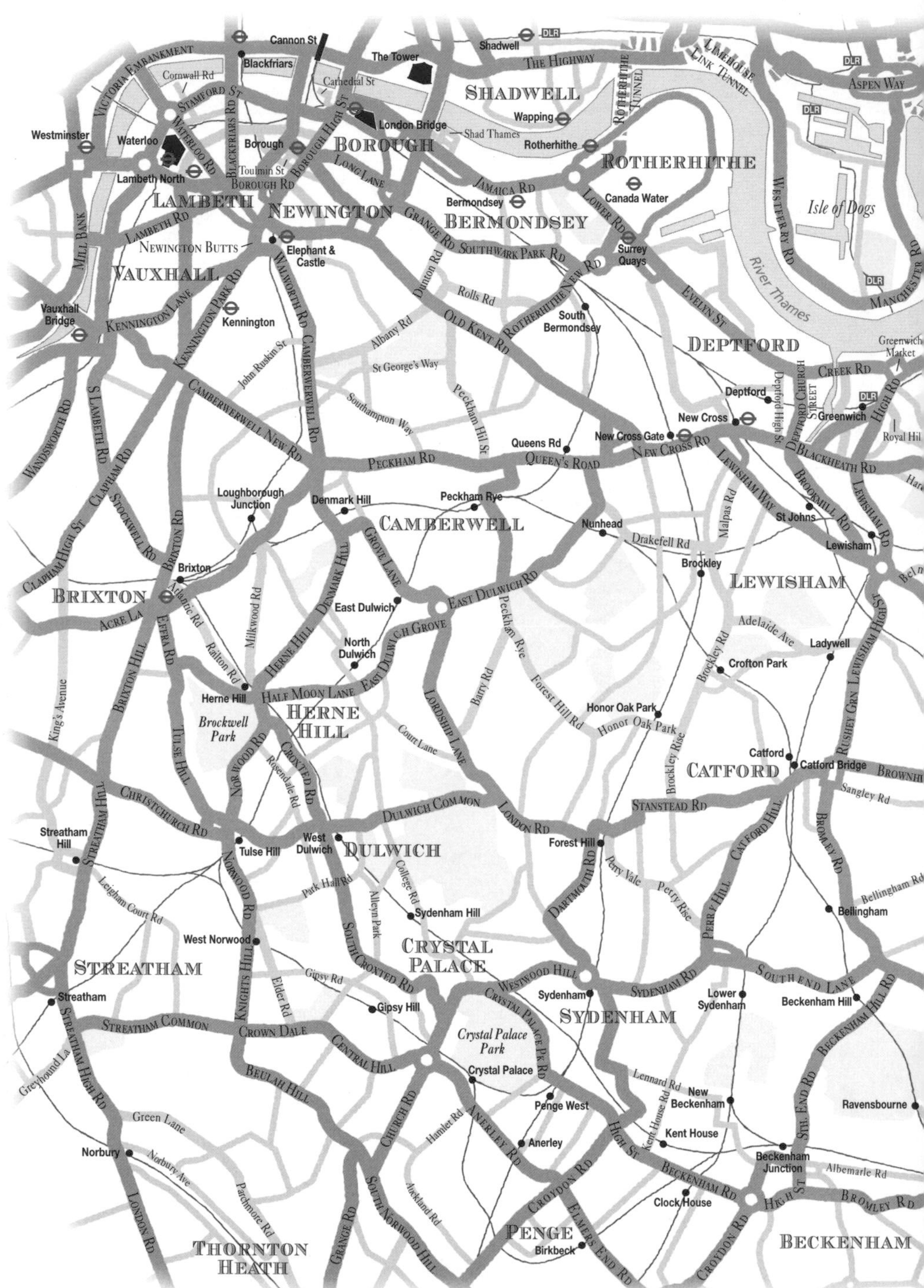

Cannon St
Shadwell
DLR
The Tower
Victoria Embankment
Blackfriars
The Highway
Limehouse Link Tunnel
Cornwall Rd
Cathedral St
Shadwell
Rotherhithe Tunnel
Aspen Way
Stamford St
Wapping
Waterloo Rd
Westminster
Waterloo
London Bridge
Shad Thames
Borough
Borough High St
Borough
Rotherhithe
Blackfriars Rd
Toulmin St
Rotherhithe
Lambeth North
Borough Rd
Long Lane
Jamaica Rd
Westferry Rd
Canada Water
Lambeth
Newington
Bermondsey
Lower Rd
Isle of Dogs
Mill Bank
Lambeth Rd
Grange Rd
Bermondsey
Newington Butts
Elephant & Castle
Southwark Park Rd
Surrey Quays
Vauxhall
Walworth Rd
Dunton Rd
Rotherhithe New Rd
Evelyn St
River Thames
Manchester Rd
Vauxhall Bridge
Kennington Lane
Kennington Park Rd
Kennington
Rolls Rd
South Bermondsey
Kennington Rd
Albany Rd
Old Kent Rd
Deptford
Greenwich Market
John Ruskin St
Camberwell Rd
St George's Way
Creek Rd
Deptford
Deptford Church Street
Deptford High St
Wandsworth Rd
S Lambeth Rd
Camberwell New Rd
Southampton Way
Peckham Hill St
New Cross
Greenwich
High Rd
Royal Hil
Clapham Rd
Queens Rd
New Cross Gate
New Cross Rd
Peckham Rd
Queen's Road
Blackheath Rd
Lewisham Way
Stockwell Rd
Loughborough Junction
Denmark Hill
Peckham Rye
Brookmill Rd
Clapham High St
Brixton Rd
Camberwell
St Johns
Lewisham Rd
Nunhead
Drakefell Rd
Malpas Rd
Lewisham
Brixton
Grove Lane
Brockley
Clapham High St
Denmark Hill
Lewisham
Brixton
Atlantic Rd
Milkwood Rd
East Dulwich
East Dulwich Rd
Acre La
Efra Rd
Adelaide Ave
Ladywell
North Dulwich
East Dulwich Grove
Peckham Rye
Railton Rd
Herne Hill
Brockley Rd
Crofton Park
Lewisham High St
Brixton Hill
King's Avenue
Herne Hill
Half Moon Lane
Barry Rd
Forest Hill Rd
Honor Oak Park
Brockwell Park
Herne Hill
Lordship Lane
Court Lane
Honor Oak Park
Rushey Grn
Tulse Hill
Norwood Rd
Rosendale Rd
Croxted Rd
Brockley Rise
Catford
Catford Bridge
Catford
Brownhi
Streatham Hill
Christchurch Rd
Dulwich Common
London Rd
Stanstead Rd
Sangley Rd
Streatham Hill
Tulse Hill
West Dulwich
Dulwich
Forest Hill
Catford Hill
Bromley Rd
Norwood Rd
Park Hall Rd
College Rd
Perry Vale
Perry Rise
Leigham Court Rd
Allyn Park
Dartmouth Rd
Perry Hill
Bellingham
Bellingham Rd
Sydenham Hill
West Norwood
South Croxted Rd
Crystal Palace
Streatham
Knights Hill
Gipsy Rd
Westwood Hill
Sydenham
Sydenham Rd
Southend Lane
Streatham
Elder Rd
Crystal Palace Pk Rd
Lower Sydenham
Beckenham Hill
Beckenham Hill Rd
Gipsy Hill
Sydenham
Streatham Common
Crown Dale
Crystal Palace Park
Central Hill
Streatham High Rd
Crystal Palace
Beulah Hill
Lennard Rd
New Beckenham
Sth. End Rd
Ravensbourne
Greyhound La
Penge West
Green Lane
Church Rd
Hamlet Rd
Kent House Rd
Kent House
Anerley Rd
Anerley
High St
Norbury
Norbury Ave
Beckenham Junction
Albemarle Rd
Croydon Rd
Beckenham Rd
Parchmore Rd
Auckland Rd
South Norwood Hill
Clock House
High St
Bromley Rd
London Rd
Grange Rd
Penge
Elmers End Rd
Croydon Rd
Beckenham
Thornton Heath
Birkbeck

South East

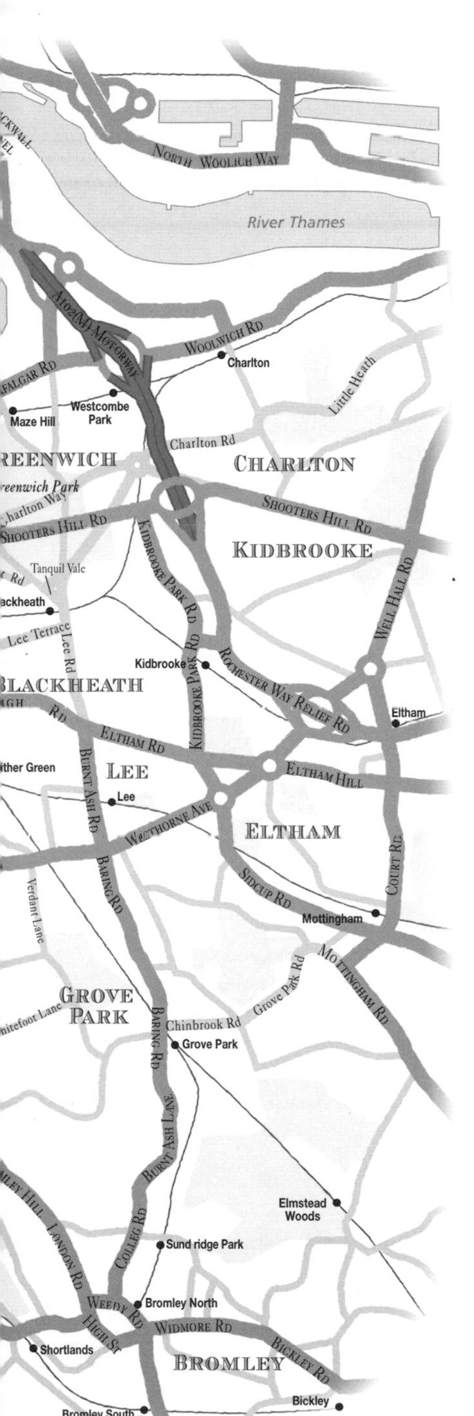

LEGEND

	Motorway
	Main Road
	Other Road
Highbury & Islington •	Railway Station
⊖	Underground
	Waterways
	Parks
DLR	Docklands Light Railway

0 1000m

0 1000yd

Beckenham

Cheese shop
Delicatessen

JAMES'S

188 High Street, Beckenham, Kent BR3 1EN
Tel: 020 8650 3335
Open: Mon-Fri 9am-5.30pm, Sat 9am-5pm **Closed:** Sun and Bank holidays **Mainline station:** Beckenham Junction **Bus:** 54, 227, 367 **Payment:** cash, cheques, Delta, MasterCard, Switch, Visa

This used to be the British cheese affineur, James Aldridge's shop, and his matured cheeses, notably Tornegus, are still stocked here. In fact cheeses, not surprisingly, still have pride of place in this specialist shop, which also sells beers, cider and wine, along with some organic products. Most of the cheese selection is British, but there are also varieties from France, Switzerland, Norway and Denmark, a few of which are imported directly from the producers. A good chance to try something new is on Saturdays, when the owners host cheese and cider tastings. Other offerings include breads from Delice de France, jams for diabetics and Christmas hampers, containing biscuits, chocolates and Port.

Sausages

VILLAGERS FINE SAUSAGES

91 High Street, Beckenham, Kent BR3 1AG
Tel/Fax: 020 8325 5475
Open: Mon-Sat 8.30am-5.30pm **Closed:** Sun **Mainline station:** Beckenham Junction **Bus:** 54, 276, 227 **Payment:** cash, cheques, Amex, Delta, MasterCard, Switch, Visa
Catalogue, takes orders

The old-fashioned appearance of this shop simply reinforces an old-fashioned approach to making traditional, handmade sausages without any additives or preservatives. With a selection of 65 varieties always available, and up to 300 varieties available on request, owner Ron Etheridge claims to offer the largest selection of bangers in the south of England. Along with traditional Cumberland and Lincolnshire flavours, for example, you will find venison, wild boar and vegetarian spicy cabbage. The international selection also includes vegetarian and gluten-free offerings. Homemade pickles, chutneys, sauces and South African biltong are also sold, along with prepared meat dishes such English leg of lamb, boned and stuffed with Toulouse sausage meat.

Bermondsey

Food Hall

LE PONT DE LA TOUR FOODSTORE

360d Butler's Wharf, Shad Thames, London SE16 2YE
Tel: 020 7403 4030
Fax: 020 7357 0968
Open: (Summer) Mon-Fri

Neal's Yard

Borough branch – *see page 156*

Rogg's

Tower Hamlets – *see page 69*

Lisboa Pâtisserie

Notting Hill – *see page 98*

Chalmers & Gray

Notting Hill – *see page 91*

DAILY FISH PRICES
CRABS
LOBSTERS
per lb
WILD SALMON 5.60
FARM SALMON 3.60
TURBOT
HALIBUT 3.90
7.40
9.40
DOVER SOLE 10.20
LEMON SOLE 6.20
GREY MULLET —
RED MULLET 8.90
PLAICE FILLETS 6.90
—
COD FILLET 5.20
HADDOCK FILLET 5.20
SKATE
MONKFISH 10.60
HAKE 9.60
SARDINES 3.50
SQUID 6.50
TUNA
SWORDFISH 10.80
RAW KING PRAWNS 15.60
SNAPPER 6.80
16.80

Freshlands

Camden branch – *see page 109*

8.30am-8.30pm (Winter) Mon-Fri 8.30am-7.30pm, Sat-Sun 10am-6pm **Closed:** 25, 26 Dec., Good Friday
Tube: London Bridge or Tower Hill **Bus:** 42, 47, 78, 188 **Mainline station:** London Bridge
Payment: cash, cheques, Amex, Delta, MasterCard, Switch, Visa
Food-to-go

Style guru Terence Conran's version of the corner shop. Everything is intended to combine visual appeal with top quality in this cornerstone of Conran's Gastrodome complex. ('We seek out the more unusual products that not only taste great but look fab in your kitchen', says a manager.) Along with the attractively packaged groceries, there are plenty of foods to take away, from filling sandwiches made with bread baked daily on the premises, to Italian antipasti, farmhouse cheeses and top-quality charcuterie. Or, buy fresh poultry, meat, fish and season game to cook at home.

Oils
Spices

THE OIL & SPICE SHOP
Butler's Wharf Building, Shad Thames, London SE16 2YE
Tel: 020 7403 4030
Fax: 0207 357 0968
Open: Mon-Sun noon-6pm
Closed: 25, 26 Dec., Good Friday **Tube:** London Bridge, Tower Hill **Bus:** 42, 47, 78, 188
Mainline station: London Bridge
Payment: cash, cheques, Amex, Delta, MasterCard, Switch, Visa

A foodie treasure trove in the restored historic spice quay along the Thames, with all the signature hallmarks of Terence Conran's sleek style. More than 80 different extra-virgin olive oils, 50 from Italy, fight for shelf space with a huge range of balsamic vinegars, wine vinegars and fresh fruit. As you would expect, this is the place for difficult-to-find spices from around the world, along with the more common ones. For inspiration, a good range of cookery books are also sold.

Blackheath

Delicatessen

HAND MADE FOOD
40 Tranquil Vale, London SE3 OBD
Tel 020 8297 9966
Fax: 020 8265 0235
Open: Mon-Fri 9am-6pm, Sat 9am-5.30pm **Closed:** Sun and Bank holidays **Mainline station:** Blackheath **Bus:** 53, 54, 75,108
Payment: cash, cheques, Delta, MasterCard, Switch, Visa
Food-to-go

This is a high quality, traiteur-style delicatessen, well kept and friendly, where everything is attractively displayed. They offer a delicious and extensive range of ready-made starters, salads, main courses and puddings all of which are cooked on the premises. The kitchen at the back of the shop exudes the most wonderful cooking smells. The dishes are not limited to just traditional French fare, in fact, the owners describe themselves more as global cooks. The menus change with the seasons so there is always something new to try. Choose from a traditional coq au vin to a Moroccan lamb tagine or a Thai curry. They also produce their own pâtés and terrines and stock a good range of farmhouse cheeses, salamis, and dry goods from Carluccio's (see page 29), including a wonderful selection of pastas, olive oils and sauces. Well worth a visit to stock up your fridge or freezer.

Borough

Fishmonger

★ ABERDEEN SEA PRODUCTS

Unit 2, Toulmin Street, London SE1 1PP
Tel: 020 7407 0247
Fax: 020 7407 0248
Open: Mon-Fri 5.30am-12.30pm, Sat 5.30am-10am
Closed: Sun and Bank holidays
Tube: Borough **Bus:** 35, 40, 133, 344, P3 **Mainline station:** London Bridge **Payment:** cash, cheques, Amex, MasterCard, Visa
Bespoke deliveries to Central/SE London (min order £30)

The first thing that strikes a visitor to this essentially wholesale enterprise is the bareness of the warehouse-style entrance; the next impression is of a barely perceptible, sea-fresh smell and pristine cleanliness. You won't see much fish on display, though there's a constant buzz of activity and piles of polystyrene boxes in the preparation room. But a scan of the list will tell you that almost anything can be found here, from cod to Kingfish, prawns to Venus clams, smoked wild salmon and potted shrimps, even caviar. Best bets, perhaps, are the Japanese sushi-grade (ultra fresh and unblemished) salmon, seabass, red snapper and tuna. Indeed the tuna is the freshest, most perfect 'uniformly pigeon blood red' I've ever seen. Orders from restaurants flow thick and fast, and virtually all stock arrives straight from the coast and leaves the prep room on the same day, though a small quantity is kept frozen. You don't need to phone through for most varieties of fresh fish, though it would be as well to if you're after exotics or seasonal shellfish. Despite those restaurant-trade early hours, this reviewer at least is unlikely to be buying fish elsewhere following this discovery.

Fishmonger

★ fish!

Cathedral Street, Borough Market, London SE1 9AL
Tel: 020 7407 3801
Fax: 020 7407 3804
Open: Mon-Fri 9.30am-7pm, Sat 9.30am-3.30pm, Bank holiday Mon 9.30am-3.30pm **Closed:** Sun **Tube:** London Bridge **Bus:** 35, 40, 43, 47, 48, 133, 149

Borough Market

Open: 9am-5pm **Tube:** London Bridge **Bus:** 35, 40, 43, 47, 48, 133, 149
Mainline station: London Bridge

During the week, and early in the morning, the west side of Borough High Street is lined with stalls which sell magnificent fruit and vegetables, mostly in wholesale quantities. Every Friday and Saturday, however, a food market is held in tandem with the weekday market. Various growers, farmers, wholesalers and food producers come in from around the country to sell their wares, often on a wholesale basis, although smaller buys can be negotiated. There are some thirty-five stalls at present, which offer a variety of foods: olives and oils, prepared sauces, terrines and preserves, breads, coffee, organic beef, venison, smoked eel and salmon, organic (and bio-dynamic) fruits, vegetables and juices, cheeses, herbs and ice-creams. There was a sumptuous display of wild mushrooms at the end of August. A market has existed in the area for at least 300 years (originally sited on London Bridge), but the food market started fairly recently (1998).

WORTH A DETOUR

Vinopolis City of Wine, 1 Bank End,
London SE1 9BU
Tel: 020 7940 8301

Mainline station: London Bridge
Payment: cash, cheques, Amex, Delta, MasterCard, Switch, Visa
Catering, delivery , mail-order

Dine and shop at the same time at fish!, the fishmongers with a diner attached in trendy Borough market. Fishmonger William Black, perhaps best known as food writer Sophie Grigson's husband and co-author of 'Fish', is the consultant and it's part of a chain that owns the respected Jarvis fish shop in Kingston upon Thames. fish! offers organic farmed salmon, GM-free farmed fish, scallops from Scotland and a selection of fish smoked at the shop in Kingston, along with a long list of seasonal fresh fish and poultry and game. You can select your fish at the shop or telephone for UK mainland delivery. Or, have fresh fish packed up while you eat and just pay one bill.

Bakery
Pâtisserie

KONDITOR & COOK

22 Cornwall Road, London
SE1 8TW
Tel: 020 7261 0456
Fax: 020 7261 9021
Open: Mon-Fri 7.30am-6.30pm, Sat 8.30am-2.30pm **Closed:** Sun and Bank holidays **Tube:** Waterloo **Bus:** 26, 68, 76, 168, 171, 176, 188, 341 **Mainline station:** Waterloo **Payment:** cash, cheques, MasterCard, Switch, Visa
Bespoke wedding cakes

Give your sweet tooth a treat at this stylish bakery, a favourite with Jerry Hall, Mick Jagger, Tina Turner and actors from the nearby National Theatre and Old Vic. Only natural butter and free-range eggs are used in Gerhard Jenne's irresistible cakes, cookies and pastries. 'Glamorous' and scrumptious' are just 2 adjectives used to describe the stunning-looking baked goods, which can include prune buns, plum tarts, whisky-and-orange bombe and 'magic' cakes. The customised wedding cakes have graced many top-society weddings. Or, if you're in the mood for something less sweet, try the lunch time snacks to take away.

Branch: 10 Stoney Street, London
SE1 9AD
Tel: 020 7407 5100

Cheese shop

NEAL'S YARD DAIRY

6 Park Street, London SE1 9AB
Tel: 020 7403 9544

Main shop: see Covent Garden, page 30

Brixton

Delicatessen

A & C CO.

3 Atlantic Road, London
SW8 8HX
Tel: 0207 733 3766
Open: Mon-Sat 8am-8pm **Closed:** Sun **Tube:** Brixton **Bus:** 2, 3, 35, 41, 59, 109, 133, 196 **Mainline station:** Brixton **Payment:** cash, cheques

Cyprus meets Portugal in this well-presented neighbourhood shop. The shop started life as a Cypriot deli but was taken over by the friendly Portuguese couple who still own it today, so it has an eclectic mixture of stock, from Spain, Italy and Portugal, as well Cyprus and Greece. Francisco Cardosa and his wife, Dina, sell fresh filo, olives, oils, Spanish and Italian cheeses, chorizo sausages, bread and lots of dried pulses and pasta, and sweet Italian biscuits.

Grocer
Greengrocer
Wholefoods
Organic

BRIXTON WHOLEFOODS

59 Atlantic Road, London
SW9 8PU
Tel: 020 7737 2210
Open: Mon, Fri 9.30am-6pm, Tue-Thu, Sat 9.30am-5.30pm **Closed:** Sun and Bank holidays **Tube:** Brixton **Bus:** 2, 3, 35, 45, 109, 118, 133, 159, 196, 250 **Mainline station:** Brixton **Payment:** cash, cheques

Hillary Waterfield's health-food shop is a popular spot in lively Brixton Market. It's crammed with organic fruit and veg, teas, cheese, butter, oil, balsamic vinegar, wine, rice, pasta and pulses, as well as Rachel organic milk and Rocombe ice cream. Vegetarians will find a range of tofu, soya chunks, TVP, GM-free and vegetable sausage and burger mixes, and sheep's milk and gluten-free vegetables are also available for anyone on restrictive diets. Regulars like the large jars of herbs and spices where they serve themselves – at 20p an ounce this works out much less expensive than buying packaged varieties. Some of the more unusual offerings include dried nettles, hops, rosehips, limeflower and bee pollen.

L. S. MASH AND SONS

Fishmonger

11 Atlantic Road, London SW9 8HX
Tel: 020 7274 6423
Open: Mon-Sat 7am-6.30pm
Closed: Sun, Bank holidays **Tube:** Brixton **Bus:** 2, 3, 35, 45, 109, 118, 133, 159, 196, 250 **Mainline**

Brixton Market

Electric Avenue, Brixton Station Road
Open: Mon, Tue, Thu-Sat 8.30am-6pm, Wed 10am-3pm **Closed:** Bank holidays
Tube: Brixton **Bus:** 3, 36, 109, 133, 159 **Mainline station:** Brixton

Between Brixton Road and Coldharbour Lane, a plethora of roads and covered arcades make up one of the most vibrant, ebullient and entertaining markets in the capital. Centred originally on Atlantic Road and Electric Avenue (so-called because it was one of the first shopping streets to be electrically lit), it is reputed to be the largest market in Europe for Caribbean and African foods, reflecting the needs of a large proportion of the locals, immigrants who settled the area in the late 1940s, early 1950s. Amidst stalls of apples, tomatoes and potatoes, there are strikingly exotic displays of yams, okra, dried pulses, unfamiliar nuts and leaves, plantains and guavas. Butchers in the area specialise in offal and Halal meat; some offer mutton and goat. Fishmongers - of which there are several, principally in Granville Arcade - offer fish from all over the world, among them croakers, snappers and tilapia, gleaming crabs and large raw prawns. There are also bacon, spice and bread, old clothes, household goods, vinyl and wig shops and stalls. The atmosphere is electric as well, especially on Fridays and Saturdays when the market is busiest: everyone is buying for the week ahead, bargains are being touted, jokes and gossip exchanged, and competing rhythms - calypso, jazz, reggae and gospel among them - thump from all sides.

station: Brixton **Payment:** cash, cheques over £20

'I don't think there is a fish we don't sell,' says Lorne Mash the second generation of his family to run this friendly, neighbourhood shop catering for the local Caribbean and Portuguese communities. The diverse selection of seafood on offer comes fresh daily from Billingsgate Market and the south coast and includes West Indian and Portuguese favourites such as Jamaican snapper, talapia, red fish, octopus and salt fish. More conventional offerings are cod, mussels, trout, sprats and prawns.

Italian Delicatessen

PIACENZA DELI

2 Brixton Road, London SW9 6BU
Tel: 020 7735 2121
Open: Mon-Sat 9am-6.30pm Sun 10am-1.30pm **Closed:** Bank holidays **Tube:** Oval **Bus:** 3, 36, 109, 133, 159 **Mainline station:** Elephant & Castle **Payment:** cash, cheques

Edorodo Coda and his family have built up a friendly neighbourhood Italian delicatessen like the ones you would expect to find in his native Piacenza, south of Milan. That's the region of renowned hams, so not surprisingly the shop stocks San Daniele ham, along with a selection of salamis. Specialities are Signora Coda's home-made tortelloni with vegetable stuffing, and a selection of fresh pasta sauces - familiar basil pesto, as well as a red pesto with a hint of chilli, walnut sauce and Sicilian pasta with almonds, sun-dried tomatoes 'and lots and lots of chillies and garlic.' Just stir the cold sauces into a pot of hot pasta and you have the makings of an authentic Italian meal. The shelves are stocked with Italian '00' flour for bread- and pizza-making, as well as de Cecco and Emiliane dried pastas. Coffee is freshly ground for the wonderful flavour.

Deptford

Fishmonger

DEPTFORD CODFATHER

47 Deptford High Street, London SE8 4AD
Tel: 020 8692 3292
Open: Tue-Sat 6am-4pm **Closed:** Sun, Mon, day following a Bank holiday Mon **Mainline station:** Deptford **Bus:** 47, 53, 177, 225, X53 **Payment:** cash only

A small fishmonger geared up to serving the local community, particularly the Caribbean and Chinese populations. Norwegian salt cod, rolled to the hardness favoured by Caribbean cooks, is a speciality and remarkably inexpensive. Indeed all the fish, from cheaper lines such as coley and mackerel, to more exotic red bream, sea bream, squid, cuttle and even luxurious bass are both very affordable and very

Deptford High Street Market

Open: Wed, Fri, Sat 8.30am-5pm **Mainline station:** Deptford **Bus:** 47, 53, 177, 225

A friendly local market which lines the high street south of Deptford railway station to Deptford Broadway and meanders off west into what many describe as a separate market, in Douglas Way and Douglas Square. Prices are low, whether for fruit and vegetables, or for household goods, clothes, tapes or CDs. Many Afro-Caribbeans live in the area, and the market stalls reflect this ethnic diversity, as do many shops in the street. There are several good grocers selling African specialities, a few butchers who offer goat and cows' feet, and a fishmonger with a fine selection of tropical fish and shellfish. There are two traditional pie and mash shops in the area, if hunger strikes.

fresh, bought 'straight from the coast'. A small stock of frozen fish includes snapper and freshwater catfish.

Dulwich

AU CIEL

Chocolate
Pâtisserie

1a Calton Avenue, London SE21 7DE
Tel/Fax: 020 8488 1111
Open: Mon-Sat 8.30am-5.30pm, Sun 8.30am-2pm **Closed:** Bank holidays **Mainline station:** West Dulwich (10 mins.) **Bus:** P4, P13, P15 **Payment:** cash, cheques

Persian artist Hamideh Bayley realised a long-held dream in creating this 'experience' of an elegant chocolaterie/boulangerie in the very likely, but otherwise fine food bereft, location of Dulwich Village. Every element of the shop, from movable display-panel stairwell storage, to local foundry-wrought cast iron chairs, glass-topped shelves and tables, and even clever plastic sweet dispensers for jelly-bellies and the like, has been custom made with both pragmatism and aesthetics in mind. Thus the chocolates (by Valrhona) rest on fluted, washed-clay dishes that both prevent condensation and display them to irresistible perfection. Hamideh's own-designed calla and sunflower clay dishes and mirror boxes, in which she creates further chocolate displays, have proven so popular they are sold in their own right. Her skills are further expressed in the creation of chocolate sculptures (delicate cabbages, bunches of grapes, bouquets and the like) and favours for weddings. Locals are, however, particularly delighted to find the full range of & Clarke's breads (see page 86) and De Baere pâtisserie and boulangerie (see page 91) on sale daily, in addition to a small range of carefully selected preserves (Dartington spiced cherries, peaches, green figs and ginger, for example), glacé fruits and Ackermans' novelties (see page 129). Hamideh's bubbly personality adds to the pleasure.

Cheese shop
Delicatessen

THE CHEESE BLOCK

69 Lordship Lane, London
SE22 8EO
Tel: 020 8299 3636
Fax: 020 8516 1154
Open: Mon-Fri 9.30am-6.30pm, Sat 9am-6pm **Closed:** Sun
Mainline station: East Dulwich
Bus: 40, 176, 185 **Payment:** cash, cheques, MasterCard, Switch, Visa

Although this shop is not large, it's a Mecca for cheese-lovers in this part of south London with an average of 250 different cheeses. And, with such a selection from the UK, France, Italy, Spain, Holland and Switzerland there tends to be something for everyone - traditional farmhouse cheeses, organic cheeses and the increasingly difficult-to-find unpasteurised ones.

As Christmas approaches, the range increases to more than 300. The shop also stocks many products you would expect to find at any good deli – olives, pâtés, hams, salume, oils, vinegars, dried pasta, coffee and breads. Local produce includes lime pickle, honey from Dulwich Park and homemade organic breads.

Italian
Delicatessen

LA GASTRONOMIA

86 Park Hall Road, London, SE21 8BW
Tel: 020 8766 0494
Open: Mon-Sat 9am-6pm
Closed: Sun and 3 weeks in Aug
Mainline station: West Dulwich
Bus: 3 **Payment:** cash, cheques, Amex, Delta, MasterCard, Switch, Visa
Catering, food-to-go

Visiting this popular deli is like travelling to Italy without the hassle of international travel. You'll find savoury dishes, vegetable salads and cakes, all prepared daily. You'll also find the dried pastas, fresh breads, olive oils and well-stocked charcuterie counter you would expect, along with meat and vegetable pâtés, grilled and marinated vegetables (including olives) and pasta sauces. Try the San Leo *prosciutto crudo*, which owner Daniele Policane claims to be even better than Parma or San Daniele. The shop also sells 50 international cheeses and an impressive range of organic

We need to learn to change the way we shop, to understand that value for money means getting good quality, not just cheap produce. 

Sophie Grigson

groceries. At Christmas it is filled with up to 30 varieties of Italian biscuits, as well as panettone, pandoro and panforte.

Greengrocer
Wholefoods
Organic

SMBS FOODS

75 Lordship Lane, London
SE22 8EP
Tel: 020 8693 7792
Open: Mon-Fri 9am-7.30pm, Sat 9am-6pm, Sun 9am-5pm **Closed:** Bank holidays **Mainline station:** East Dulwich **Bus:** 12, 40, 176, 185, 312 **Payment:** cash, cheques, Delta, MasterCard, Switch, Visa

Under the same ownership as the better-known Cheese Block (see page 160) and located just a couple of doors along, this shop is an eclectic treasure-trove of high quality foods. The outdoor display of fruits and vegetables in excellent condition is accessible enough, as is the indoor chill cabinet packed with organic greengrocery, but beyond that you will have to hunt a little (or request friendly assistance) along a couple of high-stacked and somewhat narrow passageways to find whatever you are looking for. This might be anything from organic breads, biscuits, baby food, dairy produce, meats fresh and frozen, to any number of ethnic foods – salt cod, plantain crackers, preserved black beans, palm sugar, *umeboshi* – and spices, no matter how abstruse, generally in good value packets. Grains include the likes of biodynamic risotto rice, freekeh, quinoa and Hopi blue popping corn. Bakers will appreciate the almond oil, rosewater, fresh organic yeast and Himalayan lotus and wildflower honey. The healthily self-indulgent can choose from a wide range of organic ices (Yeo Valley, Green & Black, Rocombe, Swedish Glace) and chocolate truffles. In short, the perfect out-of-town grocery store.

Elephant & Castle

Columbian Grocer

LA BODEGUITA

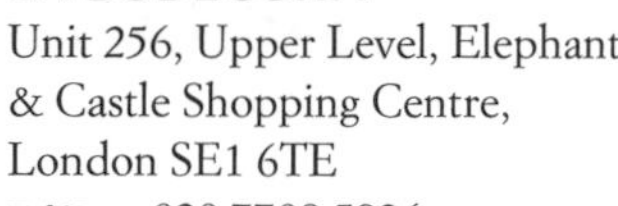

Unit 256, Upper Level, Elephant & Castle Shopping Centre, London SE1 6TE
Tel/Fax: 020 7708 5826
Open: Mon-Sat 8.30am-8pm
Closed: Sun and Bank holidays
Tube: Elephant & Castle **Bus:** 1, 12, 35, 45, 53, 63, 68, 168, 171, 176, 188, 344, C10 **Mainline station:** Elephant & Castle
Payment: cash only
Food-to-go

This recently opened café-cum-kiosk located in the somewhat bleak setting of the Elephant and Castle Shopping Centre is something of a welcome gathering spot for the local Latin American community, but is also of considerable interest to anyone seeking out authentic Colombian ingredients. These include PAN maize flour, *yuca harina* (tapioca starch), pastry and *buñuelos* mixes, frijoles beans, chocolate to grind for drinks and cooking, panella molasses and preserved figs. Equally fascinating is the ever-changing range of home-cooked foods to eat on the spot or take away: *Cuchuco de trigo, Aborrajados*, Colombian *Empanadas* and almost-familiar *Queso* (cheesecake). Enjoy a cup of good, strong coffee whilst you shop.

Spanish Grocer

LA CORUNA

103 Newington Butts, London SE1 6SF
Tel: 020 7703 3165
Open: Mon-Fri 9am-6pm, Sat 10am-6pm **Closed:** Sun and Bank holidays **Tube:** Elephant & Castle **Bus:** 1, 12, 35, 45, 53, 63, 68, 168, 171, 176, 188, 344, C10
Mainline station: Elephant & Castle **Payment:** cash, cheques

This little shop-cum-café, situated right by the Elephant & Castle complex, is not quite the gem it once was: salt cod, Paolo Ribecca explained, is now too expensive for him to stock regularly. Still, it remains a social centre for the local Hispanic community and does stock some rather good Spanish and Italian produce: there is, for instance, tinned *bacaloa alla Vizcaina* by the reputable Miau company - a very popular line, Paolo notes. Other conserves include Callos Madrileña and Spanish-style chickpeas. You will find Asturiana lentils and paella rice among the dried goods. There is a good range of sweetmeats, as one might expect: a good many varieties of *turròn*, plus sugared almonds, tiny dried figs and rows of sweet biscuits. Charcuterie includes the anticipated chorizos, salume and Parma ham.

Greenwich

Cheese shop

THE CHEESEBOARD

26 Royal Hill, London SE10 8RT
Tel: 020 8305 0401
Open: Mon-Wed and Sat 9am-5pm, Thu 9am-1pm, Fri 9am-

Greenwich Market

Off Stockwell Road

Open: Sat 10am-4pm **Mainline station:** Greenwich **Bus:** 53, 53X, 180, 199

A visit to Greenwich deserves at least a day: there is the National Maritime Museum, a host of wonderful historic buildings, the Cutty Sark, the Millennium Dome – and the markets. Sunday is the most popular day for the latter, which offer antiques, bric-à-brac, crafts, books, new and old clothes in a variety of locations, both under cover and in the open air. Saturday, though, is the day to go for food. By the side of the Village Market, off Stockwell Street, some half dozen or so traders offer organic foods - olives and olive oil, eggs, cheese, Longwood Farm sausages and meat (also at Portobello Organic Market on Thursdays, see page 23), fruit and vegetables; the Celtic Baker sells 20 different types of organic bread.

5.30pm **Closed:** Sun **Mainline station:** Greenwich **Bus:** 53, 53X, 180, 199 **Payment:** cash, cheques, MasterCard, Visa **Free local delivery on orders over £20, mail-order**

This pretty corner shop is the first in a charming row of little shops with old frontages situated just outside the main throb of Greenwich centre. They offer a range of over 150 cheeses from all over Europe and specialise in farmhouse cheeses many of which are unpasteurised. The cheeses range from the classic English farmhouse stiltons, Caerphilly and cheddars to more unusual Spanish cheeses, quality mozzarella and a vast selection of French cheeses such as St Agur, Vignotte and wonderful goat's cheeses. Over the years the shop has built up an excellent reputation and a solid clientele. They also sell freshly baked breads including French and Italian breads, Jewish Bagels and Chollas, and other speciality breads from & Clarke's (see page 86). Cheese-related foods such as chutneys, mustards, pickles, biscuits and ports, wines and champagnes add to the groaning shelves. Regular cheese tastings are held.

THE DAB HAND

Fishmonger

20 Royal Hill, London
SE10 8RT
Tel 020 8858 2268
Open: Tue-Sat 9am-5pm, Sun

10am-4pm **Mainline station:** Greenwich **Bus:** 53, 53X, 180, 199 **Payment:** cash, cheques **Catering service, food-to-go, mail-order**

Although decorated rather in the fashion of an old-style fish shop, this is very much a modern-day fish delicatessen and is one of three pretty Georgian-fronted shops just outside Greenwich centre. Inside is a wet fish counter with a fine selection of fish and shellfish plus butters and sauces to accompany the fish. They also have a blackboard showing the availability of a selection of ready meals, from Bouillabaisse to Jambalaya. Quiches, pies charcuterie, pâtés and sausages can be bought here, too.

Butcher
Sausages

DRINGS

22 Royal Hill, London
SE10 8RT
Tel: 020 8858 4032
Open: Mon-Sat 8am-5pm, Thu 8am-1pm **Closed:** Sun **Mainline station:** Greenwich **Bus:** 53, 53X, 180, 199 **Payment:** cash, cheques

Established in 1910 this is one of London's few remaining traditional family butchers (it even has sawdust on the floor). Trade is good and that's not surprising. The Dring brothers, David and Robert, offer friendly, personal service; they seem to know most of the customers by name, and claim that between them there is nothing that they don't know about meat. There's a wide selection of quality meat on offer, but the sausages are the real speciality. Anything unusual can be ordered in advance and they will cut the meat to any specification. Although they don't have any organic meats they do offer free-range meats.

Delicatessen

SAUCE FOR THE GOOSE

66 Royal Hill, London
SE10 8RT
Tel: 020 8692 3010
Fax: 020 8694 8861
Open: Mon-Wed 10am-6pm, Thu 10am-1pm, Fri-Sat 10am-6pm, Sun 10am-3pm **Closed:** Bank holidays **Bus:** 177, 180, 199 **Mainline station:** Greenwich **Payment:** cash, cheques **Catering service, food-to-go**

A very welcome recent addition to the sparse fine-food scene in Greenwich, this useful little deli is located just a few doors along from The Cheeseboard (see page 162). While it does not, therefore, sell cheese, it does stock bread from the London Bread Factory and, more interestingly, pastries and teabreads from Didier Pâtisserie. Owners Lucy Sigurdsson and Zsa Zsa Barton were already catering prior to opening the shop, and the most popular items – home-baked gammon on the bone; frozen meals including Roman lamb with marsala and beef-orange-and-barley; vegetables salads and interesting pasta sauces – reflect this aspect of the operation. Beside these, there is a carefully chosen range of fresh and canned delicacies: Simply Sausages, Denhay hams, Alejandro chorizo; Calasparra and Carnaroli rice; Il Saraceno flours, Spanish and Italian bottled peppers and artichokes; and a good range of olive oils. Sweetmeats have an Italian emphasis: torroncini, cantucci and coffee amaretti, but the locally baked cakes are thoroughly British.

Herne Hill

French
North African
Delicatessen

MIMOSA

16 Half Moon Lane, London SE24 9HU
Tel: 020 7733 8838
Fax: 020 8678 6915
Open: Tue-Fri 9am-7pm, Sat 9am-5.30pm, Sun 10am-3pm **Closed:** Mon **Mainline station:** Herne Hill **Bus:** 37, P15
Payment: cash, cheques
Catering, food-to-go, mail-order

Vibrant Mediterranean flavours from France, Morocco and the Lebanon permeate the fresh food on offer at this bright and appetising-looking traiteur – brochettes of Moroccan chicken along and quiches are examples of the *plats du jour*. Pâtisserie baked on the premises has a distinctively French style, featuring *crême brulées*, fruit tarts and meringues, along with homemade chocolate truffles. The shop also stocks French cheese and three of the best of British - Montgomery and Keen's Cheddars and Colston Basset Stilton. You'll also find a selection of smoked and plain hams, olive oils, vinegar, pasta, freshly squeezed organic juices and Moroccan pottery from the owner's native village. The catering arm of the business provides everything from food to equipment to staff.

West Norwood

Fishmonger

GUNN FISHERIES

326 Norwood Road, London SE27 9AF
Tel: 020 8670 0880
Open: Tue-Sat 9am-5pm **Closed:** Sun **Mainline station:** West Norwood **Bus:** 2, 68, X68
Payment: cash, cheques

As soon as you walk in this ordinary-looking high street fishmonger you can smell a wonderful oak smoke from the smokery at the back of the shop. Gunns have been in business for 30 years now, and they know their plaice! They don't sell anything fancy, but their fish is very good quality, the best that is in the market that day. They smoke their own fish: trout, haddock, kippers, mackerel and some salmon, which is extremely popular. They will do special orders if asked. They have built up a good reputation over the years, and practically all of their custom is from regulars. For good quality fish, friendly service and to experience some freshly smoked fish it is well worth a visit.

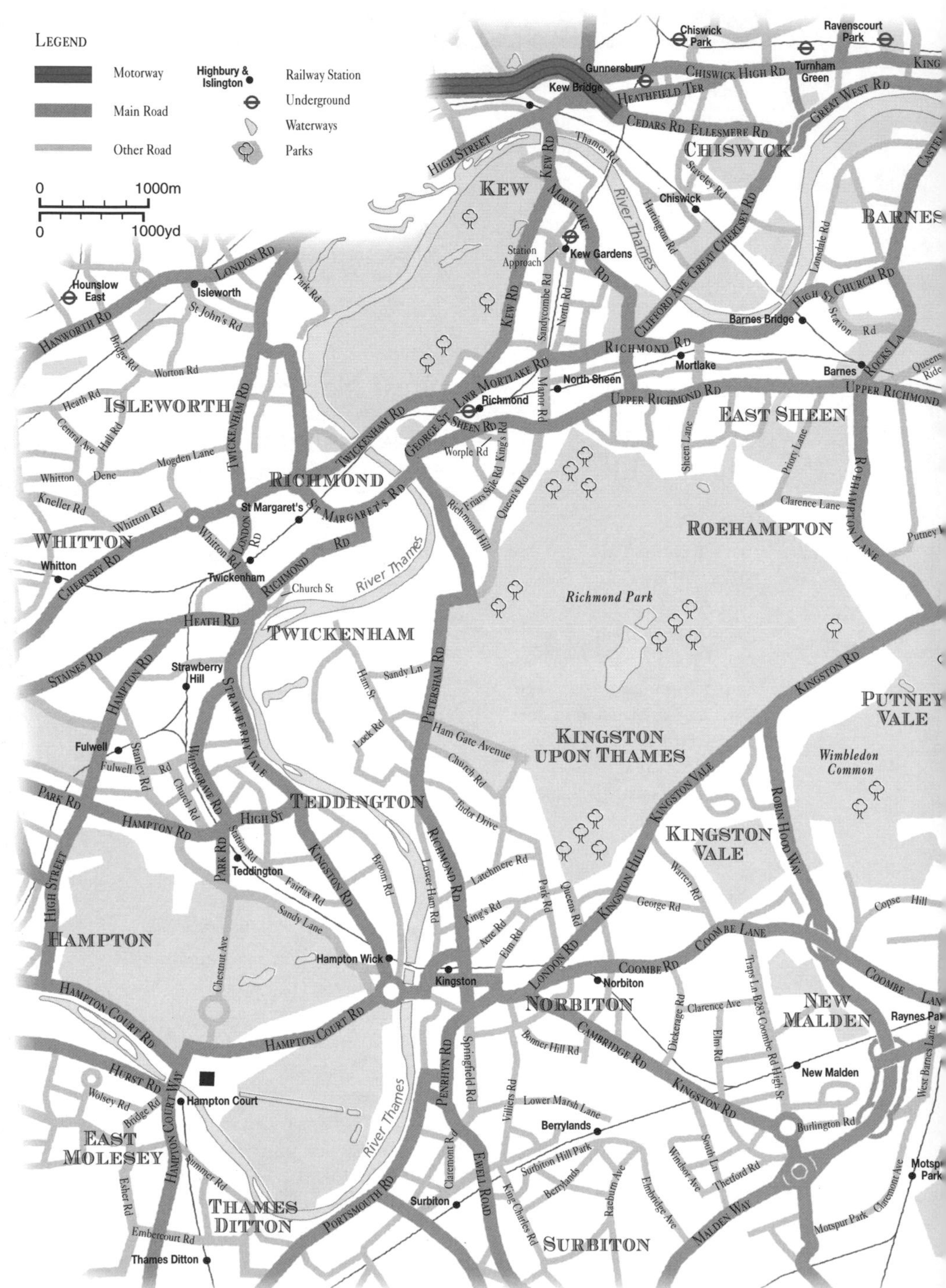
Legend
Motorway
Main Road
Other Road
Highbury & Islington
Railway Station
Underground
Waterways
Parks
0
1000m
0
1000yd
Chiswick Park
Ravenscourt Park
Gunnersbury
Chiswick High Rd
Turnham Green
Kew Bridge
Heathfield Ter
Great West Rd
Cedars Rd
Ellesmere Rd
Chiswick
High Street
Kew Rd
Thames Rd
Kew
Mortlake
River Thames
Staveley Rd
Harrington Rd
Barnes
Station Approach
Kew Gardens
Great Chertsey Rd
Clifford Ave
Lonsdale Rd
London Rd
Hounslow East
Isleworth
Park Rd
Sandycombe Rd
North Rd
St John's Rd
Church Rd
High St
Barnes Bridge
Station Rd
Hanworth Rd
Bridge Rd
Richmond Rd
Mortlake
Rocks La
Queens Ride
Worton Rd
Lwr Mortlake Rd
North Sheen
Barnes
Heath Rd
Isleworth
Twickenham Rd
Richmond
Manor Rd
Upper Richmond Rd
East Sheen
Central Ave
Hall Rd
George St
Sheen Rd
King's Rd
Worple Rd
Mogden Lane
Sheen Lane
Priory Lane
Whitton
Dene
Richmond
Friars Stile Rd
Queen's Rd
Roehampton Lane
Kneller Rd
Whitton Rd
St Margaret's
St Margaret's Rd
Richmond Hill
Clarence Lane
Whitton
Roehampton
Putney
Twickenham
Chertsey Rd
Church St
Richmond Park
Heath Rd
Twickenham
Staines Rd
Hampton Rd
Strawberry Hill
Strawberry Vale
Ham St
Sandy Ln
Petersham Rd
Kingston Rd
Putney Vale
Lock Rd
Ham Gate Avenue
Kingston upon Thames
Fulwell
Stanley Rd
Fulwell Rd
Church Rd
Waldegrave Rd
Wimbledon Common
Kingston Vale
Park Rd
Hampton Rd
Teddington
Tudor Drive
Robin Hood Way
Kingston Vale
Kingston Hill
Warren Rd
Latchmere Rd
Broom Rd
Lower Ham Rd
Park Rd
Queens Rd
George Rd
Copse Hill
Fairfax Rd
Sandy Lane
King's Rd
Acre Rd
Elm Rd
Hampton
Chestnut Ave
Coombe Lane
Hampton Wick
Coombe Rd
Traps Ln
B283 Coombe Rd
High St
Kingston
Norbiton
New Malden
Raynes Park
Hampton Court Rd
Norbiton
Dickerage Rd
Clarence Ave
Elm Rd
Cambridge Rd
Bonner Hill Rd
Penrhyn Rd
Springfield Rd
West Barnes Lane
Hurst Rd
Hampton Court Way
Hampton Court
Wolsey Rd
Bridge Rd
Villiers Rd
Lower Marsh Lane
New Malden
East Molesey
Berrylands
Burlington Rd
Summer Rd
Claremont Rd
Ewell Road
Surbiton Hill Park
Windsor Ave
South Ln
Thetford Rd
Motspur Park
Esher Rd
Thames Ditton
Portsmouth Rd
Surbiton
King Charles Rd
Berrylands
Raeburn Ave
Elmbridge Ave
Malden Way
Motspur Park
Claremont Ave
Embercourt Rd
Thames Ditton
Surbiton

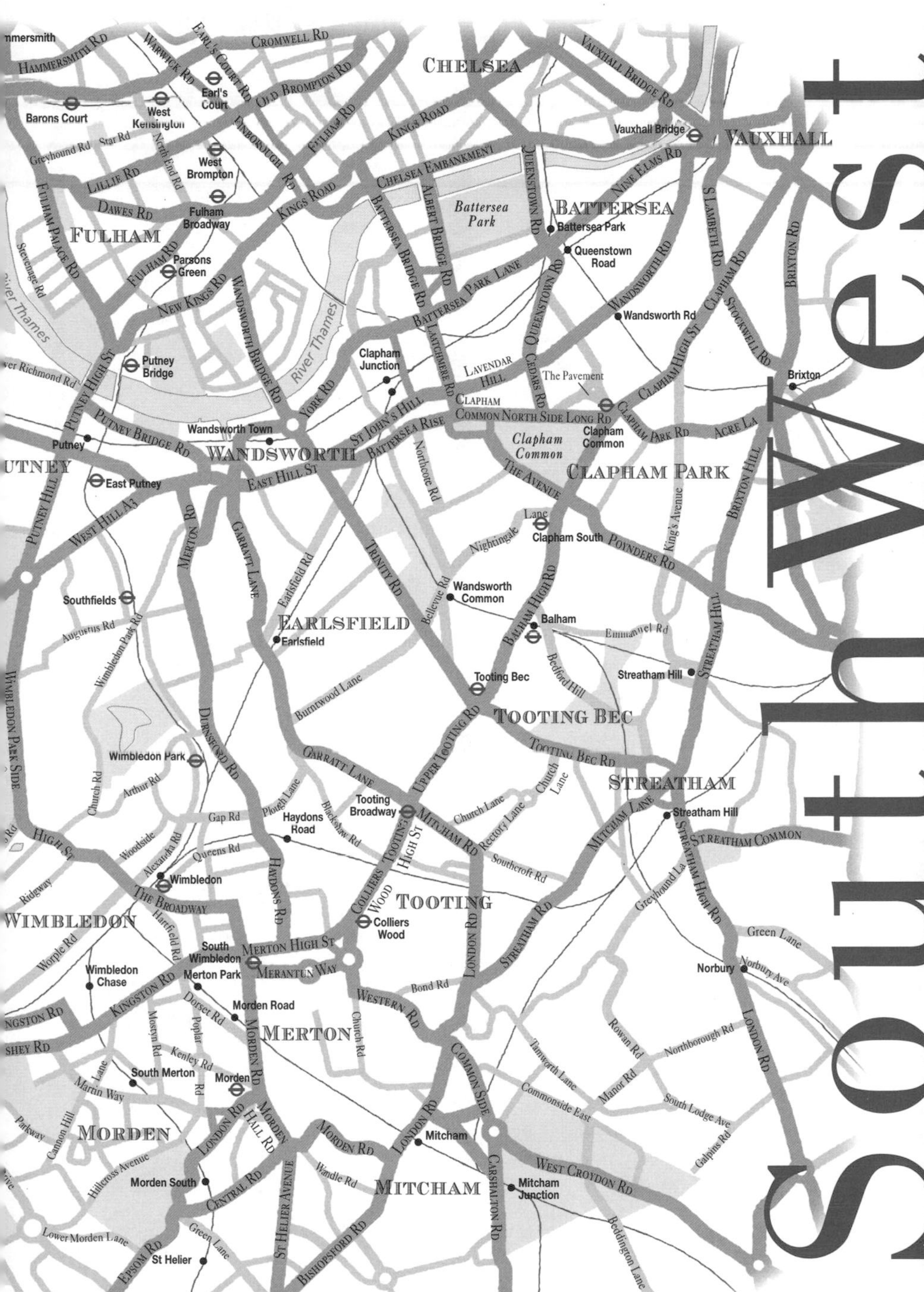
South West
Hammersmith
Hammersmith Rd
Warwick Rd
Earl's Court Rd
Cromwell Rd
Chelsea
Vauxhall Bridge Rd
Earl's Court
Old Brompton Rd
Barons Court
West Kensington
Fulham Rd
Kings Road
Vauxhall Bridge
Vauxhall
Greyhound Rd
Star Rd
North End Rd
Finborough Rd
West Brompton
Chelsea Embankment
Queenstown Rd
Nine Elms Rd
Lillie Rd
Dawes Rd
Fulham Broadway
Kings Road
Battersea Bridge Rd
Albert Bridge Rd
Battersea Park
Battersea
Fulham Palace Rd
Fulham
Fulham Rd
Parsons Green
Queenstown Road
S Lambeth Rd
Brixton Rd
Stevenage Rd
Wandsworth Rd
Clapham Rd
River Thames
New Kings Rd
Wandsworth Bridge Rd
Battersea Park Lane
Stockwell Rd
Wandsworth Rd
Putney Bridge
River Thames
Clapham Junction
Latchmere Rd
Lavendar Hill
Cedars Rd
The Pavement
Clapham High St
Brixton
Lower Richmond Rd
Putney High St
York Rd
St John's Hill
Clapham Common North Side
Long Rd
Clapham Park Rd
Acre La
Putney Bridge Rd
Wandsworth Town
Battersea Rise
Clapham Common
Putney
Wandsworth
Northcote Rd
Putney
East Hill St
The Avenue
Clapham Park
East Putney
Brixton Hill
Putney Hill
West Hill A3
Merton Rd
Garratt Lane
Trinity Rd
Nightingale Lane
Clapham South
Poynders Rd
King's Avenue
Earlsfield Rd
Bellevue Rd
Wandsworth Common
Balham High Rd
Southfields
Augustus Rd
Wimbledon Park Rd
Earlsfield
Earlsfield
Balham
Emmanuel Rd
Bedford Hill
Streatham Hill
Streatham Hill
Tooting Bec
Burntwood Lane
Wimbledon Park Side
Upper Tooting Rd
Tooting Bec
Durnsford Rd
Wimbledon Park
Tooting Bec Rd
Garratt Lane
Church Rd
Arthur Rd
Church Lane
Streatham
Plough Lane
Tooting Broadway
Church Lane
Rectory Lane
Mitcham Lane
Streatham Hill
Gap Rd
Haydons Road
Blackshaw Rd
Mitcham Rd
Tooting High St
Streatham Common
High St
Woodside
Alexandra Rd
Queens Rd
Southcroft Rd
Wimbledon
Haydons Rd
Colliers Wood
Streatham High Rd
Greyhound La
Ridgway
The Broadway
Tooting
Wimbledon
Hartfield Rd
Colliers Wood
Streatham Rd
London Rd
Green Lane
Worple Rd
South Wimbledon
Merton High St
Norbury
Norbury Ave
Wimbledon Chase
Kingston Rd
Merton Park
Merantun Way
Bond Rd
Western Rd
Kingston Rd
Dorset Rd
Morden Road
Mostyn Rd
Poplar Rd
Morden Rd
Merton
Church Rd
Rowan Rd
Northborough Rd
London Rd
Bushey Rd
Kenley Rd
Common Side
Tamworth Lane
Manor Rd
South Merton
Morden
Lane
Martin Way
Commonside East
South Lodge Ave
Morden
London Rd
Hall Rd
Mitcham
Galpins Rd
Parkway
Cannon Hill
Morden
Morden Rd
London Rd
West Croydon Rd
Hillcross Avenue
Morden South
Central Rd
St Helier Avenue
Wandle Rd
Mitcham
Carshalton Rd
Mitcham Junction
Lower Morden Lane
Green Lane
Epsom Rd
St Helier
Bishopsford Rd
Beddington Lane

Barnes

Fishmonger

ALEXANDER & KNIGHT

18 High Street, London
SW13 6TY
Tel: 020 8876 1297
Open: Tue, Thu, Fri 8am-5pm, Wed 8am-1pm, Sat 8am-4pm
Closed: Mon, Wed afternoons, Sun, Bank holidays **Mainline station:** Barnes Bridge **Bus:** 33, R69, 209 **Payment:** cash, cheques
Food-to-go

Chris Lofthouse's bustling friendly fishmonger is one of the several high-quality shops along the high street that contribute to this leafy south London suburb's desirablity. He has been here since 1984 and the range of farmed and wild seafood on offer is impressive, whether you're after some mackerel or haddock for a family supper, or dinner party fare, such as black bream, loin of tuna, cod for roasting, or tiger prawns. His bass is from Newlyn, the herrings come from Orkney and the oysters from Ireland. Cockles and clams are available in season and occasionally they sell the more unusual razor-shell clams and sea urchins. The smoked fish range includes cod's roe, eel fillets and mackerel. When you don't want to cook, try the salmon fish cakes, dressed crabs, or a jar of French fish soup.

Barnes Market

Essex House Surgery, opposite Barnes Pond, at the junction of the High Street and Church Road
Open: Sat 12noon-4pm **Mainline Station:** Barnes Bridge **Bus:** 33, R69, 209

Established in October 1999 by Tim Dimond-Brown, the market has twelve to twenty stalls (which may grow in number in 2000), offering fruit and vegetables, superb organic meat (from Somerset Level Organic), cheeses and yogurts, poultry and game, wet and smoked fish, jams and other preserves, wines, ciders and breads. A speciality is pies, savoury and sweet (an apple pie with the lightest shortcrust pastry, made by Limetree Pantry, apparently is appreciated in the highest circles in the land). Many farmers' markets insist on every ingredient being grown or produced by the supplier; the rules here are less strict, and if a jam is homemade, even though the maker has not grown the fruit involved, it can be sold.

Sausages

ARKWRIGHTS

20 High Street, London
SW13 9LW

Tel: 020 8878 1520
Open: Mon 12noon-6pm, Tue-Fri 9am-6pm, Sat 9am-5.30pm
Closed: Sun **Mainline station:** Barnes Bridge **Bus:** 33, R69, 209
Payment: cash, cheques

This bespoke sausage shop may be small, but it sells a range of traditional as well as more exotic flavours that must cater for all tastes. Organic sausages are chorizo, Taunton Toulouse and a basic banger, while the non-organic range encompasses traditional venison and Cumberland flavours. But if you want to give your taste buds a wake-up call, try Thai 5-spice flavour or Caribbean, with chillies and brandy. Napoletans are pork sausages with prunes for sweetness, while beef sausages flavoured with stout capture the tastes of Ireland. You will also find vegetarian sausages, Urchfont mustard and piccalilli, as well as a growing range of organic products, such as eggs and chutneys.

Bakery
Pâtisserie

BOTTICELLI

The Blue Door Yard,
74 Church Road, London
SW13 0DQ
Tel: 020 8741 4230
Fax: 020 8741 3287
Open: Fri-Sat 10am-4.30pm
Closed: Sun-Thu and Bank holidays **Mainline station:** Barnes Bridge **Bus:** 33, R69, 209
Payment: cash, cheques
Catering

This is a tiny shop whose main business is catering and pastry orders, hence the restricted opening hours. They make a range of sweet fruit and savoury tarts each week – red pepper-and-onion, goat's cheese, pepper-and-spinach, and ham-and-broccoli, to name a few. & Clarke's breads and pastries (see page 86) are also stocked. Small selections of Italian olive oils and balsamic vinegars are on sale (they use the same brands in their cooking) including an unfiltered extra virgin olive oil and 5- and 10-year old balsamic vinegars. Christmas specialities include a luxury plum pudding sold in a china basin and wrapped in calico, and a traditional Christmas pudding, wrapped in brown paper, both made specially for Botticelli by a supplier in Dorset. They also sell Panettone and Swedish *knacke brot*.

The Kitchen Shop

17 High Street, London SW13 9LW
Tel: 020 8876 3775

In the Area This upmarket shop sells top of the range items, including Sabatier knives. You will find a full range of cooking utensils, pots, pans and baking equipment, alongside a limited range of crockery and glassware.

Butcher

J. SEAL BUTCHERS

7 High Street, London
SW13 3LW
Tel: 020 8876 5118
Open: Mon-Tue, Thu-Fri 6.30am-5.30pm, Wed 6.30am-1.30, Sat 6.30am-4pm **Closed:** Sun, Bank holidays **Mainline station:** Barnes Bridge **Bus:** 33, R69, 209 **Payment:** cash, cheques, Delta, MasterCard, Switch, Visa

An ox-blood red exterior

welcomes you to this family-run, old-fashioned butcher and delicatessen. There has been a butcher's shop on this site since 1850 and the Harrison family has been at the helm for more than 40 years, with a son training to take over. They sell grass-fed prime Aberdeen Angus beef, grass-fed lamb from Dorset, free-range pork from Suffolk, free-range chickens, game in season and organic turkeys and geese at Christmas (expect long queues). If you want organic chicken or beef, you should order in advance, Mr Harrison says, because it sells fast. He will prepare crown roasts and guards of honour, again to order. Also on offer are cooked pies that just need re-heating from the Real Pie Co., including steak-and-kidney, steak-and-mushroom and vegetarian leek-and-potato.

French
Italian
Delicatessen

SONNY'S FOOD SHOP

92 Church Road, London SW13 0DG
Tel: 020 8748 8541
Fax: 020 8748 2698
Open: Mon-Sat 10am-6pm **Tube:** Hammersmith **Bus:** 9, 209, 33, 72 **Mainline station:** Barnes
Payment: cash, cheques, Delta, MasterCard, Switch, Visa
Catering, food-to-go

This tiny delicatessen is crammed with goodies, from France and Italy in particular. A speciality is the extraordinary *pane carasau*, or *carta da musica*, a paper-thin dried bread from Sardinia (see above). There are delicious cakes and breads from Miller's bakery, and breads imported from Poilâne, the famous Parisian baker. They stock a good range of Carluccio's products (see page 29), as well as fine preserves, including own-label marmalades, jams and pickles, Tamarind chutneys, quality olive oils and vinegars. Their appetizing take-away homemade dishes, freshly prepared in their own kitchen, are especially good – the late-autumn range included lamb stew, blackbean chilli, lasagne, and beef stew. Always on offer is a grilled vegetable salad and mustard-glazed ham. The shop stocks a good range of baked goods including sausage rolls and Cornish pasties – both meat and vegetarian varieties – and a small range of cheeses.

Carta da Musica

This flat Sardinian bread resembles old music manuscript, hence the name. It is sold in carefully packaged boxes – it's very fragile – of 10 to 20 slices. Sardianians eat the bread either soaked in water and served with ripe tomatoes and grated Pecorino cheese, or brushed with oil, garlic and rosemary and briefly heated in a hot oven until very crisp. Alternatively, it can be softened and layered with a filling, as for lasagne, sprinkled with Parmesan cheese and baked.

Greengrocer
Organic

TWO PEAS IN A POD
85 Church Road, London
SW13 9HH
Tel: 020 8748 0232
Open: Mon-Sat 8am-5.30pm, Sun 10am-1pm **Closed:** Bank holidays **Mainline station:** Barnes Bridge **Bus:** 209 **Payment:** cash only
Home delivery

With more than five customers in the place at a time, this well-established, pint-sized shop begins to get crowded. But don't be put off, the range and quality of produce within is good. Fruit and vegetables from all over the world include plenty of seasonal British produce, herbs from the Channel Islands and soft fruit from Scotland. The customer base is local and loyal, and the staff are on first-name terms with many of them. 'If you can't see it in the shop, we'll get it in for you straightaway', they say. 'The whole world is going organic', says owner Malcolm Louis 'and look, everything's getting dirtier!' Sure enough, the unevenly shaped, earth-covered organic potatoes and carrots look just how vegetables used to look.

Battersea

Butcher
Pies

DOVES
71 Northcote Road, London
SW11 6PJ
Tel: 020 7223 5191 (24 hour answerphone)
Open: Mon 8am-1pm, Tue-Sat 8am-5.30pm **Closed:** Sun, Mon pm, Bank holidays **Tube:** Clapham South **Bus:** G1, 319 **Mainline station:** Clapham Junction **Payment:** cash, cheques, Delta, MasterCard, Switch, Visa
Free local delivery

Three generations of master butchers have run this popular local butcher since 1889. It specialises in free-range and organic meat, especially Aberdeen Angus, Highland and Welsh Black beef, grass-fed Welsh lamb, cooked ham and the much sought-after bronze turkeys at Christmas, as well as sausages, homemade pâtés and fishcakes. Also popular - especially with dinner-party hostesses short on time - are the

> "Pies have always been convivial food, timeless and fun. Now they score on the grounds of convenience and growing internationalism, too."

Philippa Davenport writing for *Country Living*

pies baked daily by the owner's wife, Linda. They are made without preservatives or colouring, and the flavours include steak-and-claret, steak-in-Guinness, venison-in-cider and chicken-ham-and-leeks in a creamy tarragon sauce.

French Delicatessen

FILERIC

12 Queenstown Road, London SW8 3RX
Tel: 020 7720 4844
Fax: 020 7207 3176
Open: Mon-Sat 8am-8pm, Sun 8am-4pm **Tube:** Clapham Common **Bus:** 137 **Mainline station:** Battersea Park, Queenstown Road **Payment:** cash, cheques, Amex, MasterCard, Switch, Visa
Catering, food-to-go, mail-order

Francophiles flock to this French traiteur-delicatessen for a genuine taste of France. Inside there is a wonderful smell of freshly baked bread, as they bake their own baguettes on the premises. You can also buy everything you need for a snack lunch or quick dinner as well as for a special dinner party: from bread to cheeses to ready-made dishes such as soups, salads, cassoulets, pizzas and quiches. The cheese counter is well stocked: there are over 60 cheeses from all over France, from small farmhouse cheeses to Roquefort and St Agur. Salume, charcuterie and terrines, plus beautifully presented pâtisserie line the remaining shelves. And to finish, don't miss the homemade sorbets of honey, champagne or elderflower.

Wholefoods Organic

THE GRAIN SHOP

567 Battersea Park Road, London SW11 3BJ
Tel: 020 7801 9131

Main shop: see Notting Hill, page 94

Cheesemonger

HAMISH JOHNSTON

48 Northcote Road, London SW11 1PA
Tel: 020 7738 0741
Open: Mon-Fri 9am-7pm, Sat 9am-6pm **Tube:** Clapham Common **Bus:** 319, G1 **Mainline station:** Clapham Junction **Payment:** cash, cheques, Amex, Delta, MasterCard, Switch, Visa
Free local delivery, mail-order

For one of the largest selections of British and Irish farmhouse cheeses in the area look no further than this fine cheese shop. They offer over 120 British and French farmhouse cheeses, with wonderful names such as Lincolnshire Poacher and Cropwell Bishop Stilton. The range of Irish cheeses has increased recently, to include the camembert-like St Killian from County Wexford and a mature (mature being the operative word) Coolea, a 14-month old cheese that is somewhere between a Gouda and a Parmesan. Tasting is encouraged and every Saturday there is a sampling of cheeses and olive oils. On the shelves bowls are brimming with fresh olives, and there are huge flagons of olive oils from which you can fill your own container. The oils are from Italy, South Africa, California, France and Spain. There are also pickles and relishes, mustards, speciality breads and biscuits. Other fine foods include terrines, rillettes and pâtés from Gascony and dried *cèps.*

Branch: see Clapham, page 176

Honey

THE HIVE HONEY SHOP
93 Northcote Road, London SW11 1PA
Tel: 020 7924 6233
Open: Mon-Fri 10am-5pm, Sat 10am-6pm **Tube:** Clapham Common **Bus:** 319, G1 **Mainline station:** Clapham Junction
Payment: cash, cheques, Delta, MasterCard, Visa
Mail-order

In this small shop (previously situated in Webbs Road) you will find the largest selection of honeys and honey products in London. The main attraction are the honeys produced from the owner's, James Hamill, own hives which are dotted around the country, but mostly around London and the South East. His honeys are flavoured with ginger, cognac and rum and raisin, he does a Bell Heather honey and a Wandsworth's own Floral honey. Candles, cosmetics, mustards and cough and cold cures are also packed on the shelves. Bee-keeping equipment and books are available, and the owner runs bee-keeping courses. Most startling of all is the 5-foot-high glass-fronted working hive of 20,000 bees which stands in the middle of the shop. Staff is enthusiastic and knowledgeable.

Northcote Road Market

Open: Mon-Sat 7am-6.15pm
Tube: Clapham Common **Bus:** 319, G1
Mainline station: Clapham Junction

Not far from Clapham Junction railway station, this excellent local market lines one side of Northcote Road - which has become rather foodie in orientation - as it bisects Battersea Rise. Most of the thirty or so stalls specialise in fresh fruit and vegetables, some of which is everyday stuff, but there are a lot of Afro-Caribbean lines as well. It is busier and more atmospheric on Saturdays.

Delicatessen

MISE-EN-PLACE
21 Battersea Rise, London SW11 1HG
Tel: 020 7228 4392

Branch: see Clapham, page 176

Italian Delicatessen

SALUMERIA NAPOLI

69 Northcote Road, London SW11 1NP
Tel: 020 7228 2445
Open: Mon-Sat 9am-6pm **Closed:** Sun and Bank holidays
Mainline station: Clapham Junction **Bus:** G1, 319 **Payment:** cash, cheques

You get a real taste of Italy at this well-established delicatessen, as Salvatore Maggiulli imports most of his Italian products directly. As well as a good selection of Italian biscuits, olives and pasta sauces, you will find a choice of regional olive oils, including some organic ones, and about every shape of dried pasta you can imagine. The breads - focaccia, ciabatta and casareccio toscano - are supplied daily by Sicilian bakers, and tortelloni is made fresh daily. Mozzarella di bufala and pecorino romano are just two of the Italian cheeses to choose from, and you also find a small selection of other European cheeses.

LA CUISINIÈRE

81-83 Northcote Road, London SW11 6PJ
Tel: 020 7223 4487

In the Area

A friendly if somewhat overcrowded shop. You will find all manner of cutlery, crockery, pots, utensils and baskets, as well as more unusual items such as pre-packed picnic back-packs, titanium pots, specialist utensils and cheerful china from Italy and France. Helpful and friendly staff are on hand to profer advice.

Delicatessen

WAINWRIGHT & NEILL

284 Battersea Park Road, London SW11 3BT
Tel: 020 7350 2035
Open: Mon-Fri 9.30am-7.30pm, Sat 9am-6pm, Sun 10am-7pm
Closed: 25, 26, Dec. **Mainline station:** Clapham Junction, Battersea Park **Bus:** 344, 44
Payment: cash, cheques

One of the signs of a 'good' deli are its homemade prepared foods. This neighbourhood shop - owned by two friends and their families - always has a selection of homemade pâtés, cheeses, cakes and tarts. The most popular quiche is goat's cheese-and-roasted vegetables, and the range of pâtés on the day we visited included chicken liver with pistachios, mackerel, tuna and salmon. The shop also sells homemade sausages, such as Cumberland, lamb-and-mint, and pork-and-sage, along with a variety of olives and a small selection of Spanish, Italian and Hungarian salume. You will also find organic products and the more usual deli goods and wines.

Clapham

Delicatessen

BON VIVANT DELICATESSEN

59 Nightingale Lane, London SW12 8ST
Tel: 020 8675 6314
Open: Mon-Fri 8.30am-8pm, Sat 8.30am-7pm, Sun 9.30-12.30pm; open on occasional Bank holidays **Closed:** 25, 26,

Dec., 1 Jan. and sometimes other days between Christmas and New Year **Tube:** Clapham South **Bus:** G1, 319 **Payment:** cash, cheques, Delta, MasterCard, Switch, Visa

A selection of about 30 cheeses is one of the reasons Simon Robertson's shop has been popular since it opened in 1987. The deli counter also stocks olives, salume and hams, and you will find packaged pâtés, including foie gras, as well as breads, biscuits, jams, teas and coffees. The olive oils collection includes varieties from South Africa as well as from European countries. The organic range is expanding, and includes handmade bread from the local Post Office Bakery.

Fishmonger

★ CONDON FISHMONGERS

363 Wandsworth Road, London SW8 2JJ
Tel: 020 7622 2934
Open: Mon, Thu 8.45am-1pm, Tue, Wed, Fri Sat 8.45am-5.30pm **Closed:** Mon, Thu afternoons, Sun, Bank holidays **Tube:** Stockwell **Bus:** 77, 77A, 322 **Mainline station:** Vauxhall **Payment:** cash, cheques

Don't let appearances deceive you. This unassuming shop supplies the ultra-fashionable River Café restaurant and Sonia Stephenson, as well as a steady

WILD OR FARMED? KNOW YOUR SALMON

Stocks of wild salmon are dwindling at an alarming rate, which accounts for the high prices of the genuine article in the shops. The Soil Association is now working with selected farms in order to set up organic farmed salmon, so look out for the new label 'transitional organic'.

Sometimes unscrupulous traders will pass farmed fish off as the real thing, so here are a few hints on what to look out for. Fresh wild salmon are sleek, firm creatures, with large triangular, rudder-like tails and well-rounded fins; their noses will be 'as streamlined as a torpedo', says Matthew Fort. Whereas farmed fish will have a much flabbier flesh, dullish skin, a rather humped back, sad, raggedy tails and fins, and a somewhat blunted nose resulting from overcrowding in cages.

Sea Trout (also called Salmon Trout) is generally somewhat cheaper to buy than non-farmed salmon. These wild creatures have only a short season - from about March to July. Allow around 225g per person if you are buying a whole fish.

stream of regular customers. Ken Condon runs the family business that has been in this shop since 1902, when the smokehouse commemorating Edward VII's coronation was built. It's still in regular use and shellfish is also boiled in the shop. The large selection of fresh fish (including Dover soles, monkfish, sea bass and turbot the day we visited) is bought daily at Billingsgate Market, and oysters are imported directly from the supplier on the West Coast of Ireland. If you are planning a seafood feast, Condon also lends fish kettles, fish plates, oyster knives and oyster plates - as well as selling you the main course!

Cheese shop

HAMISH JOHNSTON

48 Abbeville Road, London SW4 9NF
Tel: 020 8673 5373

Main shop: see Battersea, page 172

Delicatessen
Organic

MISE-EN-PLACE @ PAMELA PRICE

26 The Pavement, London SW4 0GA
Tel: 020 7622 4051
Fax: 020 7622 6818
Open: Mon-Sat 8am-10pm, Sun 8am-8pm **Closed:** 25, 26, Dec. **Tube:** Clapham common **Bus:** 37, 88 **Mainline station:** Clapham High Street **Payment:** cash, cheques, MasterCard, Visa
Catering, food-to-go

There is a strong vegetarian influence to this well-established delicatessen and shop that was the first of its kind in the area when Pamela Price opened it in the 1970s. Recently she has gone into partnership with the owners of Mise-en-Place, a Battersea delicatessen (see page 173), where the *plats du jour* - spicy chick peas, pork brochette, and fishcakes, on the day we visited - are prepared. Organic products, including baby food, are popular, as are homemade pasta sauces, cheeses from Barstow & Barr (see page 86), Sandwich Farm ham from Dorset and Mrs O'Keefe's sausages. For something out of the ordinary, try the Central American sauces made from hot banana wax peppers, jalapeno peppers or yellow sweet peppers.

Branch: see Battersea, page 173

Butcher
Organic

M. MOEN & SONS

24 The Pavement, London SW4 OJA
Tel: 020 7622 1624
Fax: 020 7622 1626
Open: Mon-Fri 8.30am-6.30pm, Sat 8am-5pm **Closed:** Sun and bank holidays **Tube:** Clapham Common **Bus:** 37, 88 **Mainline station:** Clapham High Street **Payment:** cash, cheques, Delta, MasterCard, Switch, Visa
Local delivery

This is the place for organic and free-range rare breeds of pork, lamb and beef, and prime Scottish beef from the Duke of Beccleauch's estates. Garry Moen runs his family's business, which after 20 years in an old-fashioned-style shop has just moved to new, light and airy premises. This gives them a better chance to showcase their 15 flavours of homemade sausages, cheeses - including Denhay Farm's mature Cheddar - and the wonderful selection of breads, including German dark rye, speck bread and onion bread, which they offer. They also sell a small amount of seasonable vegetables - wild mushrooms, squashes and asparagus, all when they are at their best.

Earlsfield

Organic Grocer

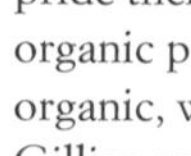

ORGANIQ

607 Garratt Lane, London SW18 4SU
Tel: 020 8947 1087
Fax: 020 8947 6490
Open: Mon-Wed 10am-6pm, Thu 1-7pm, Fri-Sat 10am-6pm
Closed: Sun and Thu am and Bank holidays **Mainline station:** Earlsfield **Bus:** 44, 77, 270
Payment: cash, cheques, Amex, Delta, MasterCard, Switch, Visa
Bespoke delivery in south-west London; free for orders over £25

Gillian Jakeway and James Carr pride themselves on only selling organic products. 'If it isn't organic, we don't have it,' Gillian says. The selection includes cereals, baby food, jams, biscuits, oils, vinegars and pasta, and meat to order. (Plans are afoot to expand into the shop next door so as to put in a deli counter.) This small, friendly shop also stocks everyday items that range from toothpaste to toilet paper. Deliveries are made twice weekly to the SW postal codes.

East Sheen

Chocolate

SANDRINE

239 Upper Richmond Road West, London SW14 8QS
Tel/Fax: 020 8878 8168
Fax: 020 8874 9198
Open: Mon-Sat 10am-5.30pm
Closed: Sun and Bank holidays
Mainline station: Mortlake **Bus:** 33, 337 **Payment:** cash, cheques, Amex, Delta, MasterCard, Switch, Visa

Irish-born owner Jean Bradley's fine arts background is evident in the design of the packaging, from the strong blue and yellow wrapping and ties to the handmade boxes. Rightly proud of her stock, she specialises in handmade Belgian chocolates, many of which are made specifically for her – 'natural ingredients only'. Most of the stock comes from the Ghent chocolatier, Du Barry - look out for his avocaat-and-brandy cherries - but she also sells some English chocolates and fudge. In the summer, she says, people tend to favour the fresh creams and fondants, while pralines and truffles take over in winter. Generally, says Bradley, the English prefer milk (45% chocolate) and white (cocoa butter only) chocolates, to plain (75% chocolate). Particularly delicious are her orange-and-pistachio-flavoured marzipan, and her almond-praline-and-advocaat.

Branch: see Twickenham, page 186

Italian
Delicatessen
Grocer

VALENTINA

210 Upper Richmond Road, London SW14 8AH
Tel: 020 8382 9127
Open: Mon-Fri 9am-5pm, Sat 8.30am-6pm, Sun, Bank holidays 9.30am-3pm **Closed:** 25, 26, Dec. **Mainline station:** Mortlake **Bus:** 33, R69, 337
Payment: cash, cheques, Amex, Delta, MasterCard, Switch, Visa
Catering, food-to-go

Sergio Borfecchia's popular double-fronted Italian emporium, named after his daughter, has been here a decade; he has recently enlarged the kitchen so they can cook a larger range of prepared dishes and do more outside catering. He stocks the comprehensive selection of the hams, cheeses, salume and wines you would expect, but the highlights are his wife Anna's cooked ready-to-go dishes that can include *petti di pollo milanese*, cannelloni, lasagna, *melanzane parmigiana, frittata di zucchini*, stuffed peppers, roasted baby chickens and *tiramisu*, along with grilled and marinated vegetables (look out for the semi-soft marinated sundried tomatoes) and quality pâtés. There is fresh pasta every day, with a selection of sauces, bread from Molino bakery in Wandsworth and homemade pizza on Fridays and Saturdays. For Italian cooking with a twist, try the fresh (not cured) Parma ham roasted with herbs, or the boned and rolled pork flavoured with herbs. Bargain-hunters claim his white truffles in season are the cheapest in London.

Kew

Wholefoods
Organic
Grocer
Delicatessen

★ OLIVER'S WHOLEFOOD STORE

5 Station Approach, London TW9 3QB
Tel: 020 8948 3990
Open: every day 9am-7pm **Tube:** Kew Gardens **Bus:** 33, R69, 391
Mainline station: Kew Gardens
Payment: cash, cheques, Delta, MasterCard, Switch,Visa,

This 1999 winner of the Best Community Shop award has been trading for over a decade in the heart of Kew village. It is a mecca for high-quality produce of all kinds, including foods for those on special diets. Inside the front door, the fridges bulge with fresh organic fruit and vegetables, while those at the rear contain a good range

> “We are, after all, designed to enjoy sumptuous mood-boosting food, not to eat pellets. If you think about the sensory aspects of the food, your body will gain more happiness from food that looks and tastes delicious. 
>
> Jane Clarke, Nutritionist

of fresh and dairy produce. The shelves throughout the shop are packed with things organic, from herbs and spices to pulses, grains, dried fruits, sauces, vinegars, pasta, cakes, chocolates, breads, coffee, preserves, herbal teas, condiments and much more (including wines and spirits). Bread (from soda bread to spelt sourdough) comes from Cranks, the Village Bakery, Celtic Bakers and other top-quality suppliers. Frozen yoghurt, Hill Station and Rocombe organic ice cream can be found in the freezers at the back of the shop, At Christmas, Oliver's stocks free-range geese, organic bronze turkeys, free-range ducks, organic gammons and hams, plus smoked salmon, sausages and sausage meat to order. There is also a natural remedies department which sells books and other related products and most days, therapists are on hand to give dietary advice.

THE KEW CHEESE

French
British
Cheese shop

227 Sandycombe Road, London TW9 3LU
Tel: 020 8940 2944 retail
020 8940 1944 mail order
Open: Mon-Fri 9.30am-6pm
Closed: Sun and Bank holidays
Tube: Kew Gardens **Bus:** 33, R69, 391 **Mainline station:** Kew Gardens **Payment:** cash, cheques, Delta, Switch, MasterCard, Visa

The Kew Cheese opened in September 1999 and is situated just around the corner from Kew village. The shop houses an impressive array of more than 100 cheeses in wall-mounted, glass-fronted refrigerated cupboards. The cheeses are mostly unpasteurized and proportionately 40% British and 40% French, with the remainder coming from other European countries. With each purchase you are given a card with details of the cheese maker, the style of the cheese, how it is made, and how to store and serve it. Advice is given and time taken to help customers make their purchase. The Kew Cheese also sells loose,

SUPERMARKETS

JUST HOW SUPER ARE THEY?

A few facts and figures to chew on:

■ More than 70 per cent of all food sales in Britain are made at the Big Five supermarkets

■ Our Office of Fair Trading is conducting investigations into why we appear to have the most expensive food in Europe

■ With the growth of out of town shopping centres which tend to be built around the huge supermarket chains, we now make more than 30 per cent more car journeys for shopping than we did two decades ago - and the trips are twice as long

■ Nearly all stock sold via supermarkets comes from distribution centres, so even our own home-grown food will be travelling 50 per cent farther to get to us compared to a generation ago

■ Food air freight tonnage doubled in the Eighties and is currently growing even faster now - but this cannot possibly last because of the impending crisis in the availablility of fossil fuels

fresh English butter and unsalted Normandy butter, biscuits for cheese, pickles and chutneys as well as port and wine, decanters, carafes and corkscrews. They will also hire out raclette and fondue equipment.

Branch: The Teddington Cheese, 42 Station Road, Teddington, Middlesex TW11 9AA
Tel: 020 8977 6868

Putney

Thai
Delicatessen
Grocer

★ TALAD THAI

326 Upper Richmond Road, London SW15 6TL
Tel: 020 8789 8084
Fax: 020 8789 8601
Open: Mon-Sat 9am-10pm, Sun 8.30am-2pm **Closed:** Bank holiday **Tube:** Richmond **Bus:** 33, 337, 371, R69 **Mainline station:** Richmond **Payment:** cash, cheques, Delta, MasterCard, Switch, Visa

A favourite of cookery writer, Sri Owen, though rather unprepossessing from the outside, this well-stocked shop sells mostly Thai ingredients, but stocks other oriental items, too. There are many types of Thai and Indian curry pastes, fish sauce, preserved fish, dried beans, noodles, teas as well as essential ingredients such as palm sugar, dried mushrooms, pickled greens and tamarind paste. You will also be able to find Japanese dried seaweed, including wakame and nori, for sushi and other dishes. The freezers are well stocked with spring roll pastry, fish and other seafood (including dried shrimp) and ready-to-cook food such as shrimp, dumplings or shrimp on sugar canc sticks. The open refrigerator carries a good range of fresh oriental greens, long beans, ready-prepared beef balls for soup, white aubergines, galangal, green mangoes, fresh tofu, beansprouts, rice noodles and the like. For keen cooks, they sell large, traditional mortars and pestles and a range of oriental cookbooks. Demonstrations of Thai cooking are given at 11am most Sundays during the school term (telephone ahead to check) for a modest fee, and you can order take-away food from their restaurant, just two doors away, during its opcning hours (11.30am-3 pm and 5.30-10pm)

Richmond

French
Bakery
Pâtisserie

MAISON BLANC

27B The Quadrant, London
TW9 1DN
Tel: 020 8332 7041

Main shop: see St John's Wood, page 127

Butcher
Game dealer
Organic

ORGANIC WORLD

23 Friars Stile Road, London
TW10 6NH
Tel: 020 8940 0414
Fax: 01444 443480
Open: Mon-Sat 7.30am-5.30pm
Closed: Sun and Bank holidays
Tube: Richmond **Bus:** 33, 391, R69 **Mainline station:** Richmond
Payment: cash, cheques, Delta, MasterCard, Switch, Visa

After trading as The Natural Mcat Company for almost 10 years, owner Steve Sains has now gone completely organic. He sells a wide range of produce, although the core stock is meat and poultry, game in season, and frozen wild rabbit and vension all year. (If you want a peacock or a whole stag, Steve says he can get it for you.) The shop was refitted in autumn '99 for a more modern look of stainless steel and pale wood. He and his friendly staff sell a good range of homemade sausages, Greek-style marinated lamb for making kleftiko and specially marinated meats and poultry for barbecuing in the summer. Bronze turkeys are a speciality at Christmas. The greengrocer next door is handy as is Oddbins across the road.

Delicatessen

VIVIAN'S

2 Worple Way, London
TW10 6AF
Tel: 0208 940 3600
Open: Mon-Fri 9am-8pm, Sat 8.30am-6pm, Sun 8.30am-2pm
Closed: Bank holiday Sun and Mon **Tube:** Richmond **Bus:** 33, 337, 371, R69 **Mainline station:** Richmond **Payment:** cash, cheques, Delta, MasterCard, Switch, Visa
Food-to-go

Richard Craig, an ex-chef and wine grower, has now bought himself a gem of a shop with an established customer base and a high reputation for quality; Vivian's can hold its own with the very best delis in central London. With its knowledgeable and enthusiastic staff, this is a very pleasant place to visit. Trying out the cheese and other fresh produce is positively encouraged, with no pressure to buy, and at weekends wine is generally freely available to taste (they have a good and unusual range, competitively priced for daily and special occasions). Gabriel, a French chef (ex-Ivy and Partridges) makes the prepared foods upstairs - typical traiteur meals include *boeuf bourgignon*, rabbit in mustard, paella, tortillas, homemade pâtés and terrines (including fresh foie gras at Christmas). The rest is a foodie's wish list: 150 international cheeses, most of which are unpasteurised; Hill Station organic ice cream; dried chillies from the Cool Chile Co. (see page 190); organic smoked salmon, trout, eel, ham; breads from Miller's Bespoke Bakery; and a wide selection of roasted preserved vegetables, extra-virgin olive oils (also available by the litre - bring your own bottle), sauces, vinegars, preserves, biscuits and cakes. Christmas specialities include the Carved Angel Christmas pudding and Museum Street Café Christmas Cake. Some fruit and vegetables are also available. As we go to press, they are planning to open other branches in the near future.

Roehampton

ST. MARCUS FINE FOOD

South African
Butcher
Sausages
Grocer

1 Rockingham Close, Priory Lane, off Upper Richmond Road, London SW15 5RW
Tel: 020 8878 1898
Fax: 020 8876 0761
Open: Mon-Sun 9am-6pm **Tube:** East Putney **Bus:** 10, 337
Mainline station: Barnes Common **Payment:** cash, cheques, Delta, MasterCard, Switch, Visa
Mail-order

This is perhaps one of the oddest food shops in London and is certainly not for the faint-hearted. Situated on the corner of a parade of shops, just along from Richmond rugby ground, this South African butcher – a member of the Guild of Master Butchers – and food shop has been established for 16 years. Enter the shop and you are confronted with a forest of brownish-black stalactites hanging from the entire ceiling. These are sticks of biltong – salted, dried meat, a favourite with South Africans and becoming increasingly popular in this country – in various stages of air-drying – 7 days for a soft texture to 21 days for brittle sticks. The meats in question include ostrich, impala and kudu as well as beef. Also on sale is a range of high-quality meat and game including the best Scottish Aberdeen Angus beef, beef from Zimbabwe, plus springbok, wild boar and Scottish venison. Another speciality are the gourmet sausages – 54 varieties are currently made on the premises – including bratwurst, chorizo, merguez, boerwors, Chinese duck, Cajun and venison, as well as the more prosaic English varieties, such as Lincolnshire and Cumberland. The deli section sells South African herbal teas, preserves, chutneys and tinned foods. Often they are very busy on rugby match days and on Saturdays. Plans for enlarging the premises were being finalized at the time of going to press.

Streatham

Central European Delicatessen Kosher

KORONA DELICATESSEN

30 Streatham High Road, London SW16 1DA
Tel: 020 8769 6647
Open: Mon-Fri 9am-7pm, Sat 9am-6pm, Sun 9am-1.30pm **Closed:** Bank holidays **Mainline station:** Streatham Hill **Bus:** 109, 118, 133, 159, 205 **Payment:** cash, cheques, Delta, MasterCard, Switch, Visa

This charming shop continues the tradition of a continental delicatessen at this site for 50 years, with the present friendly Polish owners since 1982. It's not surprising Henrietta Green named it one of the Best Shops in London in 1998 - it's like the best of Eastern European delicatessens, with delicacies from Italy, Spain and South Africa thrown in as well. You will find everything from salume, hams and sausages to jars of stuffed cabbage and bigos. The baked goods are abundant and authentic - German breads baked by Germans with German flour, Polish ryes, Ukrainian breads from a Ukrainian bakery in Bradford, along with cheesecakes (plain and poppy seed), doughnuts, biscuits and cakes. There is also a large kosher section, and Mediterranean specialities such as taramasalata and houmous.

Italian Delicatessen

ROSTICCERIA ROMA

152 Streatham Hill, London SW2 4RU
Tel: 020 8674 1901
Open: Mon-Fri 9.30am-8pm, Sat 9.30am-6pm **Closed:** Sun and Bank holidays **Mainline station:** Streatham Hill **Bus:** 45, 109, 133, 159 **Payment:** cash, cheques, Amex, Delta, MasterCard, Switch, Visa
Food-to-go

With the owner from Palermo, Sicily, you can be confident of finding a real taste of Italy here. The shop stocks only Italian food and wine, with the to-be-expected range of pasta, pasta sauces, hams, salume and cheeses, including buffalo mozzarella. Examples of the take-away food prepared daily includes roast chicken, rigatoni with tomato sauce, *pollo cacciatore*, four-cheese pasta and risotto.

Tooting

Butcher
Sausages

COPPIN BROTHERS

276 Mitcham Road, London SW17 9NT
Tel: 020 8672 6053
Open: Tue-Sat 7am-4.30pm
Closed: Sun, Mon **Tube:** Tooting Broadway **Bus:** 44, 77, 133, 155
Mainline station: Tooting Junction **Payment:** cash, cheques, Amex, Delta, MasterCard, Visa
Local delivery available

People come from far and wide to this traditional family butcher founded over 100 years ago by James Coppin and now run by his grandson. Here you will find Scotch beef, English lamb and wonderful hams; some of the meat is free-range. Home-cooked meats, all prepared on the premises, include tongue, salt beef, roast beef and home-cooked hams, for which they hold gold awards. They also make their own sausages and have over 10 different types including Cumberland, spicy tomato and pork-and-apple. What they are particularly famous for, however, is their Victorian Royal Roast, a boned goose stuffed with a boned duck, then a boned pheasant, then a boned chicken and finally a boned quail. They are one of the few butchers in London to offer this. Service is friendly and staff are knowledgeable and always happy to offer advice.

Indian
Food Hall

DEEPAK FOODS

953-959 Garrett Lane, London, SW17 0LW
Tel: 020 8767 7819 & 020 8767 7810
Fax: 020 8767 9002
Open: Mon-Sat 9am-8pm, Sun 10am-4pm **Tube:** Tooting Broadway **Bus:** 77, 282 **Mainline Station:** Tooting **Payment:** cash, cheques, Delta, MasterCard, Switch, Visa

This large utilitarian-looking shop resembles an Eastern bazaar inside, and stocks an amazing array of food and drink from India and the Caribbeans. You will find every kind of dried pulse, a wide range of rice, flour, oils, butter and vegetable ghee. The range of spices, pastes and pickles, including dried mixes for chicken masala, chicken passanda and ginger garlic, along with rose petal spread and mango jam, seem endless. Frozen food ranges from halal lamb burgers, kofta kebabs, whole tilapia and king fish steaks to ready-made tagine. Frozen vegetables include fresh blackeye peas, pigeon peas, bitter melon and whole artichoke bottoms. Fresh vegetables such as baby aubergines, long beans, sweet potatoes, yams, cassava and chow chow were on display at the time of our visit. The shop also stocks a wide and varied range of Indian breads.

Asian
Afro-
Caribbean
Grocer

NATURE FRESH

126-128 Upper Tooting Road, London SW17 7EN
Tel: 020 8682 4988

Greengrocer

Open: Mon-Sun 8am-7pm **Tube:** Tooting Broadway **Bus:** 155, 219, 355 **Mainline station:** Tooting **Payment:** cash, cheques

An impressive display of fresh fruit and vegetables is piled high at the front of this self-service greengrocer, where tomatoes, watermelons, garlic, chillies, custard apples, persimmons, mooli and huge bunches of fresh herbs fight for space. English, Afro-Caribbean and Asian communities are all catered for, and prices are competitive. Inside you can find an exhaustive range of *kulfi* (Indian ices), sugar cane, fresh tamarind, spices, biscuits and Asian breads.

Asian Grocer

PATEL BROTHERS
187-191 Upper Tooting Road, London SW17 7EN
Tel: 020 8767 6338 and 020 8672 2792
Open: Mon-Sat 8.30am-7pm, Sun 9.30am-6pm **Tube:** Tooting Broadway **Bus:** 155, 219, 355 **Mainline station:** Tooting **Payment:** cash, cheques

Established in 1972 Patels claims to be the first Asian grocery store in South London. Local competition is now hot, but they still seem to offer what people want, which is an enormous range of Indian and Asian goods ranging from pistachios to curry pastes, good quality hand-washed grains, rices, beans and pulses. Most of these can be bought in whatever quantity is required, from a 400g pack to 32kg sacks, all packed specially for Patel Brothers, imported directly from India and very good value. Service is friendly and there is always someone who will help the uninitiated. The choice can be daunting; there are shelves upon shelves of seasonings, spice mixes, sauces, pickles,

Tooting Market and Broadway Market

Open: Mon, Tue, Thu-Sat 9am-5.30pm, Wed 9am-1pm, **Tube:** Tooting Broadway **Bus:** 155, 219, 355 **Mainline station:** Tooting

Two indoor markets, adjacent to each other on Upper Tooting Road, near Tooting Broadway tube station. The food stalls include excellent fishmongers offering familiar and unfamiliar seafoods, several vegetable and fruit stalls (with everyday and exotic produce), Afro-Caribbean groceries, Halal and conventional butchers, and a multitude of household goods. There are some good snacks to be had in both markets, and fantastic food bargains when it is time to close up shop on Saturdays.

ready to make snacks, and tins of unusual fruits and vegetables. One side of the shop is reserved for the bulk goods where you can buy huge tins of cashew kernels, oils of every sort and sacks of flours and grains. You can also buy fresh Asian groceries such as fresh turmeric roots, baby aubergines, white radish, spinach and fenugreek.

Butcher
Fishmonger
Halal

RAINBOW
201 Upper Tooting Road, London SW17 7EN
Tel: 020 8672 7771
Open: Mon-Fri 9am-7pm, Sat 8.30am-6pm, Sun 9am-6pm
Tube: Tooting Broadway **Bus:** 155, 219, 355 **Mainline station:** Tooting **Payment:** cash, cheques

The local ethnic community crowd to this halal meat, poultry and fish shop in their droves. Saturdays will often see a queue up the street. Behind the counter is a sea of butchers in red and white aprons, weighing, cutting, chopping, slicing. The counter display has mounds of chicken wings, fresh goat meat, chickens, steak and mutton. All the meat and fish is of high quality and service is fast. Prices are exceptional.

Twickenham

Chocolates

SANDRINE
38A Church Street, Twickenham TW1 3NR
Tel: 020 8744 9197
Main shop: see East Sheen, page 177

Fishmonger
Poulterer
Game dealer

SANDY'S
56 King Street, Twickenham, Middlesex TW1 3SH
Tel. 020 8892 5788
Open: Mon-Sat 8am-6pm
Closed: Sun and Bank holidays
Mainline station: Twickenham
Bus: 267, 281 **Payment:** cash, cheques, Delta, MasterCard, Switch, Visa
Food-to-go, mail-order

Right on a busy main road, this large, bustling white-tiled shop has been run by 'The Big Fella', Ray Sandys, for over 12 years now. Specializing in seafood and game, he stocks a wide range of fresh fish and shellfish as well as smoked salmon (including Forman's famous London smoked salmon, see page 191), trout, halibut, tuna, shark and marlin. In the refrigerators, you will find Gressingham and Barbary ducks, fresh pigeon breast, whole guinea fowls, venison and wild boar, as well as a range of homemade sausages. At Christmas there are free-range geese and bronze turkeys, while for Hogmanay or Burns Night, they stock MacSweens famous haggis. To complement all these goodies, there is a range of exotic groceries on offer. Furthermore, large platters of home-cooked salmon and seafood, beautifully decorated, are available to order.

New Covent Garden Market

Nine Elms Lane
Open: Mon-Fri 3am-11am, Sat 4am-9am **Closed:** 24 Dec.- 5 Jan **Tube:** Vauxhall
Bus: 2, 77, 77a, 88, 322, 344 **Mainline station:** Vauxhall

Perhaps the oldest market in the city, it began in medieval times, when the produce of the Abbey of Westminster's 'Convent Garden' was sold to the public. A formal square was later built to house the rapidly growing market, designed in part by the architect Inigo Jones, and this, now the fashionable heart of a regenerated Covent Garden, is where the market remained until 1974. Now located at Nine Elms in Vauxhall, the wholesale market was forced into purpose-built efficiency. Some 300 companies trade from two principal buildings - the Fruit and Vegetable Market, with its annexe, the Pavilion, and the Flower Market. Some 70 per cent of the foods available are imported from abroad, so you could find almost anything in the world here in its due season. It is primarily a wholesale market, but the public are welcome so long as they buy in wholesale quantities (but that can be as little as a kilo of mushrooms). On Sundays, when the main market is closed, there is a small retail food market which offers meats, cheese, eggs, breads and some fruit and vegetables.

Wandsworth

Delicatessen

FOX'S OF WANDSWORTH COMMON

14 Bellevue Road, London SW17 7EG
Tel: 020 8767 3131
Fax: 020 8767 1011
Open: Mon-Fri 8.30am-8pm, Sat and Sun 8.30am-6pm **Closed:** 24 Dec.- 5 Jan. **Tube:** Tooting Bec
Bus: 689, 690 **Mainline station:** Wandsworth Common
Food-to-go

This neighbourhood shop caters for the locals with an extensive range of cheeses and impressive range of olive oils, along with fresh fruit and vegetables and speciality breads -as well as foie gras, caviar and fine wines. Food-to-go includes a huge selection of olives, char-grilled vegetables, salads and homemade cakes.

Branch: 509 Old York Road, London SW18 1TF
Tel: 020 8870 5655

Wimbledon

Delicatessen

BAYLEY & SAGE

60 High Street, London
SW19 8EE
Tel: 020 8946 9904
Open: Mon-Sun 8am-9pm **Tube:** Wimbledon **Bus:** 93, 200
Mainline station: Wimbledon
Payment: cash, cheques for £5 and over, MasterCard, Switch, Visa

'Great food' is the main emphasis of this friendly, well-stocked deli, according to Manager Andy Charman. You can't help but notice the attractive range of fresh produce just inside the door - in the autumn, for example, it has an abundant selection of wild mushrooms, such as *pieds bleu*, chanterelles and *trompettes-de-mort*. You'll find all the hams, salume, cheeses and breads that you would expect in a good deli, but the more unusual stock includes Albert Roux's pistachio oil, the Go range of organic pasta sauces, coffee from Zimbabwe, Celtic organic wholemeal and white breads, Hill Station ice creams, Stapleton's flavoured yoghurts and puddings from Cartmel in Cumbria.

Bakery
Delicatessen

FRANKONIA

79 High Street, London
SW19 5EG
Tel: 020 8947 9911
Fax: 020 8947 1242
Open: Mon-Wed, Fri 9am-6pm, Thu 9am-6.30pm, Sat 8.30am-6pm, Sun 10am-4pm **Closed:** Easter and Christmas **Tube:** Wimbledon **Bus:** 93, 200
Mainline station: Wimbledon
Payment: cash, cheques, Delta, MasterCard, Switch, Visa

There's a real Continental flavour to this popular deli in the heart of pretty Wimbledon Village, with a selection of products from just about every country in Europe. A French pâtissier makes the cakes; a German baker uses German flour to bake speciality German breads; as well as a whole range of other breads - Irish soda bread, French *pain-au-lait*, English coarse wholemeal, Mediterranean-style fig-and-date and olive-and-rosemary loaves, and a walnut bread that makes a perfect accompaniment to the small selection of good-quality cheeses on sale. Other specialities include a Black Forest ham made from organic pigs raised on acorns, smoked salmon pâté from Argyll and Richard Woodall's bacon and sausages from Waberthwaithe. You'll also find olive oils, Seggiano Italian vegetables in jars for antipasto, French fish soups, East European pickled vegetables and Italian pastas and sauces.

Mail order and delivery services

"The supermarkets have been quicker than most to jump onboard the organic train. But what indulgence to have a box of freshly picked, as Nature intended, vegetables, delivered to your doorstep every week."

Claire Phipps

Organic Greengrocer

ABEL & COLE

Tel: 0800 376 4040
e-mail: sales@abel-cole.co.uk
Open: Mon-Fri 9am-5pm; 24-hour answerphone **Closed:** Sat-Sun, Bank holidays **Payment:** MasterCard, Switch, Visa **Order:** 24 hours ahead **Minimum order:** None **Delivery:** Free
Catalogue

When this pioneering organic food delivery service started in 1988 it catered only for Londoners, but now it delivers anywhere within the M25.

All produce is bought directly from the producers or is traceable back to its farm of origin. The essential vegetable box contains 8 seasonal varieties, and it comes in three sizes to cater for all households. Along with the fruit and veg boxes, they supply beef and pork from Higher Hacknell Farm in Devon, along with pork, chickens, bread and milk. There is even a baby-weaning box. Each postal code has a delivery day; one-off orders are accepted, but they prefer standing orders, tailoring them to your needs in terms of frequency and content.

Afro-Caribbean Sauces

CARIBBEAN STYLE

Tel/Fax: 020 8694 1898
Open: every day, 24 hour answerphone **Payment:** cash, cheques **Minimum order:** 4 jars **Delivery :** £6 minimum for P&P

Yvonne Goulbourne creates home-made Afro-Caribbean sauces, marinades, seasonings, pickles and oils which are completely free of artificial colourings or preservatives. The chilli-and-garlic and the ginger-garlic-and-coriander sauces are the most popular. Her particular speciality is Jamaican Jerk marinade, which is available in three different quantities (65g, 180g and 260g) and is very reasonably priced.

Organic Wholefoods

CLEAR SPRING DIRECT

Tel: 020 8746 0152
Fax: 020 8811 8893
e-mail: mailorder@clearspring.co.uk
Web site: www.clearspring.co.uk
Open: 9am-5pm Mon-Fri; 24-hour answerphone **Closed:** Sat-Sun, Bank holidays **Payment:** cheques, Delta, MasterCard, Switch, Visa **Order:** 24 hours ahead **Minimum order:** None
Delivery: Free if order over £25, otherwise £6

High-quality vegetarian and macrobiotic ingredients from Europe, Japan and the States - including handmade Japanese pastas and a large range of sea vegetables - are available from this mail-order wholefood supplier. Everything is sugar- and dairy-free, and many ingredients are also organic and/or gluten-free. Order via the web site or on the telephone, and your order should be with you the next day if you are in the UK.

Chocolate

THE CHOCOLATE CLUB

Tel/Fax: 020 7267 5375
Open: Mon-Fri 9am-5.30pm (24 hour answerphone for orders)
Closed: Bank holidays, 24th Dec-4th Jan **Payment:** cheques, Amex, Diners, Mastercard, Switch, Visa **Order:** By 11th December for Christmas
Minimum order: £10 **Delivery:** Free if order is over £60, otherwise £3.50

The Chocolate Club won two awards in the 1999 Great Taste Awards: Gold for its after dinner chocolate mints and Bronze for its Ackerman chocolate bars. A glossy catalogue shows an endless variety of delicious-looking chocolates in all shapes, sizes and prices, including well known-names such as Ackermans, Lessiter, Lindt and Godiva. In addition there is a selection of Turkish Delight, glacé fruits, nougat and traditional *panforte*. Children can enjoy chocolates shaped as dolphins, cats, bears and can even play chocolate dominoes. Diabetics are catered for. In the unlikely event that you are unable to find something to tempt your taste buds, gift vouchers are available in £10 and £20 denominations, valid for 4 months. Orders can also be sent abroad. Allow 7 days for delivery except at Christmas, when it will take a minimum of 14 days.

Christmas Cakes

THE CHRISTMAS CAKE

Tel/Fax: 020 229 6722
Open: Anytime **Payment:** cash, cheque **Order:** For a big order, there is an Easter deadline, otherwise October for Christmas **Minimum order:** None
Delivery: £6 P&P

Sisi Edmiston creates succulent, alcoholic, Christmas fruit cakes, encrusted with nuts and glazed fruit. The end results look almost too good to eat. Her family recipe contains vast quantities of raisins and sultanas liberally drenched in cognac or apricot brandy. Dried fruit such as apricots and peaches are added with a minimal amount of flour to bind the delicious mixture together. Cooking is long in a slow convection oven, but the process starts much earlier, at Easter, when the fruit is marinated in spices for months. The meticulous preparation that goes into creating these cakes ensures a product which is both pleasing to the eye and the tastebuds.

Chillies

COOL CHILE CO.

Tel: 0870 902 1145
Fax: 0870 056 2288
e-mail: dodie@coolchile, demon.co.uk
Open: 24-hour answerphone
Payment: cheques, Delta, MasterCard, Switch, Visa
Minimum order: None **Delivery:** Free if order for over 4 items, otherwise £1.60

Mail Order

Want to spice up mealtimes? Dodie Miller is the person for you! She imports more than 20 dried chillies from Mexico, and can tell you everything there is to know about chillies, from which are the hottest or mildest to how the flavours vary. (The fainthearted should look for the *nora*, very mild with a smooth, sweet fruit flavour; try the *habanero* to blow your head off.) She also sells hot or mild starter packs as introductions to chilli appreciation and other authentic Mexican ingredients, such as powdered chillies, dried corn husks, dried avocado leaves and blue cornmeal. The brochure contains a wealth of information and recipe ideas.

Branch: Market stall
77 Portobello Road,
London W11 2QB

Organic
Greengrocer
Grocer

FARM-A-ROUND ORGANIC

Tel: 020 7627 8066
Fax: 020 7627 4698
email: homedelivery@farmaround.co.uk
Web site: farmaround.co.uk

Open: Mon-Fri 9am-5.30pm ; 24 hour answerphone **Closed:** Sat-Sun, Bank holidays **Payment:** cash at door, cheques, MasterCard, standing orders, Switch, Visa (surcharge for using debit and credit cards) **Minimum order:** £6.20 (fruit box) **Delivery:** £1

This company delivers bags of organic produce as well as other ingredients. You can order a bag which will include 9 types of vegetables, such as potatoes, carrots, onions and other seasonal produce, or one which offers 11 types of vegetables. Fruit also comes in two different sized bags. A salad bag includes leafy greens, herbs and tomatoes; the Mediterranean bag has pasta, sauce and vegetables – everything you need for an Italian meal. Other products you can order are eggs, wines, olive oil and fruit juices.

French
Italian
Delicatessen

FIORELLA'S DELICATESSEN

Tel: 020 8969 6034
Fax: 020 8969 6250
e-mail: fiorella.clinf@freeserve.co.uk

Web site: www.whitewine.co.uk **Open:** Mon Fri 9am 6pm **Closed:** Sat, Sun **Payment:** cash, cheques, Delta, MasterCard, Visa **Minimum order:** None **Delivery:** unless you live in W10 or W11, and your order is over £25, delivery costs £5.

Specialising in French and Italian produce, which she sources and imports, Fiorella includes among her clients Marco Pierre White and Anton Mosimann. Her product list offers a variety of organic goods: flours, dried fruits, nuts, preserves and cereals. Italian delicatessen products such as *antipasti*, cheese, sauces, biscuits and cakes are available, as well as various types of pasta, and a selection of truffle. Delivery is the next day. A special arrangement can be made if you need same day delivery.

Shopping service

THE FOOD FERRY

Tel: 020 7498 0827
Fax: 020 7498 8009
e-mail: sales@foodferry.com
Web site: www.foodferry.com
Open: Telephones manned Mon-Fri 8.15am-10.15pm, Internet and fax orders taken 24 hours **Closed:** weekends and Bank holidays **Payment:** BAC payment for corporate clients, cash, cheques, Delta, MasterCard, Switch, Visa **Minimum order:** £20 **Delivery:** £2-£5.50

Fans of The Food Ferry think of it as a 'fairy' godmother because this shopping service eliminates the drudgery of supermarket shopping, delivering groceries to your door - even if you live in a top floor flat. Just phone, fax, e-mail or order via the web site, specifying a delivery time (11am-4pm or 5.30-9.30 pm; orders before 10.15am are delivered that evening) and your shopping is done. One of the reasons for the popularity of this service is the range of 2500 food items, including top major brands, on offer. Specialities include cookery writer Lady Clare Macdonald's Gourmet Meals, Mrs Gill's Frozen Curries, Bigham's Cook-it-Yourself Meals and free-range and organic meat.

SMOKING THEIR OWN

There is no doubt that the best Smoked Salmon comes from wild fish. Quite a lot more expensive than farmed salmon, more salty and smoky tasting, with a firmer texture and most probably a darker colour. H. Forman & Son (see page 194 for mail order details) is London's leading smoker, with a business dating back to the turn of the century. They dry-salt their fish for 12 hours then wash it and dry it for four. Next follow 12 more hours of cool-smoking, East European fashion, before the final drying process which again takes four hours. The fish finally emerges moist on the inside and quite crisp on the outside. Forman is now also selling its own London Smoked Haddock, using Icelandic fillets which are briefly cured in sweetened brine before being cold-smoked for about three hours. No additives or artificial flavouring here.

"To me, the things I look forward to with extreme passion are the first broad beans and the first peas. 

Sir Terence Conran

Fishmonger
Kosher

H. FORMAN & SON

Tel: 020 8985 0378/4321
Fax: 020 8985 0180
e-mail: info@formans.co.uk
Web site: www.formans.co.uk
Open: Mon-Fri 5am-3pm **Closed:** Sat, Sun **Payment:** cheques, Amex, MasterCard, Visa
Minimum order: None **Delivery:** P&P depending on weight

Britain's oldest established salmon smoker, and supplier of 'London Smoke' salmon, both farmed and wild, to London's top shops and restaurants, is thoroughly geared up to both national and international mail order and distribution. Indeed, most of their business comes from wholesale trade, but they are perfectly happy to sell to individuals either via mail order or call-in at the smokery/office premises at Hackney Wick. Expect to pay retail prices if calling in; it's best to phone before calling, and to travel by car in the early hours. Smoked salmon apart, you can buy sturgeon, salmon and herring caviar, plus smoked eel, halibut, marlin, shark and swordfish, all beautifully presented.

THE FRESH FOOD CO.

Greengrocer
Organic
Grocer

Tel: 020 8969 0351
Fax: 020 8964 8050
e-mail: organic@freshfood.co.uk
Web: www.freshfood.co.uk
Open: 9am-6pm, 24-hour telephone **Payment:** Amex, Delta, MasterCard, Switch, Visa
Minimum order/Delivery: depends on products purchased

This successful husband and wife team have created an extensive catalogue providing a wide variety of organic produce with a nation-wide overnight delivery service. In 1995 they won The Soil Association Fresh Produce Award and Josa Young writes recipes accessible on the company's web site. Their sources are 70% UK-based, with the rest coming from France, Italy and Spain. With the standard boxes of mixed fruit and vegetables, you can request more exotic items:

avocado, artichoke, kiwi and mango. Regular weekly orders of the 'main' boxes receive a 5% discount. A particular speciality are the fish boxes, which arrive fresh, on ice, from Cornwall, and can include monkfish, plaice, cod, sea bass, scallops, red mullet and fresh or smoked salmon. Meat boxes are also available. A 'Dry Goods List' offers an assortment of essential household items ranging from toothpaste to tea bags, and the 'Wine List' includes 200 different wines, beers and spirits. Ordering can be on-line, freepost or by telephone, with a subscription set up for regular deliveries to your door. These can be changed at any time and cancelled at one week's notice.

Afro-Caribbean Sauces

GERALDINE'S KITCHEN

Tel/Fax: 020 8802 8797
Open: 24 hours answerphone
Payment: cash, cheques, postal orders **Minimum order:** 2 jars (approx. £5) **Delivery:** approx. £5 for p&p

Specializing in chilli-hot relishes, pickles, chutneys, sauces and oils, Geraldine sells her deliciously spicy products at Spitalfields market every Sunday from 9am-5.30pm, as well as by mail order. Hailing from Nevis in the Caribbean, she says her best-sellers include jerk marinade for chicken and pork, chow-chow pickle (extra hot and made with Scotch bonnet peppers) and sweet chilli jelly.

Afro-Caribbean Sauces

GRAMMA's

Tel: 020 8470 8751
Fax: 020 8548 8755
Open: Mon-Sat 9am-6pm
Closed: Sun **Payment:** cheques, postal orders **Minimum order:** None **Delivery:** P&P

Based on the ancient Afro-Carribean tradition of using chillies and spicy food to promote health benefits, Dounne Alexander started manufacturing a concentrated hot-pepper herbal sauce in 1987 as a tribute to her herbalist/spiritualist grandmother. Today her range also includes concentrated herbal seasonings (with original, curry, Creole and hot-and-spicy flavours) and a selection of herbal teas and drinks. None of the products contain colourings, anti-caking agents, thickeners or fillers. They are also gluten- and yeast-free, and are suitable for anyone following a vegetarian or vegan diet.

Organic Grocer Greengrocer

GREENSHOOT

Tel: 020 7259 2261/ 0793 047 0072
Fax: 01483 203179
e-mail: rboswell@globalnet.co.uk
Open: Every day 9am-5pm
Payment: cash, cheques **Orders:** 3 days in advance **Minimum order:** £16 **Delivery:** £1.50

This home delivery service provides a wide variety of certified organic produce ranging from the usual grocery and dairy products to more diverse choices such as tea, pasta, chocolate, bread, water and even shampoo. Wherever possible these come from local UK sources. Specialist needs and requirements such as vegan, wheat-, gluten- and GM-free foods are catered for. Robin Boswell creates regular boxes of mixed fruit and vegetables (small – 14 varieties, standard – 17 varieties and family size – 17 varieties) but greater quantity and made-to-measure boxes to suit individual tastes can be arranged. Packaging is recycled and customers are invited to leave their old boxes out for collection. Orders may be weekly or fortnightly, or whenever suits you.

Organic
Greengrocer

JUST ORGANIC

Tel/Fax: 020 7704 2566
Open: Anytime (answerphone otherwise) **Payment:** Cash, cheques **Minimum order:** £10
Delivery: free

This is a Soil Association accredited organic box scheme, run by Mike and Dee Adams. They deliver fruit and vegetables which are seasonal and UK-grown. A typical box contains 8 vegetables and 3 fruit, or 6 vegetables and 2 fruit. Customers tastes are catered for - you can choose what goes into the box, ie. the fruit/veg balance. Delivery to your home is free of charge, in the evenings, from Tuesday to Thursday.

LA DOLCE VITA

Italian
Pâtisserie
Food-to-go

Tel/Fax: 020 7916 3198
e-mail: postmaster@bianca.demon.co.uk
Open: 24 hour answerphone
Payment: cash, cheques
Minimum Order: None **Delivery:** £5 minimum unless local to King's Cross

This is a small home-based outlet specialising in Italian pâtisseries and Mediterranean catering. Sheila Douglas researches her products thoroughly, creating many delicacies which have a strong regional flavour and are based on old local Italian traditions and techniques. Celebration cakes are a particular speciality and often come heavily laden with alcohol - the ever-popular *umbriaca* is soaked in rum and vermouth. Everything is custom-made and thus Ms Douglas is able to be flexible in meeting customers' needs and requirements, such as vegetarian, GM-free foods and organic produce. Ever-ready to offer suggestions, she generally takes orders by telephone and can happily cope with orders of a substantial nature (catering for up to 100 people), given a few days' notice. There is a delivery charge unless you are local to the King's Cross area, but most people do the collecting themselves.

"I have had many fair-to-middling avocados, but the really good ones are so soft, nutty and smooth that you don't mind that eating them is something of a hit-and-miss experience."

Nigel Slater

Delicatessen

MOREL BROS., CORBETT AND SON

Tel: 020 7346 0046
Fax: 020 7346 0033
e-mail: info@morel.co.uk
Web site: www.morel.co.uk
Open: Mon-Fri 9 am-5.30 pm (answerphone outside office hours) **Closed:** Bank holidays
Payment: cheques, Amex, MasterCard, Switch, Visa **Order:** Min. 10 days in advance – by 10th December for Christmas
Minimum order: None **Delivery:** £3.95 standard, £7.95 for fresh food

This company, dating back to the 19th century, provides a sumptuous selection of fine delicatessen foods, which may be perused either by catalogue or internet. Essentially the range consists of fish, cooked meats, preserves, sauces and confectionery. Particular delicacies include caviar, game pies, brandy butter, truffles and Christmas pudding. Wheat-free and organic produce are available. In addition you can order seasonal hampers, as well as 'Gift Selections' (the latter consists of a Greek spice grinder and three types of peppercorns, for example). The company aims to deliver within 21 days of your order, and can deliver abroad.

Indian Pickles

MRS BASSA'S INDIAN KITCHEN

Tel: 020 8871 4460
Fax: 020 8543 7194
e-mail: Mbikltd@aol.com
Open: Mon-Fri 10am-3pm
Closed: Sat-Sun, public holidays
Payment: cheques, Delta, MasterCard, Switch, Visa
Delivery charge: p&p

Whether you are settling down for a quick take-away in front of TV, or have made your own curry, Mrs Bassa's condiments will give your meal an authentic touch. Made following Indian family recipes, these dips, pickles, salsas and pastes couldn't be more real if you were buying them in Delhi. The top-seller is garlic pickle, made with whole cloves, and the Sathot chilli sauce is for anyone with an asbestos throat. The latest addition to the range is a smooth paste of fresh coriander and mint, just as delicious for a sandwich spread as for flavouring a chicken curry.

Organic Greengrocer

THE ORGANIC DELIVERY COMPANY

Tel: 020 7739 8181
Fax: 020 7613 5800
e-mail: info@organicdelivery. co.uk
Website: www.organicdelivery.co.uk
Open: Mon-Fri 9am-6pm, Sat-Sun 10am-5pm **Payment:** cheques, Amex, Delta, MasterCard, Switch, Visa **Order:** By 5pm night before delivery **Minimum order:** None **Delivery:** Free for a box, otherwise £3.95

This Soil Association registered company delivers a range of organic products in the London area (including Richmond and Kingston) during the evenings, either weekly, fortnightly or as a one-off. Their produce is all from organic growers in Devon. They offer standard mixed fruit and vegetable boxes: small – 6-7 varieties, medium – 8-9 varieties, and large – 10-11 varieties. Bread can also be baked to order by bakers at The Old Post Office.

Spanish Delicatessen

QUALITY FOODS DIRECT

Tel/Fax: 020 7603 3335
Open: 24hours **Closed:** Bank holidays **Payment:** cheques **Minimum order:** None **Delivery:** Free

This newly set up, small company run by Miguel Carmosa, will deliver Spanish hams, chorizo and a lesser known sausage, *salchichón*, which is thin and resembles the Italian pepperoni. Mr Carmosa does stock other items, such as olive oils, but these are exclusively for the bulk-buying restaurants and are not yet available on mail order. However, this outlet is friendly and flexible and may well be persuaded to expand their choice in the future - they are already considering providing thin, slightly sweet *fuet* sausages.

Chocolate

SARA JAYNE TRUFFLES

Tel: 020 8874 8500
Fax: 020 8874 8575
email:sarajaynestanes.academy@ virgin.net
Open: Telephones manned Mon-Fri 9am-6pm ; answering machine out of hours **Payment:** cheques only **Minimum order:** £12.50 **Delivery :** £4

Cookery writer Sara Jayne Stanes, who is also a director of the Academy of Culinary Arts, makes no bones about why she thinks her rich, handmade chocolates stand out from all others – 'apart from the quality of the chocolate and the cream, the most important ingredient is love' – she says, with each one being piped and dipped by people who adore chocolate. The end result, she maintains, 'is as smooth as a kiss'. She offers 8 flavours, including the unusual combination of bitter chocolate with tequila and chilli. Venus Nipples has a rich coffee liqueur inside ivory chocolate with a coffee bean and dark couverture coating. The truffles will keep in the fridge for up to 4 weeks.

Organic Grocer

SIMPLY ORGANIC
Tel: 0845 1000 444
Fax: 020 7622 4447
Website: www.simplyorganic.net
Open: Mon-Fri 8am-8pm, Sat 9am-2pm **Closed:** Sun **Payment:** cheque, Delta, MasterCard, Switch, Visa **Minimum order:** None **Delivery:** £5
Catalogue

This company deals with, amongst others, products from the Stamp Collection (founded by Elizabeth Buxton in collaboration with Terence Stamp) and Space Food. Both offer breads, cheeses, chocolates and confectionery which are organic, and the Stamp Collection products are wheat- and dairy-free.

Food-to-go

TUCK BOX
Tel: 020 7720 1476
Fax: 020 7720 3060
Open: Mon-Fri 10am-5pm **Closed** : weekends
Payment: cheque, Amex, Delta, Diners Club, MasterCard, Solo, Switch, Visa **Order:** by 16th December for Christmas
Minimum order: 50 picnic boxes otherwise pay surcharge
Delivery: £15 for picnic box, otherwise P&P

For an alternative to a wicker hamper for grand-event picnics, or for special gifts, send for Dagny Bain's catalogue. 'Gourmet' picnics come packed in attractive, coloured, high-gloss, embossed boxes; they are ideal for a day at the races or *al fresco* concerts, and consist of sandwiches, quiches, spicy chicken drumsticks, creamy potato salads, homemade tarts or cakes and fruit, with the optional extras of champagne, wine and fruit juices. Gift boxes feature Belgian chocolates, fruit cakes, champagne and liqueurs. They come tied with gold ribbon and a personal message on the gift tag.

"Let food be your medecine... ... and medecine be your food"

Hippocrates

READER'S REPORT FORM

Please use this page either to recommend shops of outstanding quality within Greater London, that you feel ought to be included in our next edition, or add comments on quality of products, service, prices, etc. on existing entries.

Shop's name

Address

Tel. no.

☐ YES include ☐ NO don't include ☐ Deserves excellence award

Comments:

Shop's name

Address

Tel. no.

☐ YES include ☐ NO don't include ☐ Deserves excellence award

Comments:

I am not connected in any way with management or proprietors.

Your name:

Address:

Tel. no.

READER'S REPORT FORM

Please use this page either to recommend shops of outstanding quality within Greater London, that you feel ought to be included in our next edition, or add comments on quality of products, service, prices, etc. on existing entries.

Shop's name

Address

Tel. no.

☐ YES include ☐ NO don't include ☐ Deserves excellence award

Comments:

Shop's name

Address

Tel. no.

☐ YES include ☐ NO don't include ☐ Deserves excellence award

Comments:

I am not connected in any way with management or proprietors.

Your name:

Address:

Tel. no.

Index

Page numbers in **bold** indicate a shop's main branch.

*Denotes mail-order and delivery service only

Index

Index

Index

Index

Index

ACKNOWLEDGEMENTS

The publishers would like to thank the following for their help with this publication: all the proprietors and staff of the shops and businesses listed; The Guild of Food Writers, and especially Rosemary Moon, Jill Norman and Miriam Polunin; Liz McMahon and the Guild of Fine Food Retailers; and finally Antonio Carluccio for agreeing to write the introduction to this guide and imparting to us his invaluable insight into the world of food.